The Management and Marketing of Services

The Management and Marketing of Services

Second edition

Peter Mudie

and

Angela Cottam

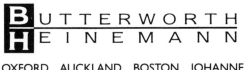

OXFORD   AUCKLAND   BOSTON   JOHANNESBURG   MELBOURNE   NEW DELHI

Butterworth-Heinemann
Linacre House, Jordan Hill, Oxford OX2 8DP
225 Wildwood Avenue, Woburn, MA 01801–2041
A division of Reed Educational and Professional Publishing Ltd

℞ A member of the Reed Elsevier plc group

First published 1993
Reprinted 1993, 1994, 1995, 1998
Second edition 1999

HD 9980.5

.M83

1999

British Library Cataloguing in Publication Data
Mudie, Peter
  The Management and Marketing of Services. – 2nd ed.
  1. Service industries – Marketing 2. Service industries –
  Management
  I. Title II. Cottam, Angela
  658.8

ISBN 0 7506 3594 0

Composition by Genesis Typesetting, Laser Quay, Rochester, Kent
Printed and bound in Great Britain by
Biddles Limited, Guildford and King's Lynn

PLANT A TREE

British Trust for
Conservation Volunteers

FOR EVERY TITLE THAT WE PUBLISH, BUTTERWORTH-HEINEMANN
WILL PAY FOR BTCV TO PLANT AND CARE FOR A TREE.

Contents

Preface to the second edition

For the second edition we have retained the structure of the book as we believe in its continuing appeal and representativeness of service industry issues. However, significant sections of the first edition have been reviewed and updated as evidenced by the inclusion or expansion of topics such as blueprinting, quality control, pricing, yield management, customer retention, lifetime value and employee loyalty.

Peter Mudie
Angela Cottam

Preface to the first edition

We live in a service society. An increasing proportion of GNP comes from our consumption of services. An increasing number of the workforce are employed in this sector. The management literature and training, however, have continued to be dominated by product management and marketing techniques.

The distinctive characteristics of services merit their own management framework. Service management is more complex. Consumers buy something that is intangible. In most cases they are not entirely certain what they will receive in exchange for their money. The service provider is often none the wiser. The interactive roles played by the server and the served mean that service provision and consumption vary enormously.

This in turn changes the role of marketing. It must embrace functions traditionally regarded as the responsibility of operations or human resource management. For example, in services the traditional function of promotion must embrace such issues as the design of the physical environment and the motivation and appearance of personnel.

We believe that the best way to manage a service company is to develop a corporate culture, the management structures and the operations systems that recognize the sector's uniqueness.

In writing this book our aims were as follows:

- To provide a comprehensive treatment of the subject matter.
- To highlight the problems that service providers are likely to confront.
- To demonstrate a range of concepts and techniques for solving these problems.
- To present the solutions within a theoretical and practical framework to facilitate their application to a variety of service industries.

Peter Mudie
Angela Cottam

Acknowledgements

Invaluable contributions to the text were made by Les Mitchell of Edinburgh College of Art (Chapter 4 on the service setting), and David Windle, Department of Mathematics, Napier University.

Invaluable contributions were made to the presentation of the book by those organizations that kindly gave us permission to reproduce artwork or illustrations. In this context we would like to mention: Avis, British Airways, British Gas, Kwik-Fit, Legal and General, Life Association of Scotland, Prudential, Reed Employment and Toys 'R' Us. We would also like to thank *Marketing Magazine* for allowing us to reproduce Peter Plant's cartoon.

For granting copyright clearance we are grateful to the following: Bowling Green State University for Figure 2 from R. Larsson and D. E. Bowen, 'Organisation and Customer: Managing Design and Coordination of Services', *Academy of Management Review*, vol. 14, no. 2, 1989, © Bowling Green State University 1989; Harvard Business School Press for Exhibit 1 from G. Lynn Shostack, 'Designing Services that Deliver', *Harvard Business Review*, Jan–Feb 1984, © President and Fellows of Harvard College, 1984; Sage Publications Inc for Figure 3 from M. Levine, 'Placement and Misplacement of You-are-here Maps', *Environment and Behaviour*, vol. 16, no. 2, 1984, © Sage Publications Inc 1984; *Cornell HRA Quarterly* for Exhibit 3 from W. B. Martin, 'Measuring and Improving Your Service Quality', *Cornell HRA Quarterly*, May 1986, © Cornell HRA Quarterly 1986; Gower Publishing Company Ltd for Figure 15.6 from T. Gillen, *Twenty Training Workshops for Customer Care*, 1990, © Gower Publishing Company 1990; Academic Press Inc (London) for Table 2 from G. H. Bower, J. B. Glack and T. J. Turner, *Scripts in Memory for Text, Cognitive Psychology II*, 1979, © Academic Press Inc (London) 1979; Pergamon Journals Ltd for Table 1 from S. D. Ball, K. Johnson and P. Slattery, 'Labour Productivity in Hotels: An Empirical Analysis', *International Journal of Hospitality Management*, vol. 5, no. 3, 1986, © Pergamon Journals Ltd 1986; The Marketing Journal and Publishing Company for Table 1 from G. H. G. McDougall and D. W.

Snetsinger, 'Items, Products and Services, and Scenarios', *Journal of Services Marketing*, vol. 4, no. 4, Fall 1990, © The Marketing Journal and Publishing Company 1990; Chartered Institute of Marketing for Figure 5 from R. Brown, 'Marketing – a Function and a Philosophy', *The Quarterly Review of Marketing*, vol. 12, nos 3 and 4, 1987, © Chartered Institute of Marketing 1987; MCB University Press Ltd for Figure 2 from G. L. Shostack, 'How to Design a Service', *European Journal of Marketing*, vol. 16, no. 1, 1982, © MCB University Press Ltd 1982; The American Marketing Association for Figure 1 from A. Parasuraman, V. A. Zeithaml and L. Berry, 'A Conceptual Model of Service Quality and its Implications for Future Research', *Journal of Marketing*, vol. 49, Fall 1985, © The American Marketing Association 1985; MCB University Press Ltd for Table 1 from D. A. Tansik and W. L. Smith, 'Dimensions of Job Scripting in Service Operations', *International Journal of Service Industry Management*, vol. 2, no. 1 1991, © MCB University Press Ltd 1991.

Chapter 1

Introducing services

Introduction

There are particular problems and challenges for those managing an organization whose major activity is providing some type of service. For the customer there may be little evidence, in advance, of what to expect. The service provider has often to produce the service under the watchful gaze of customers. Finally, both parties may fail to agree on what constitutes quality service.

To produce and deliver a service, management needs to recognize what that means in practice (see Figure 1.1). First an appropriate foundation must be laid through which the service will be channelled. If these 'bottom line' conditions of design, structure and setting are not properly thought out the prospect of providing a quality service is reduced.

The next stage involves the actual delivery of the service. People, materials and equipment must be deployed and managed to attract and serve customers in accordance with their needs and preferences. It is essentially a process in which customer and service interact in a variety of ways. Throughout that process the organization needs to demonstrate a commitment to service quality by setting appropriate standards and ensuring their implementation.

Finally, to test the success of that commitment, service performance must be monitored and evaluated. This must be an ongoing process that enables management to detect and rectify any deficiencies.

The goods–services continuum

In 1966 John Rathmell[1] observed that most marketers have some idea of the meaning of the term 'goods'; they are tangible economic products that are capable of being seen and touched and may or may not be tasted,

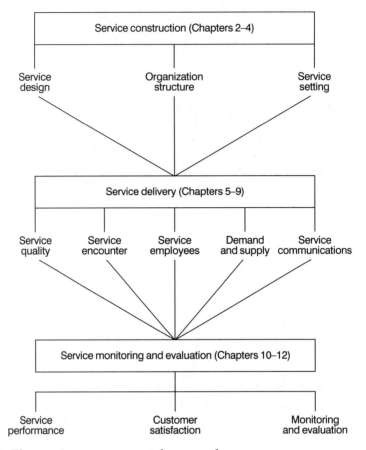

Figure 1.1 The service management framework

heard, or smelled. As for services, Rathmell asserted that there was no clear understanding. He sought to change this by defining a good as a thing and a service as an act; the former being an object, an article, a device or a material and the latter a deed, a performance, or an effort.

Another distinction between a good and a service, according to Rathmell, lay in the nature of the product's utility. Does the utility for the consumer lie in the physical characteristics of the product, or in the nature of the action or performance? From such tests Rathmell concluded that there were very few pure products and pure services. Economic products were to be regarded as lying along a goods–services continuum with pure goods at one extreme and pure services at the other, but with most of them falling between these two extremes (see Figure 1.2). Rathmell stated that some are primarily goods with service support, whereas others are primarily services with goods support. Most goods are a complex of goods

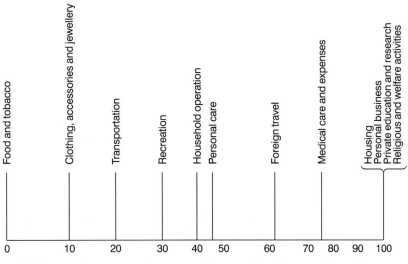

Figure 1.2 Personal consumption expenditure related to services. *Source:* Rathmell (1966)[1]

and facilitating services; most services are a complex of services and facilitating goods. He applied the measuring rod of personal consumption to distinguish between goods and services. For the food and tobacco category, percentage personal consumption expenditure on the services was nil. For recreation it was 33 per cent and for religious and welfare activities, 100 per cent.

Sixteen years later Shostack[2] developed a refined version of the original continuum (Figure 1.3) and it remains a valuable perspective for understanding the nature of services. The essence of the continuum is that tangibility (ability to see, touch, smell, hear prior to purchase) decreases as one moves from left to right. Tangible entities are in evidence, such as the equipment used by the nurse but, in general, they cannot be owned or possessed like salt or dog food. Every organization on the continuum delivers some degree of service as part of its total offer. However, it is the organizations to the right which deliver most in the way of service and can therefore truly bear the hallmark 'service organizations'. It is important to make a distinction between those for whom service is part of the overall offer (e.g. computer manufacturer, car dealer, fashion retailer) and those for whom service is the offer (e.g. hotels, banks, airlines, accountants), as the latter exhibit particular characteristics that merit attention.

In addition, there is another aspect that singles out services from other organizations. Marketing plans are usually structured around what is commonly known as the '4 Ps', namely product, price, promotion and place. But when it is service that is being marketed three more Ps – people,

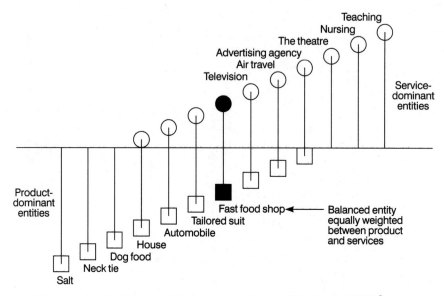

Figure 1.3 A scale of elemental dominance. *Source*: Shostack (1982)[2]

physical evidence and process must be added, making 7 Ps in all. As the additional three Ps figure prominently throughout this text, a brief description of each will suffice at this stage:

People: Service personnel and customers, e.g. appearance, attitudes, social skills, etc.

Physical evidence: Everything from the appearance, design, layout of service setting to brochures, uniforms, cheque books, etc.

Process: Just as raw materials are converted through a process into finished goods, services likewise go through a process, converting inputs to outputs. The process will involve, among other things, policies, procedures, mechanization, flow of activities, employee discretion, and customer involvement.

Employment in the service sector

One measure of the size of the service sector in the economy is the number of people employed relative to other sectors. Table 1.1 shows the number of employees in various industries in the UK. Since 1978 there has been a switch among both male and female employees away from manufacturing towards the service sector: 35 per cent of men and 22 per cent of women were employed in manufacturing in 1978 compared with only 26 per cent and 10 per cent respectively in 1997.

Table 1.1 Employees (UK): by gender and industry (%)

	Males				Females			
	1978	1981	1991	1997	1978	1981	1991	1997
Distribution, hotels, catering and repairs	15	16	19	20	24	25	25	26
Manufacturing	35	33	26	26	22	18	12	10
Financial and business services	9	10	15	16	11	12	16	19
Transport and communication	9	9	9	9	3	3	3	3
Construction	8	8	8	7	1	1	1	1
Agriculture	2	2	2	2	1	1	1	1
Energy and water supply	5	5	3	1	1	1	1	–
Other services	16	17	19	19	38	39	41	40
All employees (= 100%) (millions)	13.4	12.6	11.5	11.5	9.4	9.3	10.7	11.3

Data are at June each year.

Source: *Short-term Turnover and Employment Survey*, Office for National Statistics

In addition, the European Union, in common with most other industrialized parts of the world, has seen a long-term shift in the sectoral distribution of employment towards services and there is little sign of any slowdown in the trend shift to employment in services. (For further information see *The Eurostat Labour Force Survey and Employment in Europe* published by the European Commission.)

Characteristics of services

Services possess four key distinguishing characteristics:

Intangibility
Inseparability
Variability
Perishability.

Intangibility

Services cannot generally be seen, tasted, felt, heard or smelled before being bought. The potential customer is unable to perceive the service before (and sometimes during and after) the service delivery. For many customers of car repair, for example the service is totally intangible – they often cannot see what is being done and many indeed are unable to evaluate what has been done. Rushton and Carson[3] asked a number of service organizations whether they consciously perceived a difference between the marketing of goods and services. Several respondents pointed to the intangibility of their products with comments such as:

> We haven't got anything to show to customers like a can of baked beans.

> It's more difficult trying to explain what they [the customers] get for their money.

Implications

Intangibility presents problems in that the consumer may experience difficulty in knowing and understanding what is on offer before, and even after, receipt of the service. The challenge for the service provider is to determine the extent of intangibility and the management action required to make the service more tangible. The first task implies resort to some form of measurement, and the second task involves the provision of tangible evidence, e.g. a brochure to help consumer understanding of the service.

Measurement

A system for measuring the relative tangibility of a service organization and its offerings has been proposed by McDougall and Snetsinger.[4] A number of products and services were selected together with nine statements designed to measure tangibility (Table 1.2). Their study concentrated on the mental aspects, namely the consumer's ability to picture or visualize the service prior to purchase. Their main conclusion was that services were arrayed toward the intangible end of the continuum and most products toward the tangible end. One interesting observation was that some services (e.g. movies, fast food) were rated as more tangible than some products, and some products (e.g. used car, a new compact car) more intangible than some services.

Evidence

The ability to picture a service may be assisted by the service organization providing something tangible. This may be in the form of tangible evidence, e.g. computerized representation of hairstyles or a tangible possession, e.g. a university prospectus. The aim would be to help the potential customer form expectations before using the service. Equally, tangible evidence and possessions could assist customer judgement of the service during and after usage (see Table 1.3 on page 13).

Table 1.2 Items, products and services, and scenario

Items on the tangibility scale
1 I have a very clear image of this item.
2 The image is aroused immediately.
3 This is a very abstract item to picture.
4 This item is very tangible.
5 This is a complex item to think about.
6 This item would be easy to describe to another person.
7 This item evokes different images.
8 The item is difficult to picture.
9 I feel I have an accurate visualization of the item.

Products and services selected

Products	Services
● Carpet in bedroom	● Exercise club
● Box spring in mattress	● Television repair
● Mat for bathroom	● Lunch at fast-food restaurant
● New compact car	● Furnace overhauled
● Shampoo	● Movie
● Sweatshirt	● Accountant for income tax
● Toothbrush	● Life insurance
● Colour television	● Car oil change
● Used car	● Week's vacation in Caribbean

Example of scenario
Decision A: You have decided to buy a *new colour television*. To what extent do you agree with *each* of the following statements. The nine items in the tangibility scale were then presented (see above).

Source: McDougall and Snetsinger (1990)[4]

Inseparability (or simultaneous production and consumption)

There is a marked distinction between physical goods and services in terms of the sequence of production and consumption.

Physical goods	*Services*
Production	Sold
↓	↓
Storage	Produced and
↓	consumed at
Sold	the same time
↓	
Consumed	

Whereas goods are first produced, then stored, and finally sold and consumed, services are first sold, then produced and consumed simultaneously. For the production of many services (e.g. counselling, museums, hairdressing, rail travel, hotels), the customer must be physically present. Some services may be produced and delivered in circumstances where the customer's presence is optional, e.g. carpet cleaning, plumbing. Other services may rely more on written communication, e.g. distance learning course, or on technology, e.g. home banking. Whatever the nature and extent of contact, the potential for inseparability of production and consumption remains.

Implications

The involvement of the customer in the production and delivery of the service means that the service provider must exercise care in what is being produced and how it is produced. The latter task will be of particular significance. How teachers, doctors, bank tellers, lawyers, car mechanics, hairdressers conduct themselves in the presence of the customer may determine the likelihood of repeat business. Therefore, proper selection and training of customer contact personnel are necessary to ensure the delivery of quality.

Variability (or heterogeneity)

An unavoidable consequence of simultaneous production and consumption is variability in performance of a service. The quality of the service may vary depending on who provides it, as well as when and how it is provided. One hotel provides a fast efficient service and another a short distance away delivers a slow, inefficient service. Within a particular hotel, one employee is courteous and helpful while another is arrogant and obstructive. Even within one employee there can be variations in performance over the course of a day.

Implications

Reducing variability involves determining the causes. It may be due to unsuitable personality traits in an employee which are very difficult to detect at the selection stage. There is nothing much that can be done about this except hope that the employee decides to terminate his/her employment! However, there may be good sound reasons for variations in performance. For example, it could be due to poor training and supervision, lack of communication and information and generally a lack of regular support.

Some have argued for a replacement of labour with automation and a production line approach to service operations. This would mean a reduction in employee discretion and an increase in standardization of procedures. The operation of McDonald's restaurants is put forward as an ideal model of service industrialization.

The other source of variability is, of course, the customer, Peters and Waterman[5] in their bestseller, *In Search of Excellence*, called for staying 'close to the customer'. Unfortunately according to one view[6] this is being 'steadily undermined by the zealots of increased productivity and back room operations. The customer is in danger of being controlled to the point where customer service is becoming just another stage in a systematic manufacturing process, McDonald's being the definitive example'.

Perishability

Services cannot be stored for later sales or use. Hotel rooms not occupied, airline seats not purchased, and college places not filled cannot be reclaimed. As services are performances they cannot be stored. If demand far exceeds supply it cannot be met, as in manufacturing, by taking goods from a warehouse. Equally, if capacity far exceeds demand, the revenue and/or value of that service is lost.

Implications

Fluctuations in demand characterize service organizations and may pose problems where these fluctuations are unpredictable. Strategies need to be developed for producing a better match between supply and demand (see Chapter 8).

Classification

Classification is the act of dividing up phenomena and putting them into classes or categories. In marketing there are many classifications e.g. consumer (socioeconomic groups); product (convenience shopping, speciality); market (industrial, consumer, international, service).

Why classify?

The major purposes are threefold:

1 To determine whether certain characteristics or behaviours are so important and distinct as to merit separate treatment.
2 To determine the extent to which certain characteristics or behaviours may apply across all categories.
3 To create better understanding.

If we take the example of socioeconomic groups in marketing; does a consumer in socioeconomic group B exhibit a pattern of consumption exclusive to that group and therefore, by definition, distinct from socioeconomic group C1? Furthermore, decision making is helped by knowing that consumption behaviour is explained by the existence of certain categories and membership within them.

(*Note*: From October 1998 UK population segmented into seventeen new classes)

Classifying services

The major question is whether we can classify services in a useful manner. Consider a short list of services selected at random and then ask yourself the questions cited below:

Services

- Hotels
- Airlines
- Social services
- Banks
- Colleges
- Computing services
- Recreation services
- Legal services
- Carpet cleaning
- Car repair

Questions

- Do they have anything in common?
- Should each be treated separately?
- Should each be allocated to one of a number of clearly distinct categories?

Historically each service has been treated separately but now the trend is towards identifying categories that possess characteristics distinct from each other and for services in each category to share similar problems and opportunities.

To achieve this requires a list of characteristics that will help in determining the categories and allocating the services accordingly.

One of the most valuable sets of classification frameworks has been developed by Lovelock.[7] The basic framework classifies services according to whom or what they are directed and whether they are tangible or intangible in nature.

Tangible actions directed at people's bodies:	Health care, passenger transportation, beauty salons, exercise clinics, restaurants, hairdressers
Tangible actions directed at goods and other physical possessions:	Freight transport, industrial equipment, repair and maintenance, janitorial services, laundry and dry cleaning, landscaping/lawncare, veterinary care
Intangible actions directed at people's minds:	Education, broadcasting, information services, theatres, museums
Intangible actions directed at intangible assets:	Banking, legal services, accounting, securities, insurance

The main appeal of this approach is fourfold:

1 It highlights an important service characteristic, namely tangibility.
2 It focuses on at whom or what the service is directed.
3 It stresses the importance of a marketing perspective.
4 The categories are clearly distinct and collectively cover the entire services arena.

The above classification represents the foundation into which all services can be categorized. However, one may then proceed to build additional classification schemes (Lovelock developed four others) derived from a list of appropriate characteristics.

Customer involvement and uncertainty

What makes a service really a service according to Teboul[8] is the interface: the front office, the dining room, and the actual difference between a service and a manufacturing facility is the size of the interface. Teboul correctly identifies the main characteristics of the interface:

● The customer is physically present
● The service and the delivery process are interdependent (simultaneous production and consumption)
● When the customer is in the interface he or she is visiting the factory – the place where the service is delivered. And the larger the interface the more visible the service is

The physical presence of the customer is an important issue as it raises the questions:

- How much physical presence of the customer is necessary for the delivery of the service to take place?
- What is the nature of the customer contact and the implications for service management?

To say that a service cannot exist without simultaneous production and consumption is not strictly true. For example, a parcel delivery or data processing service is not consumed while it is being produced.

Finally, Teboul does not give an explanation of the 'size of the interface'. It could mean a number of things, e.g. physical space, amount of time, number of activities etc.

Teboul's view of service would seem to favour a counselling-type situation where the production, delivery and consumption occur simultaneously and are visible to all concerned. This is a very important view of service but it cannot be regarded as an exclusive explanation of what is meant by service.

Many organizations do however fall into a category similar to that outlined above. They can be portrayed as visible operational processes in which the customer is directly involved in some way. Unlike the purchase of a packet of soap powder where it is fairly certain that it will do the job it is intended to, a stay in a hotel is potentially full of uncertainty in that so many things can go wrong.

Uncertainty about what the customer actually wants is a key factor for organizations whose major activity is providing a service. The uncertainty can occur before, during and after the service.

Before

The customer as a major input to the service production process is regarded as a major source of uncertainty.[9] Customers may bring with them their bodies, minds, goods or information to be serviced. The uncertainty for the service provider lies in not fully understanding these customer inputs, for example:

- Physical state of a body for a fitness clinic
- Mental state of mind for an education service
- State and complexity of a car for detecting faults during a service
- Capacity of clothing and carpet fabrics to withstand chemical treatment
- Amount and nature of customer information for a medical diagnosis

In the above situations service providers are unsure about what to expect which in turn may affect their preparedness for creating and delivering an effective service.

During

Customers have been portrayed as posing problems for organizations by 'disrupting routines, ignoring offers of service, failing to comply with procedures and making exaggerated demands'.[10] The challenge for service organizations is the development of strategies to manage customer behaviour, hopefully in a way acceptable to both parties.

After

Intangibility of service means that the object of exchange is often an experience that can neither be touched nor possessed. Therefore, the customer may have difficulty understanding what has been obtained on receipt of a service. For example, what does the customer purchase when buying insurance? The more intangibility there is in a service, the greater this problem becomes. This is known as performance ambiguity.[11] As intangibility increases, the customer has less evidence available to assess the service (Table 1.3).

Table 1.3 Tangibility of the service at each stage of consumption

Usage stage	Tangible evidence	Tangible possession
Before usage	Insurance representative, computerized or photographed hairstyles	Holiday brochure, college prospectus
During usage	Security firm guard dog, restaurant interior design, fellow customers	Library book, car from car hire
After usage	Advertising by organization	College diploma, report from second-hand car dealer or car repair business

The service package

With the purchase of the tangible item like a car or a washing machine it is a relatively straightforward matter as to what customers have received and how it meets their needs. For a service it is not always quite so simple because after purchase and use customers, in many cases, have nothing tangible in their possession. Whether or not there is anything of a tangible nature, service organizations need to recognize that its package is composed of a number of elements, tangible and intangible.

Tangible elements

- Items bought by the customer, e.g. restaurant meal
- Item whose status is altered by the service, e.g. car repair, health and fitness club
- Items that are peripheral rather than main parts of the package, e.g. bank cheque book, cinema admission ticket, hospital appointment card
- Items without which the service would not exist, e.g. the bank branch, the aircraft, the car of a rental company
- Items that form part of the process, e.g. technology (computers, automatic teller machines, vending machines, etc.)

Intangible elements

- The personal contact with the service personnel
- The atmosphere generated by the service environment
- Emotions felt by the customer, e.g. peace of mind, enhanced self-esteem

What the service organization must now do is decide its core and peripheral services.

Core service

As with tangible products, the core elements beg the question, 'What are consumers really buying?' It was the late Charles Revson of Revlon who said 'In the factory we make cosmetics; in the store we sell hope'. In similar vein, a manufacturer of ball bearings is marketing antifriction devices. The message is clearly one of defining products or services in terms of customer benefits rather than emphasizing technical features. Otherwise another product or service may appear that will meet, more effectively, underlying customer needs. Many service organizations provide a range of packages rather than just one. Nevertheless attempts should be made to determine and communicate the benefits, e.g.:

Rail travel – safe and reliable transportation
Tax consultant – peace of mind
Education course – career enhancement, self-actualization
Hotel – hospitality, rest and recuperation
Hairdresser – feel more attractive, confidence booster.

In some cases, different market segments will perceive different core benefits from the same service, e.g. a keep-fit programme may be made up of people who wish to lose weight, get very fit or simply enjoy themselves.

Peripheral services

These comprise the following:

● *Facilitating services* These are a necessity as they make it possible for a customer to use the service, e.g. check-in services at an airline.
● *Supporting or augmented services* These are not necessarily required but they can differentiate an organization from the competition and give it a competitive advantage, although it has to be said that innovations in service can often be copied quickly and at little cost. An example of supporting services would be Virgin Airline's free head massages and aromatherapy kits to help overcome jet lag.

Expectations, perceptions and satisfaction

Expectations are formed prior to usage of the service and perceptions are the customer's evaluation of the service. After the service has been consumed customers compare the perceived service with the expected service and if the perceived service meets or exceeds the expected service, the customer is satisfied.

In this context it can be revealing for a service organization to ask the customer:

How do you feel about us?

How have we failed you?

Customers may respond:

You have not lived up to my expectations.

You have failed to take an interest in any of my problems.

If comments such as these are widespread and have any basis in fact they should be a matter of some concern for the management of service organizations. They need to recognize the importance of the first law of service which states:[12]

Satisfaction = Perception − Expectation

However, care must be exercised in the interpretation of the formula. For example, it is difficult to come to terms with the fact that if someone attends a hospital outpatient appointment expecting to wait needlessly for two or three hours along with other individuals who might well have been assigned an identical appointment time, then the customer is satisfied if indeed the duration is of two or three hours.[13]

Expectations have two components: a probability of occurrence (e.g. the likelihood that a service employee will be available to wait on customers) and an evaluation of the occurrence (e.g. the degree to which the employee's attention is desirable or undesirable, good or bad). Both are necessary because it is not at all clear that some attributes (service employees in this example) are desired by all customers. When these components are properly combined, 'high' and 'low' expectations can be defined:[14]

Expectations	Customer's anticipation
High	Desirable events will occur. Undesirable events will not occur
Low	Desirable events will not occur. Undesirable events will occur

To obtain a measure of customer satisfaction (or dissatisfaction) a comparison must be made between customer expectations and the actual, or customer perception of, performance.

Where perceptions are found to be lower than expectations, the customer is said to be dissatisfied. An international study of UK and US bank customers[15] uncovered gaps between perceptions and expectations, on both an intra- and intercountry basis. A number of service elements (e.g. physical features and facilities, contact staff, response to customers' needs and automated facilities) were researched and the overall findings suggested that although expectations were high, perceptions of the actual service quality delivered were equally high. Overall, customers were satisfied.

Another study of the banking industry[16] found that for the small business customer the cosmetic elements, e.g. branch decor, appearance of staff, are not perceived as indicators of quality service. Indeed, as the authors state, many took the view that they were paying for such peripherals in the form of higher bank charges. In this case it is clear that perceptions did not match up to expectations. In addition, it could be said that what the bank perceived to be important failed to find the agreement of the customer.

Measuring the consumer's perceptions and expectations is vitally important. However, the following question must be asked of the service organization: 'What does it think of customer expectations and perceptions?' To arrive at an answer, two variants of the original perceptions/expectations formula must be used. The objective is to determine whether or not any gaps exist between the customers' view and the service organization's perception of the customers' view. The formulae are:

Customer expectations – service organization's perception of customer expectations

Customer experience – service organization's perception of customer experience

A study which examined doctor/patient relationships[17] found that 'gaps can arise from inconsistent perceptions of expectations and experiences between patients and physicians'. This research was prefaced with a statement that should act as a continuing reminder for all service organizations:

> From a marketing perspective, the provider would design, develop, and deliver the service offering on the basis of his or her perceptions of client expectations. Likewise, modifications to the service offering would be affected by the provider's perceptions of client experiences. Whether these experiences exceed, match, or are below expectations can have a profound effect on future client/professional relationships.

To measure the three gaps, doctors and patients were required to indicate their agreement/disagreement with a long list of statements, e.g.

	Strongly agree	Strongly disagree
Perception – expectation: In an emergency doctor is available **Customer expectation – service organization's perception of customer expectations:**		

	Strongly agree	Strongly disagree
I expect my doctor to talk clearly, using words that I understand **Customer experience – service organization's perception of customer experience:** My doctor spends enough time with me.		

Not surprisingly, significant gaps were found. This is a profound problem for service organizations where the expectations/perceptions of one party are at odds with those of the other. There is no simple resolution to this problem. But unless greater effort is made to understand each other, the problem will remain.

Perceived risk

Buying any product or service involves risks. Consumers will consider what these risks will be, the likelihood of them arising and evaluate the possible consequences. The distinctive characteristics of services promote the feeling that greater risks are involved than for physical products.

Intangibility

Means that potential customers cannot, for example, see and touch many services prior to purchase or use. A typical thought might be 'What's it going to be like?'

Variability

A machine usually performs to a consistent standard wherever and whenever it is used. Not so human beings. The car mechanic does a perfect job one day but, for a variety of reasons, a less than perfect job the following day. The car owner's apprehension might find expression in 'My life is in your hands!'

Guarantees

Historically services have not enjoyed the protection of guarantees. You can return a faulty washing machine but not a bad haircut or a poorly taught course. However, progress is being made in this area. The difficulty is putting a monetary value on the consequences of a bad haircut or a poorly taught course (see Chapter 11).

Complexity

Services can be so technical and specialized that the consumer, through lack of experience, is unable to evaluate it properly. The unanswered question for the customer is often, 'How do I know he has done a good job?' The consumer puts his trust in the surgeon, car mechanic, financial advisor, etc., but is it well founded?

Types of risk

Jacoby and Kaplan[18] proposed a typology of risks for the consumer:

1 Performance risks – how well will the product work?
2 Physical risk – will the product harm the consumer?
3 Financial risk – will the product be worth all the costs involved?
4 Psychological risks – how will purchase of the product affect the consumer's self-esteem or self-concept?
5 Social risks – how will the consumer's image, as seen by friends, peers, etc., be affected after purchase?

A sixth type is often added:

6 Time loss – the waste in time, convenience and effort of getting a product adjusted, repaired or replaced.

The above types of perceived risk were written with products very much in mind and most of the research has concentrated on products. Very few studies have researched perceived risk for services. A recent study[19] found that consumers perceive services to be more risky than goods across several types of risk and more variable in nature.

Perceived risk will not only vary between goods and services but also according to the amount of consumer self-confidence (e.g. knowledge and experience), the degree of uncertainty felt and the importance and cost of the service.

Risk reduction

Again most of the methods of risk reduction were developed for products.[20] For services the following actions should be taken:

1 The service provider should determine the consumer's expectations prior to buying and using the service. The importance of this lies in the opportunity of adjusting expectations to perhaps more realistic levels and preparing the consumer for the outcome before the service is performed.
2 To avoid unrealistic consumer expectations developing, the provider should exercise care with promises made in any promotional literature. Such promises should only be communicated where the organization can confidently deliver.
3 As consumers may often experience difficulty in evaluating services, they should be assisted in terms of what to look for before, during and after service delivery.

4 Since services are characterized by a great deal of human interaction attention must be given to selection, training and supervision of customer–contact personnel.
5 Encourage trial of the service. This will not be possible for all types of services. For example, a consumer could be encouraged by a carpet cleaner to try out the service on an older and less conspicuous piece of carpeting or a student could be given the opportunity of experiencing a subject for the first few weeks. However, customer trial would be difficult for services such as hairdressing and dentistry.
6 Customer anxiety over variability in service delivery could be reduced by ensuring standardization of much of the procedures. Also the provision of tangible pieces of evidence before, during and after service can reduce a feeling of variability.
7 Guarantees and money-back offers – despite the problems in this area, increasing interest is being shown by service organizations.

Service organizations need to give more attention to perceived risk.

Promises

Given the nature of services and the complexities involved in the conduct of services it is important to bear in mind the central role played by promises. Customer dissatisfaction is the inevitable consequence of failure to deliver what had been promised. There are three aspects to this:

- **Making promises** – since potential customers are often unable to properly evaluate a service offer in advance of using it, organizations may make promises as to what customers can expect. Promises are made to assist the management of customer expectations. Unfortunately too many service organizations make unrealistic promises: in other words, promises that cannot be delivered. Pressures of the market and the desire to impress often make for overpromising. But for consumers, the expectation is one of promises designed to deliver rather than promises designed to impress.
- **Enabling promises** – in making promises in the first instance, organizations must reflect on the capacity of its resources and competencies to deliver. Enabling simply means putting itself in a position to deliver what has been promised.
- **Keeping promises** – the most critical stage as the customer experiences, 'what has been promised'.

There are several advantages to making promises.[21] As recipients of promises, the customers:

- Realize that the firm is interested in satisfying their expectations[22]
- Receive clear and precise information regarding the service norms of the firm (that way there are no surprises!)
- Gain valuable information which allows them to judge *a priori* (before experiencing the service) if the service norms correspond to their expectations.

In issuing promises, the company:

- Is enabled to favour a customer-centred management orientation: this strategy must originate from top management[23] and become a priority at all levels of management and for all personnel
- Is obligated to clarify the roles of the personnel in context with the clientele along with the support staff, and to reinforce the close relations which must be maintained between these two vital links in the service delivery process
- Is stimulated to reorganize the delivery process and thus satisfy the quality norms promised to the customers
- Underlines to contact personnel and the support staff, goals in terms of the level of quality of service offered
- Familiarizes its personnel with well-established norms, allowing them to identify the elements (abilities, knowledge, logistics, operations, etc.) to enhance in order to reach predefined quality goals[24]
- Spurs on the personnel to achieve a common objective, and fosters cooperation rather than competition or indifference.

Standards

Along with the making and delivery of promises, the setting of standards should be a central concern of service organizations. There is much discussion about standards e.g. they are falling. Unfortunately the amount of discussion is not matched by action aimed at developing and implementing standards. This is not wholly surprising as there can be difficulties in defining what is meant by a standard. In general terms a standard implies a level of performance that customers will find at the very least acceptable. The standards set by an organization will communicate a great deal about the quality of service on offer. Equally performance indicators (see Chapter 10) will show what standards of service customers are receiving.

Service standards should be set in accordance with customer requirements. They should not be determined by internal concerns such as productivity and efficiency. Such matters can be in conflict with customer needs and preferences and overall satisfaction (see Chapter 10).

Organizations and customers, for example, may have quite different perspectives on an appropriate time frame for resolving complaints or responding to enquiries. For the customer, the standard is expressed in terms of expectations (Figure 1.4). (Note that expectations can be viewed as either a normative standard in the sense of what a service should offer or a predictive standard in the sense of what a customer feels a service will offer. The first interpretation is used here.) The standard set is an expression of the service provider's view as to how long the process of responding to enquiries or resolving complaints should take. Service performance is the time it actually takes. The customer loses out not only in terms of failure to meet expectations but also in terms of a performance not even meeting the standard.

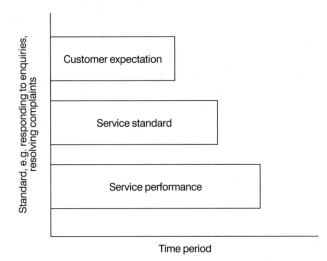

Figure 1.4 Standard: expectation and delivery

But how can such a divergence of view between customer expectations and service standards arise? Clearly this is an indication of the gap that will be found when a standard is set from a company rather than a customer perspective. The service provider may, of course, take the view that customer expectations are unreasonable or unrealistic stemming in part from a lack of understanding of the service process. On the other hand, the actual service performance may be a reflection of inefficiencies in the process.

Hard versus soft standards

Service organizations can set standards to ensure for example, that customer enquiries are attended to within a specified time period. What they find more difficult is setting standards for the courtesy level to be extended to the customer. The first type is commonly referred to as a hard measure and the second as a soft measure.

- **Hard standards** – these usually involve counts or timed actions, e.g. how many, how accurately, how quickly. Two of the five quality dimensions (see Chapter 5) are particularly receptive to hard measures. For reliability the ultimate standard is either 'right first time', e.g. correct order, delivered to customer, or 'right on time,' e.g. trains run when they are meant to run, the doctor keeps to the patient's scheduled appointment time and the dry cleaner cleans the customer's clothing by the promised date. For the second dimension, responsiveness, time or speed is what's looked for in a standard. Basically, it refers to the amount of time a customer has to wait between calling a service and receiving a call back with an answer. Even though we are dealing with something that can be objectively measured, Figure 1.4 acts as a reminder of how far apart are the views of provider and customer as to what the standard should be.
- **Soft standards** – here we are looking at areas that are much more difficult to measure objectively and agree a standard. Service customers want to experience courtesy, trust, care and understanding. These attributes are encapsulated in a further two dimensions of service quality, namely empathy and assurance. To determine the extent to which they are present during a service encounter we need to contact the customers for their opinions and perceptions. This can be done through group discussions and/or questionnaires.

Establishing standards requires a detailed assessment of the entire service process as in blueprinting or service mapping (Chapter 3). Questions can then be raised as to how far each step in the process requires specific behaviour or action to complete. The greater the degree of specificity, the easier it will be to set a standard.

Standards and standardization

Standards can be set for all services. However, the more abstract and complex the service, the greater is the challenge. In reality, many service tasks are routine, enabling specific rules and standards to be established. Where this routinization embraces the entire service process, we have a situation where scripted behaviour and actions creates highly predictable interactions between service employees and customers. This is standardization where the service is performed in a rigid, mechanical way with every behaviour and action executed in a uniform manner. Such an approach is quite acceptable for a range of service situations. The danger lies in it becoming a model for all services.[25]

Summary

Service as an activity has a very long history. However, it is only within the last thirty years that it has been marked out for special attention. More people than ever are employed in the service sector. All organizations offer service in some degree or other. However, a growing number can accurately be described as service organizations. For such organizations understanding the nature of service is fundamental.

Whether the organizations are public or private, large or small, the characteristics of intangibility, inseparability, variability and perishability need to be addressed and the implications managed. Classification systems can help in this regard.

Customer uncertainty and involvement will always be the subject of intense interest along with definitions of what the service actually offers in the form of the service package.

A key issue is that of expectations and perceptions and the gaps that seem to be present. Closing these gaps is an enormous challenge for many service organizations.

Whatever service organizations do managing their affairs there will always be an element of perceived risk in the consumption of services. Action can however be taken to minimize it.

Making promises is a crucial aspect of services marketing as customers will invariably refer to them when it comes to judging the service actually received. The question of standards is now the subject of much debate. Those that are set are invariably done in terms of a time frame, e.g. responsiveness, reliability (the hard areas). But for services, unlike manufacturing, there are many softer areas which pose a particular challenge when it comes to determining a particular standard.

References

1. Rathmell, J. M. (1966) 'What is meant by services', *Journal of Marketing*, **30**, October, 32–36.
2. Shostack, G. L. (1982) 'How to design a service', *European Journal of Marketing*, **16**(1), 49–64.
3. Rushton, A. M. and Carson, D. J. (1985) 'The marketing of services: managing the intangibles', *European Journal of Marketing*, **19**(3), 19–40.
4. McDougall, G. H. G. and Snetsinger, D. W. (1990) 'The intangibility of services: measurement and competitive perspectives', *Journal of Services Marketing*, **4**(4), 27–40.
5. Peters, T. J. and Waterman, R. H. (1982) *In Search of Excellence: Lessons from America's Best Run Companies*, Harper & Row, New York.

6. Wolstenholme, S. M. (1988) 'The consultant customers – a new use for the customer in service operations', *Proceedings of the Operations Management Association Annual. International Conference,* University of Warwick (Johnson, R. ed.), pp. 195–203.

7. Lovelock, C. H. (1996) *Services Marketing,* Prentice Hall, Englewood Cliffs, NJ.

8. Teboul, J. (1988) 'De-industrialise service for quality', *Proceedings of the Operations Management Association Annual International Conference,* University of Warwick (Johnston, R. ed.), pp. 131–138.

9. Argote, L. (1982) 'Input uncertainty and organisational coordination in hospital units', *Administrative Science Quarterly,* **27,** 420–434.

10. Danet, B. (1981) 'Client–organisation relationships', *Handbook of Organisation Design,* **2,** 382–428.

11. Bowen, D. E. and Jones, G. R. (1986) 'Transaction cost analysis of service organisation – customer exchange', *Academy of Management Review,* **11**(2), 428–441.

12. Maister, D. H. (1985) In *The Psychology of Waiting Lines. The Service Encounter* (Czepiel, J. A., Solomon, M. R. and Suprenant, C. F. eds), Lexington Books, D. C. Heath and Company, Lexington, MA.

13. Moores, B. (1989) In *Management of Service Quality. Management in Service Industries* (Jones, P. ed.), Pitman, London.

14. Oliver, R. L. (1981) 'Measurement and evaluation of satisfaction processes in retail settings', *Journal of Retailing,* **57**(3), 25–48.

15. Lewis, B. R. (1991) 'Service quality: an international comparison of bank customers' expectations and perceptions', *Journal of Marketing Management,* **7**(1), 47–62.

16. Smith, A. M. and Turnbull, P. W. (1990) 'Service characteristics and their implications for quality', *Proceedings of the Marketing Education Group Annual Conference,* **3,** Oxford Polytechnic, Oxford.

17. Brown, S. W. and Swartz, T. A. (1989) 'A gap analysis of professional service quality', *Journal of Marketing,* **53,** April, 92–98.

18. Jacoby, J. and Kaplan, L. B. (1972) 'The components of perceived risk', *Proceedings of the Third Annual Convention of the Association for Consumer Research* (Venkatesan, M. ed.).

19. Murray, K. B. and Schlacter, J. L. (1990) 'The impact of service versus goods on consumers' assessment of perceived risk and variability', *Journal of the Academy of Marketing Service* **18**(2), 51–65.

20. Roselius, T. (1971) 'Consumer rankings of risk reduction methods', *Journal of Marketing,* **35** January, 56–61.

21. Fabien, L. (1997) 'Making promises: the power of engagement', *The Journal of Services Marketing,* **11**(3).

22. Zemke, R. and Bell, C. (1990) 'Service Recovery: doing it right the second time', *Training* (June).

23. Berry, L. (1995). 'Relationship marketing of services – growing interest, emerging perspectives', *Journal of the Academy of Marketing Science,* **23**(4).

24. Ibid.

25. Ritzer, G. (1996) *The McDonaldisation of Society,* Pine Forge Press.

Chapter 2

The organizational setting

Introduction

Services are not created and delivered in a vacuum. They are produced by organizations which vary in size, structure and culture. To explain service provision we need to examine the organization in detail.

This means we need to analyse the structure, unearth the dominant and prevailing values and beliefs with a view to arriving at some explanation for the character of the service. In all of this, there must be a determination to ascertain whether, and if so what, organizational factors lead to success or failure in providing a good service. Having established the factors, reasons should be suggested for the success, or actions required to overcome failure.

It is vital that employees at or near the point of customer contact should be given a voice in any appraisal of organization structures, systems and procedures. Their understanding of how and why the organization does or does not work in the service of its customers is often vastly underrated. Researching employees' perceptions of their role, their value and how they behave can help explain lots of things about 'organizational life' and suggest whether or not there is need for change.

The organization chart

The traditional organization chart is shown in Figure 2.1. It portrays a top-down rigid hierarchy with heavy emphasis on narrowly defined functions and roles, deadening rules; procedures and controls. The appropriateness of this type of structure nowadays and in particular for service organizations where the frontline employees' role is pivotal is the subject of much debate.

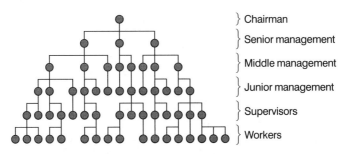

Figure 2.1 Organization chart: top-down rigid hierarchy

What the organizational chart does not reveal is:

● The informal organization structure
● The effectiveness of the prevailing communication channels
● The source and nature of power within an organization

In other words, there may be a contrast between how one envisages the organization in a formal sense on paper and how the organization operates in practice.

Arguments have been put forward in favour of turning the traditional organization chart upside down (Figure 2.2). In service organizations, the person at the point of contact is the most important person to the customer. What happens at this encounter will demonstrate either the organization's commitment to, or disregard for, the customer. Inverting

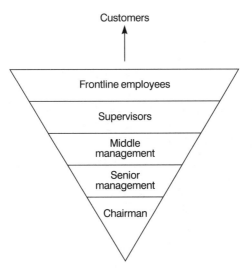

Figure 2.2 The upside-down organization chart

the organization means making all systems and support staff in the company 'work for' the frontline person to deliver the company's full capabilities at the moment of customer contact.[1] Support for this proposition grows from the technology factor whereby frontline employees sit at computers that enable them to handle a whole range of customer enquiries.

For a service organization the logic of this approach is appealing. However, the advocates of this approach fail to address the implications of their proposal. Certainly, the consumer would be much better served but only if, under their new status, the frontline employees are given the appropriate authority and responsibility. This is known as empowering frontline employees. Turning the chart upside down reverses all our thinking about status, power and authority. If frontline employees are to be given new and expanded roles, they should receive commensurate rewards. This part of the concept of empowerment is often found lacking.

Empowerment is regarded as the opposite of enslavement where one does what one is told. It is hailed as the answer to improved quality and productivity and the solution to the argument for reductions in middle management ranks. The frontline employees' authority and responsibility would be greatly enlarged. Bell and Zemke[2] regard empowerment as both exhilarating and awesome for managers with a healthy respect for Murphy's law to contemplate.

It is significant, however, that authority is often omitted from the definition. Asking people to take authority and responsibility in the area of decision making may be met with resistance, but success in achieving it will result in a more profitable and effective business.

Flattening the pyramid

Instead of an inverted structure, there is an argument to be put for a flatter structure with fewer layers of management and consequently more effective responsiveness to customer needs (Figure 2.3). In a stable and predictable environment, mechanistic rigid structures may be appropriate, but in unpredictable, dynamic circumstances, organic, flexible structures are more appropriate. Organizations in the UK tend to cluster at the mechanistic end of the spectrum.[3]

Whether the environment is stable or dynamic, the importance of structure led Peters[4] to observe that 'good intentions and brilliant proposals will be dead-ended, destroyed, sabotaged, massaged to death or revised beyond recognition or usefulness by the overlayered structures at most large and all too many small firms'.

Peter Drucker[5] recommended seven layers as the maximum necessary for any organization, while Tom Peters[4] more recently drew on the

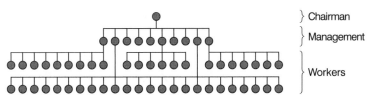

Figure 2.3 A flat organization structure

example of the Catholic Church in support of his maximum of five layers.

Federal Express, with 42 000 employees in more than 300 cities worldwide, has a maximum of only five layers between its non-management employees and its Chief Executive Officer. Direct writers in the insurance industry have flat management structures with three or, at most, four layers of management compared with around ten in a typical insurance company. 'Infinitely flat' service organizations have been achieved by the creative implementation of technology in which there seems to be virtually no limit to the reporting span (the number of people reporting to one supervisor or centre).[1]

Jan Carlzon[6] of Scandinavian Airlines demonstrated how flattening the pyramid works with the following before and after scenario:

> Let's say that you've pre-ordered a special vegetarian meal for your SAS flight from Stockholm to New York. Nervously, you approach the check-in counter to find out whether your meal has been delivered to the plane.
>
> 'I don't know', the agent sighs. 'I'm sorry but I'm too busy and I'm not familiar with the food service.'
>
> 'But what can I do?' you ask.
>
> 'You'll have to ask at the gate', she replied. 'They'll certainly be able to help you there.' The agent quickly moves on to help the next person in line. Given no alternative, you go to the gate and ask again.
>
> The gate attendant is friendly, but he doesn't know where your meal is either.
>
> 'I wish I could help, but I don't have anything to do with food service. Just check with the stewardess when you get on board and things should certainly work out.'
>
> Reluctantly you board the plane. When you ask the stewardess about your vegetarian meal, she is bewildered. She hasn't heard

anything about special food orders, but the plane is about to take off and nothing can be done now.

'You should have contacted us earlier', she reprimands. 'There would have been no problem if only we had known in time.'

In this situation, the hierarchical organizational structure has caused the airline to run three 'moments of truth' (Carlzon's term for fleeting contacts with a customer). No-one the passenger encountered had the authority to handle the specific problem, and no-one dared step out of his normal role to solve it.

Let us now suppose that the organization has changed its structure by flattening the pyramid and putting a team of people in charge of the Stockholm–New York flight from start to finish. The team has fifteen members, two of whom function as 'coaches', one indoors and one out by the plane. The indoor coach sits in on the flight crew's briefing and consults with them about preflight information such as the appropriate time to begin boarding, whether any infants or disabled people are on the passenger list, and whether anyone has ordered a special meal.

In the morning, the indoor team assembles at the check-in counters to solve passengers' ticketing problems, assign seats, hand fragile baggage and so forth. When a mother arrives with her baby, she is greeted with a smile and told that a suspended cradle has already been put on board and that the seat beside her will be kept free if at all possible.

When you arrive at check-in and ask about your vegetarian meal, you will not be hurriedly dismissed by the agent behind the counter. Thanks to the new team arrangement, your meal request becomes that agent's responsibility. She can confirm that it is already on board, or takes steps to make sure it is loaded by the time you step into the plane.

As more and more passengers check in, the SAS team gradually moves to the departure gate, where they nod to their passengers in recognition. They are well acquainted with the flight to New York and can answer all the usual questions: how to transfer from JFK to La Guardia, why there is a stopover in Oslo, the actual flight time and whether the captain will announce when they are flying over Greenland.

Problems are solved on the spot as soon as they arise. No
frontline employee has to wait for a supervisor's permission.
No passenger boards the plane while still worried or
dissatisfied. Furthermore, by giving more responsibility to the
frontline personnel, we are letting them provide the service
that they had wanted to provide all along but could not
because of an inflexible hierarchical structure.

Flattening the structure helps to eliminate the gap between customer
expectations and management perceptions of customer expectations. It
does so by:

- Increasing interaction between management and customers
- Improving upward communication from contact personnel to management
- Reducing the number of levels between contact personnel and
  management.[7]

Management should ask itself:

'To what extent does the structure create opportunities to experience first
hand what the customer wants?'

Customers should ask themselves:

'How easy is it to obtain access to a manager?'

Frontline employees should ask themselves:

'To what extent is upward communication encouraged? How often do
they see management? How often are their suggestions put into
practice?'

Frontline employees are often reticent about communicating up the
organization ladder. Several reasons for this have been given:

- Fear of losing their job
- Potential to have their job loads increased
- Their suspicion of wrong usage or under-utilization of the information they
  would provide.

Management in service organizations need to take a far greater interest
in upward communication. They need to take time to speak to employees
and find out what is required to do the job efficiently and effectively.

For service organizations, ongoing operational decisions should be
managed much lower down the organization, even to the point of the
frontline employee. Clearly the greatest competitive weapon in many

service industries is people and the way they are organized.[8] The organizational culture is critical for service organizations since so much of their activity involves human interactions. Operational decisions must still be guided by organizational policies, rules and procedures for no other reason than to facilitate smooth execution and maintain consistency.

However, service organizations need to demonstrate a willingness to depart from the 'rules' if by doing so it can be shown that customer satisfaction is achieved.

Organizational variables

According to Peters, Waterman and Phillips,[9] diagnosing and solving organizational problems means looking not merely to structural reorganization for answers but to a framework that includes structure and several related factors. Their research led to the view that any intelligent approach to organizing had to encompass, and treat as interdependent, at least seven variables:

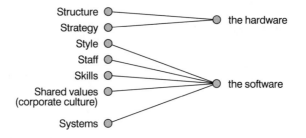

The objective was to get management to accept that the solution to understanding how organizations work lies as much in the software as it does in the hardware. For service organizations this is particularly appropriate as they are often people-intensive and the selection of particular procedures and commitment to certain values (corporate culture) play a prominent part in the final service delivered to the customer. As Peters, Waterman and Phillips[9] point out, if you want to understand how an organization really does (or does not) get things done, look at the systems (all the procedures, formal and informal, that make the organization go, day by day and year by year). How employees and customers feel they are treated is very much a reflection of organization design.

Corporate culture

Trying to understand and explain what happens in organizations can be a frustrating experience. The concept of corporate culture offers hope to the process of unravelling the mystique of organization life.

Numerous definitions of corporate culture have been proposed.[10] Here are a few:

- Observed behavioural regulations when people interact, such as the language used and the rituals around deference and demeanour
- The norms that evolve in working groups such as the particular norm of 'a fair day's work for a fair day's pay'
- The dominant values espoused by an organization such as the delivery of quality
- The philosophy that guides an organization's policy towards employees and/or customers
- The rules of the game for getting along in an organization, 'the ropes' that a newcomer must learn in order to become an accepted member
- The feeling or climate that is conveyed in an organization by the physical layout and the way in which members of the organization interact with customers or other outsiders.

All these meanings reflect the organization's culture, but the essence of culture is reserved for the deeper level of basic assumptions and beliefs that are shared by members of an organization, that operate unconsciously, and that define in a basic, taken for granted fashion, an organization's view of itself and its environment.

In brief, the corporate culture framework stresses:

- Values and assumptions prescribing what is important
- Beliefs on how things work
- Norms defining appropriate and inappropriate behaviour

For the new recruit to an organization to be told, 'This is how we do things around here', captures the notion of corporate culture in everyday language.

Types of organization culture

Culture is the key to understanding service.[11] An organization's cultural orientation will have implications for every aspect of its operations and its internal and external relationships. Organizations will have certain attitudes and styles of service.

However, the effect of culture is a separate matter from whether the service is 'good' or 'bad'. Services will differ in 'taste' and 'feel' and the definition of 'good' and 'bad' service will differ from one culture to another.

The goodness of a service must not be confused with its style.[11] A service may be warm, friendly and relaxed but that does not necessarily make it 'better' than a service which is fast, efficient and impersonal. The style of a service is very much determined by the type of service. For example, customers would expect a warm, friendly, relaxed service in a guest house. On the other hand, customers in a post office expect fast, efficient, impersonal service. One particular style does not need to be exclusively adopted. There may be a mix of styles used. It is really a question of selecting a style which is appropriate for the nature of the service. This in itself is often not an easy task. In the case of some services, for example education, disagreement may exist over which style of service to adopt.

Organizations have been classified in terms of cultural types.[12–15] No organization fits exclusively into one type. The major benefit, however, is that it helps us understand organizations. The crucial question is whether the typologies address the particular characteristics of service organizations. It has to be remembered that service organizations have the additional problem of consumers participating directly in the 'manufacture' of the output.

Cultural typologies that could represent service organizations are:

Culture	Characteristics and examples
Role	<ul><li>Large pyramid organizations</li><li>Authority based on place in hierarchy</li><li>Emphasis on roles and job titles</li><li>Fast, efficient systems designed to produce uniform and predictable outcomes</li><li>Rules and procedures predominate</li><li>Customers feel depersonalized</li><li>Uncaring, rigid, unresponsive, e.g. private and public utilities, government departments, banks.</li></ul>
Club	<ul><li>Small organization (less than 20 employees) where the owner exerts a strong influence</li><li>Emphasis on personal interaction rather than memos and meetings</li><li>Personality and speed of response often critical</li><li>Service delivery can be erratic and range from excellent to poor</li></ul>

- Demand can outstrip organization's capacity to cope, e.g. plumber, garage, hairdresser, guest house.

Task
- Organization is active and creative
- Dedicated to excellence, innovation, professional integrity
- Warm and friendly with little emphasis on hierarchy and procedure
- Challenging and questioning environment
- Staffed, usually, by young, clever energetic people, e.g. advertising agency, consulting firm.

Person
- Puts the individual rather than the organization first. Individual talent is all important
- Do not think in terms of 'organization and management'
- Employees can have considerable autonomy
- Can be chaotic, e.g. solicitor, accountant, university professor.

Support
- Compassionate, caring, responsive, receptive
- Listening to customers/clients, empathizing, responding to their concerns
- The essence of the support culture is 'what can we do for you?' e.g. the caring services like social work.

The nature of the service operation can therefore pigeonhole an organization. The National Health Service, however, is an interesting example of the clash of two cultures – the caring professionals and the business efficiency of the administrators.

The personal culture of the professionals like lawyers is giving way to more organizational disciplines. The support culture has historically been associated with the social services but any service organization or individuals within it can adopt the values of caring, responsiveness, receptivity and a sense of belonging.

Overall, what is clear is that regardless of the type of service there is a growing emphasis on areas such as organization, management, efficiency, budgets and performance measurement. Whether this means 'progress' toward a 'business culture' remains to be seen.

Role

In any organization people are required to undertake a role, e.g. supervisor, marketing manager, office secretary. The role represents the set of behaviours and activities to be performed by the person occupying that position. In service situations role behaviour is of added importance because:

- The customer is frequently in direct (face to face) or indirect (telephone) contact with organization employees
- The image of the organization is largely determined by how customers (actual or potential) are treated when, for example, making an enquiry or registering a complaint.

Much of the everyday activity of a service organization involves people. The role of the frontline team is crucial but so, equally, is that of the background personnel who are meant to provide support. Uncertainty about what one is expected to do and how one is expected to behave can be a problem for service organizations.

Consider the following expressions of feelings from service employees:[7]

> You feel like management doesn't know what you are doing. We need more support and regulation.
>
> They should give more recognition to people who are really performing. So many times you are judged by your immediate supervisor. That person may not like you. I wish other managers higher up, would know how people are performing.

If comments such as these are in any way typical, it is hardly surprising if employees take a cavalier, couldn't care less attitude to what their role should be.

The role set

The way in which a role is (or should be) performed is communicated through what is known as the role set (Figure 2.4). In trying to satisfy the various expectations and cope with the pressures and demands of the job, the catering assistant may experience role ambiguity and role conflict. Willingness and capacity to perform at an acceptable level may be reduced.

Role ambiguity

This refers to a condition where an individual e.g. the catering assistant or supervisor (see Figure 2.4) is uncertain about several matters relating to how to do a specific task, the scope of authority and responsibility, expectations of members of the role set and how performance is to be

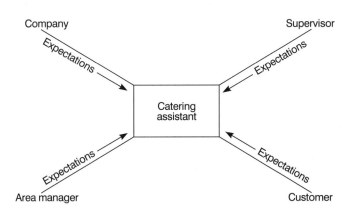

Figure 2.4 A role set for a catering assistant

evaluated and rewarded. The reduction or avoidance of ambiguity lies in providing proper training, keeping people well informed and giving feedback on performance and what is expected.

Role conflict

This refers to where an individual, in this case the catering assistant, experiences conflicting expectations from two or more members of the role set as to how the job should be performed (see Figure 2.4).

An individual may also experience conflict of another kind. A common example is when a friendship develops between the supervisor and the catering assistant. What the supervisor may be expected to do as a boss (e.g. be tough) may conflict with the behaviours expected as a friend (e.g. be sympathetic). In this case the supervisor is playing two roles and it may be difficult to fulfil the demands of both roles simultaneously.

Measurement of role ambiguity and role conflict

A more effective service can be provided for customers if role ambiguity and conflict are reduced. As a first step the organization must determine the magnitude of the problem. Items that exceed a score of 4 on the scale of 1 to 7 in Table 2.1 may warrant further investigation to establish the reasons for the ambiguity.

For role conflict the formats listed in Tables 2.2 and 2.3 may be used. Comparison of the scores of the employee and supervisor in Table 2.2 will determine the degree of conflict that exists between them.

A second format (Table 2.3) considers the extent to which frontline employees perceive any conflict between for example the supervisor and customers on how they (the frontline employees) should perform their role.

Table 2.1 Role ambiguity measurement

Item	I am certain/uncertain

1 About how I should perform my job in order to satisfy my supervisor
2 About how much authority I have
3 How my performance will be evaluated
4 About what activities in my job are most important to my manager
5 About what is expected of me
6 How much time I should spend socializing with customers
7 About company rules and regulations
8 How I should perform my job in order to satisfy my customers

Score of 1 means 'absolutely certain' and 7 means 'absolutely uncertain'

Table 2.2 Role conflict measurement

My supervisor expects me:	Employee					Supervisor				
	SA	A	N	DA	SDA	SA	A	N	DA	SDA
1 To enforce rules and regulations always										
2 To be completely honest with customers										
3 To have the knowledge to answer customers' questions										
4 To accept orders without question										
5 To think up better ways to do my job										

Scale: strongly agree (SA), agree (A), neutral (N), disagree (DA), strongly disagree (SDA)

Table 2.3 Role conflict measurement

Expectation	Perceived conflict				
	SA	A	N	D	SD
Be completely honest with customers					
Deal with complaints concerning my work performance					
Develop close relationships with customers					

Scale: strongly agree (SA), agree (A), neutral (N), disagree (D), strongly disagree (SD). The frontline employee, for example, is required to indicate whether he/she agrees/disagrees that the expectations of his/her role partners are in conflict.

For each statement employees would be asked to indicate their strength of agreement/disagreement on whether they perceive conflict between the supervisor and customers.

The above frameworks for measuring role ambiguity and conflict are simply illustrative. What is important is a willingness to investigate and act on the findings.

Role overload and underload

In addition to feelings of role ambiguity and conflict service personnel suffer from overload and underload.

- *Overload* Employees are required to do more work than they feel they can handle either in terms of the time allocated or the necessary skills and abilities to perform the job.
- *Underload* Employees spend part of their time doing nothing and the job is not felt to be mentally stimulating or challenging. (See Chapter 6 for further discussion of role.)

Defensive behaviour in organizations

Political and power-seeking behaviour is present in many organizations. For service organizations characterized by a great deal of human involvement and interaction, defensive, as distinct from offensive, behaviour is much in evidence. Understanding the reasons for defensive behaviour is not straightforward, but being aware of its existence may help explain why there is low efficiency, lack of customer loyalty and a poor image.

Customers and employees of service organizations should recognize many of the following defensive behaviours.[16]

Avoiding action

- *Overconforming* Action is often avoided by resorting to a strict interpretation of one's responsibility, e.g. 'The rules clearly say . . .' and citing supportive precedents, e.g. 'It's always been done this way'. Rigid adherence to rules can be potentially explosive in a service like social security. The situation may be defused by distancing oneself from the rules, e.g. 'I didn't make the rules', or 'Listen, if it were up to me . . .'
- *Passing the buck* Responsibility for doing something is passed to someone else, e.g. 'I'm too busy' or 'That's not my job'.

- *Playing dumb* Avoiding an unwanted task by falsely pleading ignorance or inability, e.g. 'I don't know anything about that . . .' or 'X is better able to handle that. . .'
- *Depersonalizing* Avoiding unwanted demands from clients or subordinates by treating them as objects or numbers rather than people, e.g. a doctor referring to hospital patients not by name but by their illness, talking about them in the third person, using medical terminology incomprehensible to patients, avoiding eye contact, and providing curt and patronizing answers to patients' questions.
- *Stretching* Prolonging a task so that one appears occupied or performing trivial tasks during slack periods in order to appear busy.
- *Smoothing* Masking fluctuations in effort or output to create the impression of steady productivity. Employees agree to work within specified minimum and maximum levels of output.
- *Stalling* Appearing more or less supportive publicly while doing nothing privately, e.g. a service situation where long queues are allowed to form to discourage use of the service.

Avoiding blame

- *Buffing* This term was coined to describe the practice of rigorously documenting activity or fabricating documents to project an image of competence and thoroughness. It is widely referred to as 'covering your ass'.
- *Playing safe* Avoiding situations that may reflect unfavourably on a person.
- *Justifying* Minimizing responsibility for a certain event by acknowledging partial responsibility and including some expression of remorse.
- *Scapegoating* Deflecting blame.
- *Misrepresenting* Avoiding blame by manipulating information.
- *Escalating commitment* Individuals responsible for a failing course of action often 'throw good money after bad' – the white elephant.

Avoiding change

People like to protect their own turf through actions like stalling, playing safe, overconforming, etc.

Explanation for defensive behaviour

There may be organizational and individual factors causing defensive behaviour.[16] Of particular relevance for service organizations are the following:

1. *Individual factors* Factors which may be of interest, though not exclusively to service organizations are insecurity and anxiety, emotional exhaustion and

work alienation. Employment in service organizations can be stressful due to the nature and amount of personal contact with customers. The full range of emotions must be held in check at least for frontline employees. Smiling and generally being nice is the rule. Work alienation stems from a lack of job involvement and identification with the organization. Many service occupations are simply 'dead-end jobs'. Service organizations, characterized by uncertainty and intensity of demand, are more of a pressure chamber than their manufacturing counterparts where a more orderly and less hectic routine is in evidence.

2. *Organizational factors*
   ● The specialization of tasks and formalization of rules and procedures in a bureaucracy encourage defensive-type behaviour. For example, specialization means people feel responsible for a specific, not the whole task, creating a tendency to pass the buck, play dumb, overconform and depersonalize. Formalization of rules and procedures tells people what they can and cannot do which again may promote overconforming, passing the buck, playing dumb and stalling.
   ● Defensive behaviour may, also be a means of coping with a work environment in which there is uncertainty felt over areas of responsibility and the interpretation and application of rules and procedures. People may feel that the demands of the work environment are just too great and a feeling of powerlessness only makes the capacity to cope even worse.

Organizations of the future

Charles Handy[17] sets forth his radical vision of organizations of the future. According to Handy, 'life in the core of more and more organizations is going to resemble that of consultancy firms, advertising agencies and professional partnerships. The organizations are flat, seldom with more than four layers of rank, the top one being the assembly of partners, professors or directors'. Handy envisages organizations becoming more like the shamrock. The first leaf represents the core workers made up of qualified professionals, technicians and managers who are essential to the organization. The second leaf is the contractual fringe which performs work not usual to the organization. They are paid for results not for time, in fees not wages. For example, an organization may arrange for a contractor to do much of their clerical work. The third leaf of the shamrock is the flexible labour force, all those part-time workers and temporary workers who are the fastest growing part of the employment scene. This is of particular interest for service organizations. They are not, in Handy's view, concerned about careers and job satisfaction. They will, however, require training, in some cases leading to a qualification, along with decent pay and conditions. A fourth leaf, proposed by Handy, should be of special interest to service organizations. Although not part of the formal organization structure, the practice of getting customers to do the work is growing fast. Many service organizations are now requiring customers to play a more prominent part in producing the service. Handy, perhaps optimistically, believes that all organizations will soon be shamrock organizations.

Summary

To obtain a picture of an organization the first thing we usually refer to is the organization chart. Although it is an obvious starting point, we need to 'dig much deeper' if we wish to increase our understanding of how organizations work.

For services the development of an appropriate culture is important given the numerous and direct interactions with customers. The 'way we do things around here' requires explanation and justification if we are to encourage debate about 'creating a customer-centred culture in service organizations'.

References

1. Quinn, J. B. and Paquette, P. C. (1990) 'Technology in services: creating organisational revolutions', *Sloan Management Review* (Winter), 67–87.
2. Bell, C. R. and Zemke, R. (1988) 'Do service procedures tie employees' hands?' *Personnel Journal*, September, 77–83.
3. Burnes, B. (1991) 'Barriers to organizational change: the role of culture', *Management Research News*, **14**(1/2), 24–29.
4. Peters, T. J. (1987) *Thriving on Chaos*, Knopf, New York.
5. Drucker, P. (1954) *The Practice of Management*, Harper & Row, New York.
6. Carlzon, J. (1989) *Moments of truth*, Harper & Row, New York.
7. Zeithaml, V. A., Parasuraman, A. and Berry, L. L. (1990) *Delivering Quality Service*, Free Press, New York.
8. Heskett, J. L., Sasser, W. E. and Hart, C. W. L. (1990) *Service Breakthroughs*, Free Press, New York.
9. Peters, T. J., Waterman, R. H. and Phillips, J. R. (1980) Structure is not organisation, *Business Horizons*, June.
10. Schein, E. H. (1985) *Organisational Culture and Leadership*, Jossey-Bass, San Francisco, CA.

11. Harrison, R. (1990) *Organisation Culture and Quality of Service: A Strategy for Releasing Love in the Workplace*, Association for Management Education and Development, London.
12. Mills, P. K. and Marguilies, N. (1980) 'Toward a core typology of service organisations', *Academy of Management Review*, **5**(2), 255–265.
13. Handy, C. B. (1978) *Understanding Organisations*, Penguin, London.
14. Harrison, R. (1972) 'Understanding organisations' character', *Harvard Business Review*, **5**(3), 119–128.
15. Mintzberg, H. (1991) 'The effective organisation: forces and forms', *Sloan Management Review*, Winter, 54–67.
16. Ashforth, B. E. and Lee, R. T. (1990) 'Defensive behaviour in organisations: a preliminary model, *Human Relations*, **43**(7), 621–648.
17. Handy, C. B. (1991) *The Age of Unreason*, Business Books, London.

Chapter 3

Service design

Introduction

Services require an operating and delivery system in order to function. That system should be designed in such a way as to offer effective customer service through an efficiently operated process. Needless to say, the drive to achieve efficiency and effectiveness can become unstuck to the detriment of provider and/or customer. Whatever the service, the basic design question will always be 'How should it be operated and delivered to the customer?' Design formats can, of course, vary with the type of service and even within a particular service there may be different approaches to what constitutes the best design. Whatever is decided, the design in effect is the service.

The customer mix

However, before the design of the service can take place, the marketer must decide which customers he or she will serve. Which segment of the population is the marketer aiming to satisfy? The selection of a target market is perhaps the most critical decision that is made in the design of a service.

The process that should be adopted for customer group selection depends on the current market situation. If there is no similar service already available then there is more scope for choice. The brand map lies empty. The organization proposing to launch the service will attempt to match the skills and capacity of the company with the needs of a group of consumers. The choice of customer group will, for the majority of companies, be driven by the profit motive.

In consumer services a mass market approach is often taken, e.g. high street banks and fast-food shops. In these instances the company has decided that it can function most profitably by offering a relatively undifferentiated service to a wide target market.

There is an opportunity to adopt this targeting strategy in many consumer markets. The target market may vary significantly in terms of demographics or psychographics. However, many of these differences evaporate when it comes to the variables that are key to the selection of a brand in that particular market. A supermarket may hope to attract most of the population living or working near the store. The key variable here is that of convenience, regardless of the individual's age or lifestyle.

Note that we have said in mass markets the company will offer a *relatively* undifferentiated offering. The volume of consumer demand can support a number of service companies. However, in order to survive each individual company needs to achieve a competitive advantage. The way in which each company strives for this will often affect the type of customer that it attracts. To take the example of food retailing, offering quality produce will often have a price implication (Marks & Spencer). While their concept will still have broad appeal it is probably most attractive to affluent consumers or those to whom convenience is very important.

Therefore, even in mass markets, there is generally some degree of segmentation. The competing companies will occupy different spaces on any brand map. So what makes a company select a particular group of customers? There are two key factors. First, the company believes that it can deliver what the customer wants. Second, from its understanding of the market there is a gap to be filled. For many services the opportunities presented allow the company to serve a mix of customers. Rail operators offer all their customers the same core benefit, namely safe and reliable transport. It makes the most efficient use of its resources by segmenting the travelling public and tailoring its service offering to meet their needs more precisely, e.g. pensioners and businessmen will have differing needs.

Design elements

In designing any service, eleven key factors should be taken into account.

Customer contact

● How much contact will the customer have with the service and what will the nature of that contact be?

Service mix

● What service will be provided in terms of breadth and depth? Breadth equals the number of items in each line; for example, a local authority sports and leisure service may offer the following service lines (breadth): outdoor sports, indoor sports, adventure sports and leisure activities. Within the last mentioned might be art galleries, theatres, museums and parks (depth).

Location of service consumption

- Will the customer come to a service facility (single- or multi-site) or will the service come to the customer (at home or mobile)?

Design of service facility and accessories

- What should the layout, furnishing, colours, etc. of the facility be?
- What design discussions need to be made in respect of staff (uniforms), vehicles (colour, logo), and non-personal communication (letterheadings, signs, brochures, etc.)?

Technology

- What will be the balance between technology and people, e.g. how will it apply to the employee's work and the customer's usage of the service?
- Will the technology be predominantly hard, e.g. automation or soft, e.g. pre-planned systems – pre-packaged tours?

Employees

- How many will be required?
- What will the ratio be between full-time and part-time?
- What will be the ratio between back-office and front-office employees?
- How many supervisors will be required to control frontline employees?
- What skills will be needed and how will they be acquired?
- How flexible will employees need to be?

Organization structure

- How many layers in the organization are desirable?
- How should the finance, operations, personnel and marketing functions be organized?

Information

- What information is desirable for running the organization and how easily will it be acquired?
- How will it be stored?
- How accessible will it be and who will have access?

Demand and supply management

- How much knowledge is there about demand patterns and levels?
- What strategies are known for influencing demand?
- How flexible is capacity for meeting demand fluctuations, e.g. work schedules, sub-contracting, reservation systems, stock control?

Procedures

- Will the service be mainly standardized or customized?
- How complex will the service be?

Control

- What systems will be in place and what techniques will be available for ensuring the smooth running of the operation and the provision of quality output, e.g. critical path analysis, forecasting methods, flow charts, queueing theory application?

The above listing is by no means exhaustive. Its main purpose is to signal areas that need to be addressed. Larger organizations generally adopt a more strategic approach to the area of design. The design of smaller companies' operating systems will bear the stamp of the owner's personality.

Operating systems classification

The design elements must be combined to deliver outputs required by customers. How they are combined has given rise to a particular classification of service organizations. A possible drawback is that the classification has drawn heavily on types of manufacturing organizations. For example, services can be classified depending on the extent of client contact and customization, and the degree of labour intensity. Service operating systems are said to exhibit the characteristics of a factory, mass production and a job shop. The actual terms used are service factory, mass service, service shop and professional service. The classification is as follows:[1,2]

Service factory – low in personal interaction and customization and labour intensity, e.g. airlines, hotels, resorts and recreation.

Mass service – low in personal interaction and customization and high in labour intensity, e.g. retailing, schools, retail banking.

Service shop – high in personal interaction and customization and low in labour intensity, e.g. restaurants, hospitals, car and other repair services.

Professional service – high in personal interaction and customization and high in labour intensity, e.g. doctors, lawyers, accountants.

Such a classification provides a useful basis for discussing design options in operational systems. However, problems remain:

1 It is not particularly enlightening to draw a distinction between a factory and a mass service. They are not mutually exclusive. A factory is a place where various forms of production can take place, e.g. flow production, batch production and including mass production of service. One is simply a place where various processes may occur and the other is one example of the possible processes.
2 There is no breakdown of the different processes and how relevant they may be for services. For example, flow processing systems are more characteristic of patients going through various departments of a hospital or students going through various stages in a college course. Batch processing on the other hand occurs in certain services in which availability and operation occur only when a given number or minimum number of customers are available, e.g. some entertainment services and guided bus tours.
3 The service shop is derived from its manufacturing equivalent, the job shop, where small individual orders are processed from a variety of customers. Jobs are meant to be ordered in priority and resources scheduled accordingly. However, there is no uniformity of operation across all the services that could fall into this category. Consider the contrast in operational characteristics of two services, car repair and restaurant, regarded as examples of service shops (Table 3.1). There is a greater likelihood of the garage experiencing difficulties in designing a system that will operate and deliver a service efficiently and effectively.
4 Even within the existing classification there will be argument over the examples; not only about where they are allocated but also the assumption that each service type is homogeneous, i.e. all hotels are alike, all restaurants are alike. Within any particular service, say hotels, one needs to consider:

   ● The design options in terms of operating and delivery systems
   ● Should service design be broadly similar across all hotels or is there scope for different structures.

5 Labour intensity is calculated as a cost of capital to cost of labour ratio. According to this method services like hospitals, which are thought to be very labour intensive, are in fact relatively low in labour intensity due to the

Table 3.1 Two 'service shops': a contrast in operational characteristics

Characteristics	Garage (car repair)	Restaurant
Customer access to 'production area' creating disruption	✓	
Unpredictability surrounding customer appearance (at the facility) and service requirements	✓	
Loyal customers can 'jump the queue'	✓	
Difficulties in allocating and scheduling capacity and employee skills	✓	

✓ = greater likelihood of occurring

very expensive equipment involved. The basis for calculating the ratio, namely cost, is not, however, an ideal way of revealing the respective roles of equipment and personnel in delivering the service. It is an economist's or accountant's approach that lends itself to measurement. More effort needs to be directed towards examining the contribution that equipment and personnel make to delivering customer satisfaction. The capital-ratio should not be regarded solely as a financial equation. It could act as a basis for deciding the proper balance of resources in achieving efficiency and meeting customer needs.

The front and back offices

Whatever decision is made in respect of a design classification, service organizations must address the issue of front- and back-office allocations.

The front office – that part of the system directly experienced and visible to the customer. This is where the service is performed and is thereby open to customer scrutiny, e.g. the hotel dining room.

The back office – that part of the system from which the customer is excluded, e.g. the hotel kitchen. It is often referred to as the manufacturing side of the service, not seen by the customer. However, there are instances, e.g. banks, building societies, where the back office is visible to the customer. This means that often the technical core of an organization (commonly referred to as the production process) is sealed off from any uncertainties that may occur in other parts of the organization. This is known as 'decoupling'.[3] The back office becomes separated from the front office and is allowed to work without hindrance or interference. The main objective is to enable efficiency to be maximized in the 'production processes'.

Striking the right balance between front- and back-office responsibilities can be a difficult exercise and one that many service organizations fail to achieve. As Wostenholme[4] argues, 'There is a "back office" mentality currently permeating service operations thinking. The front office is seen as a complex interactive process where the customer is variable and unpredictable. The back office, on the other hand, is controllable and affords labour cost savings by restricting the number of customer contact personnel. Further, the degree and type of customer contact is progressively moving towards the "hard" forms of contact as witnessed by the introduction of ATM's and mechanical ticket machines'. The precarious future for the front office is reflected in his comment that, 'There is undoubtedly a clearly definable trend towards the distancing of the service organisation from the source of its wealth – the customer'.

What all this means is that in the drive for operational efficiency and control (back-office supremacy), service organizations run the risk of neglecting customer expectations of what constitutes a satisfactory experience (front-office impoverishment).

A key factor in the debate over front-versus back-office dominance is customer contact. Chase[5] asserts that, 'The potential efficiency of a service system is a function of the degree of customer contact entailed in the creation of the service product'. He proposes a formula which states that:

$$\text{Potential facility efficiency} = f\left(1 - \frac{\text{Customer contact time}}{\text{Service creation time}}\right)$$

If we apply the formula hypothetically in two contrasting service situations, hotels (high customer contact) and the social security office (low customer contact), the efficiency measure might be

$$\text{For hotels: } 1 - \frac{2 \text{ hours}}{4 \text{ hours}} = 50\% \text{ efficiency}$$

$$\text{For social security office: } 1 - \frac{0.25 \text{ hours}}{2 \text{ hours}} = 87.5\% \text{ efficiency}$$

The ratio of customer contact time relative to service creation time is obviously much greater in the case of hotels but does that mean that they are that much less efficient? Furthermore, if the hotel was to take an 'inefficient 8 hours' to create the service, the resulting efficiency index would be 75 per cent! The nature, as well as the amount, of customer contact merits attention. Customer input to the hotel facility could be defined as rather passive, whereas a relatively low contact organization like a social security office may experience a significant degree of uncertainty in the form of customer disruption.

The author of the formula cited above (Chase) has subsequently reconsidered its value. The original view argued for shifting service activities to a remote back office in order to maximize efficiency. He now states:[6]

> This, after all, seemed to work well for manufacturers because it kept outside influences, that is, customers, from disturbing the production process. If a technician is assembling a widget, you don't want the customer asking him what he's doing. Or if a clerk is processing forms, talking to the customer on the phone takes her away from her job. In retrospect, this closed system philosophy overlooked the fact that there are positive benefits to both the customer and the organization by having the customer closely linked to the server, even though the job is traditionally performed in the customer's absence. From an information exchange perspective, the greater the links between consumer and producer, the easier it is to understand and respond to the customer's needs.

Whatever its deficiencies the customer contact model does represent an important advance in the thinking about service design. The extent of customer contact (whether passive or active) can have an effect on shaping the design elements listed above. In addition, it encourages development of strategies for improving and/or reducing customer contact. For example a number of widely used, commonsense heuristics have been suggested.[7]

Contact improvement

- 'Take a number' systems
- Assign contact workers who are people-oriented and knowledgeable about service system processes and policies
- Maintain consistent work hours
- Partition back office from the public service counter; do not permit work breaks in front of the customer
- Provide queueing, patterns and signs to indicate standardized and customized service channels.

Contact reduction

- Handle only exceptions on a face-to-face basis; all other transactions by phone, or better still by mail
- Use reservations or appointments-only systems
- Decentralize using kiosks with one person for information handling (this takes pressure off the main facility)
- Use drop-off points such as automatic teller machines
- Bring service to customer through postal rounds or mobile offices
- Use a roving greeter or signs outside the facility to act as buffers and information providers

As already mentioned, the Chase approach has been criticized for concentrating on the amount of customer contact. Furthermore, there is a suggestion that it offers little guidance on how to coordinate back- and front-office operations, and fails to consider customer input in the design of service work. These issues have been addressed by examining how varying forms of co-production by employees and customers affect the design and coordination of service systems. The service design options are determined by the existence and combinations of the following concepts.[8]

- Input uncertainty – refers to the service organization's incomplete knowledge of what the customer is going to bring to the service and how he or she is likely to behave during the service encounter.
- Customer willingness to participate – refers to how far customers wish to play an active part in the service. Customers' capacity to become involved can be limited by lack of knowledge, skills and understanding their role.
- Diversity of demands – refers to the uniqueness of customers' demands. Are they to be met in a customized or standardized way?
- Interdependencies – refers to different patterns with respect to division of service work (between front and back office and customer) and customization versus standardization of service actions and interdependencies.

Four service design options can now be constructed (Figure 3.1). A brief explanation of each follows:

- Sequential standardized service design – a customer-dominated design in which they serve themselves after service employees have provided the goods and facilities needed for self-service. It is a standardized service in which the front and back office can be decoupled to allow for efficient delivery of service.

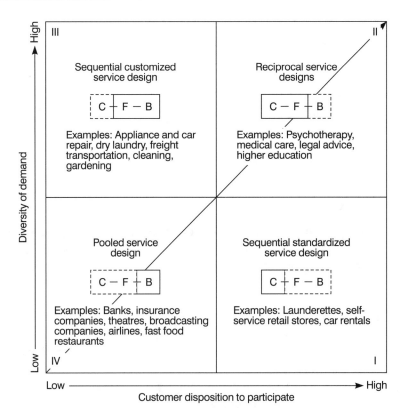

Figure 3.1 A typology of service interdependence patterns matching input uncertainty. C = customers, F = front-office employee(s), B = back-office employee(s). □ = main locus of interdependence, [ ] = supporting interdependencies. *Source*: Larsson and Bowen (1989)[8]

- Reciprocal service design – joint participation of the parties 'in which the output of each becomes the input for the others'.[3] The service is produced largely on the basis of significant interactions between front-office employees and customers.
- Sequential customized service design – the bulk of the work here is performed by the service employees in a system of strong interdependence between back and front offices.
- Pooled service design – most of the work done by an efficient back office, largely decoupled from front-office disturbances. Customers do not interact extensively with service employees but engage in the sharing of resources that makes mass service possible.

The examples given in Figure 3.1 are only examples of services that typically apply the service design illustrated. For example, it could be argued that banks, particularly at branch level, exhibit some of the characteristics of quadrant III. Equally there is sometimes a tendency for some services not to comply with what is deemed an appropriate design, e.g. customers in quadrant II might suggest that the back office plays a much greater role in reality. Recent suggestions to make social security offices open plan can be regarded as a radical departure from established approaches to service design.

Service blueprint

A service blueprint is basically a flowchart of the service process. It is a map in which all the elements or activities, their sequencing and interaction, can be visualized. There are a number of essential steps in blueprinting a service.[9]

- Draw, in diagrammatic form, all the components and processes (Figure 3.2). The service in this case is simple and clearcut and the map is straightforward. More complex services may require large, complicated diagrams.
- Identify the fail points – where might things go wrong? In Figure 3.2 the shoeshiner may pick up the wrong wax.

Figure 3.2 Blueprint for a corner shoeshine. *Source*: Shostack (1984).[9]
Reproduced by permission of *Harvard Business Review*, © 1984 by the President and Fellows of Harvard College. All rights reserved

- Set executional standards – these are tolerancies (band or range) set around each function and regarded as acceptable from a customer and cost viewpoint. Time is a good example. In Figure 3.2 the standard execution time is two minutes, and research showed that the customer would tolerate up to five minutes before lowering his assessment of quality.
- Identify all the evidence (see Chapter 4) that is available to the customer. Each item represents an encounter point.
- Analyse profitability – delays in service execution through errors or working too slowly affects profit. The shoeshiner estimates the cost of delay; anything greater than four minutes execution time and he loses money.

Consider the application and value of blueprinting for a car repair service. The perspective is that of a customer using it for the first time (Figure 3.3). Prior to making the initial contact with the garage (phoning for appointment and arrival at the garage) the customer will have formed some expectations from, for example, word-of-mouth and advertising. The telephone call and particularly arrival at the garage will go some way towards confirming or contradicting the customer's expectations, and are in fact more powerful tools once he has made contact. The customer will use various pieces of evidence (telephone response time and manner, attitudes and appearance of proprietor/employees, equipment and layout etc.) as clues to the likely quality of service. Making assumptions about service quality from the type of evidence mentioned above is understandable but has the potential to mislead. The seemingly chaotic, untidy garage manned by employees covered in oil and possessing little by way of modern equipment may be perceived as likely to render a poor service. Yet the opposite may be nearer the truth.

The diagnosis represents an encounter point where the customer may, for example, describe symptoms to assist in determining the problem. It is critical in the sense that promises made to the customer and the resource implications of the job are determined on the basis of the diagnosis. If the diagnosis is subsequently found to be incorrect, relationships with the customer may be impaired. After the initial diagnosis the customer will depart, without ever seeing the repair section.

Where the organization draws the line of visibility, distinguishing the front office from the back office, is of some significance for service organizations. The nature of the service and how it is delivered offers guidance on where to draw the line, e.g. a hairdresser's operation will be predominantly front office, while a credit card company operates a very large percentage of its service in the back office. Other services like a restaurant may feel ambivalent about where to draw the line separating the front and back office.

In making the distinction a service organization needs to address the following questions:

- How much of the service does the customer need to witness/experience?
- Will greater involvement lead to more understanding and favourable impressions, i.e. improved effectiveness?
- What effect will there be on efficiency if the customer is allowed greater access to the service process?

As already mentioned earlier in the chapter, a delicate balance may have to be struck between the need for efficiency and the desirability of customer involvement. In the case of the car repair business, allowing the customer to experience the service may create minimum disruption in terms of efficiency but maximum reward in terms of customer education and understanding.

The repair process in Figure 3.3 is sealed off from the customer but the objective must be to schedule work, deploy the necessary skills and arrange the timely availability of parts in order that promises made to the customer can be achieved.

On paper this is a good example of the construction of a service blueprint. Undertaking such an exercise provides an opportunity for the service provider to take a fresh look at the service and how it works. Stephen H. Baum, vice president of Booz, Allen and Hamilton Inc, New York, believes three factors are critical to making a pay-off.[10]

> The value delivered: what customers perceive they have actually received. The service mix: the features and levels of service the customers really care about. Plans and budgets: signals they send employees that are consistent or inconsistent with what management is trying to do.

He cites the example of a fast-food business intent on cost savings in the kitchen which was convinced that automation would result in cost reduction. 'But they were wrong', Baum said. The issue, according to Baum was not automation, but labour and time management. His analysis led him to the conclusion that 'Employees spend a lot of time waiting, walking, and doing other things that customers did not perceive as adding value. Much of the problem was caused by equipment choices, process sequences, and layout – not by employee performance'. Baum was able to show, through blueprinting, that automation would actually increase idle time and that by focusing on value-added time major reductions of in-store labour could be effected.

Blueprinting, then, can be regarded as a valuable and versatile tool in systems design. Its deployment can range from the simple design of a

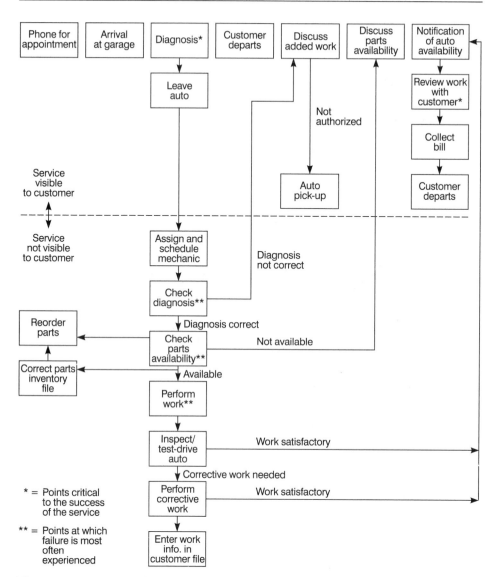

Figure 3.3 A process flow diagram for the auto repair business. *Source*: Heskett, Saser and Hart (1990)[11]

hotel bathroom through to monitoring the process flow of an important and confidential company document.[11] In developing a service blueprint it is worthwhile considering 'Who does what, to/with whom, how often, and under what conditions'.[12] Whatever the process under scrutiny the aim must always be improvements in service operation that will both deliver customer satisfaction and utilize organizations' resources efficiently. Improving the capacity, ability and willingness to serve must always be the expressed goal of any service organization. It will not be an easy task as the process moves away from the standardized design of a fast-food restaurant where time is the major design element. Clearly, performance standards, in terms of response time, are easier to set than, for example, degree of care and attention required by employees in other service situations. Of equal importance is the establishment of critical or pressure points and fail points. In many cases these are the 'moments of truth' for the customer and any vulnerability to breakdown must of necessity be minimized.

From an organizational culture perspective the blueprint allows all the employees to see their role in the process. Such an approach may bring to the surface previously unspoken tensions, but at the same time it can give, particularly the frontline employees, a voice in how the service should be delivered. Far too often the customer contact employees are simply left to 'carry out orders'. It may well be, as a result of a blueprinting exercise that the way these orders are carried out requires drastic overhauling. Management can be criticized, sometimes, for thinking they know best. Mapping out the process is as much a test of the validity and endorsement of management's belief as to how things do or should work.

A process cannot be improved until there is a clear understanding of how it works. There may well be different viewpoints as to how a process should be performed and monitored. It is advisable, therefore, that the views of management, employees and even customers should be solicited. Several types of information must be gathered and in so doing a distinction drawn between peoples' perceptions of the existing processes and their suggestions for improvement.

The areas for investigation should be:

- Process activities
- Information required to perform the process
- Products generated by the process, e.g. documents, services, etc.
- People and equipment required to perform the process
- Documents that direct how the process is to be accomplished.

Service design strategy

In the future, choice, if that is the correct word in the context of service design options will be between technology and people. As far back as 1972, Levitt[13] was berating the service sector for thinking in humanistic rather than technocratic terms. He argued that companies need to 'stop thinking of service as servitude and personal ministration if they are to effect drastic improvements in quality and efficiency'. The example of McDonald's is used to stress the benefits of an industrial mode of thinking. In effect, 'the systematic substitution of equipment for people, combined with the carefully planned use and positioning of technology, enables McDonald's to attract and hold patronage in proportions no predecessor or imitator has managed to duplicate'. The discretion and availability of service are replaced by standardization, predictability and control. Some may view the application of the McDonald's model as inapplicable at best and frightening at worst. It is, nevertheless, a constant reminder for service organizations that efficiency improvements may only be secured at the cost of the personal touch. Whether or not there is a commensurate increase in effectiveness is somewhat more problematic and one to which Levitt does not pay sufficient attention.

Technology, whether hard or soft, is being increasingly adopted by service organizations and without a doubt it does bring advantages. However, there should always be a place for the 'personal ministration' so ridiculed by Levitt.

Another 'choice' for service organizations is between greater customer or service provider input in the production process. Designing service in such a way that the customer is given a greater role can lead to benefits in terms of costs, speed and convenience. The technology that Levitt talked about is enabling this to happen. The ultimate expression of customer involvement is self-service in which the customer undertakes most of the tasks required to produce the service.

Finally, a strategic change on the part of a service organization will necessitate some adjustments to the operating system. For example a fast-food restaurant broadening its product mix may require staff training, changes in layout and revision in stock control. A garage wishing to improve the quality of its engine tuning service may involve the purchase of expensive equipment. The ambulance service has, over the years, made strategic changes in the service it offers the public and this has meant, for example, the purchase of mobile cardiac units and the development of paramedic skills. This last example raises another important point; design issues arise regardless of whether the customer comes to the service organization, the organization goes to the customer, or the service is delivered at arm's length. In fact one could argue that these are by definition design options. Refer back to service design elements and think about just how many design options there may be, not only for each element but combinations of the various elements. Service design can range from the simple and straightforward where the process is pre-packaged and standardized to the complex and variable where the process is subject to variety and customization. The options may apply to services as a whole or different parts within a particular service.

Although the design alternatives appear to be limitless, there will often be a trade-off between efficiency maximization and customer need satisfaction. Design options will also be increasingly influenced by developments in information technology. This, along with the degree and nature of customer involvement, will be the service design issues of the future.

Summary

Selecting a system is a subject of design and to arrive at a choice a range of elements must be considered. There have been, for a long time, several systems in operation. They have been developed in the manufacturing sector and attempts to apply them in services has been difficult. The problem is essentially one of finding the correct variables or characteristics that will allow service systems to be classified in design terms.

One feature that is particularly helpful in design is the idea of a front and back office. Service providers are often confronted with the dilemma of where to draw the line between operational efficiency and customer contact, the latter being a key consideration in any design decision.

The service blueprint is a valuable tool for specifying the precise details of a service. It enables the provider to determine critical/fail points the existence of which can often be attributed to a design fault.

The future for service design strategy will be between technology and people and whether services adopt a more production-line approach.

Appendix: A procedure for blueprinting a service

Select a relatively simple service, ideally one you have experience of (are familiar with) as employee and/or customer. To facilitate understanding of the process, you will probably need to draw upon the knowledge/ experiences of management, employees and customers.

Part I: Drawing a service blueprint

You will develop a blueprint of the process steps involved in creating and delivering the service you have selected. Keep your blueprint as simple as possible.

- Show the process for delivering the intended service outcome; e.g. answer the questions 'What happens first, second, third, etc.?' and 'Who performs each step or makes each decision?'.

- Which parts of the service process work well, and why?
- Where do things 'go wrong' (break down) in the service delivery, and why?
- How well does the service process deliver the key dimensions of service quality, i.e. tangibles, reliability, responsiveness, assurance, empathy?
- What measures or indicators are used/should be used to evaluate overall performance, e.g. levels of customer and employee satisfaction, revenue/profit/usage, etc.?

Part II: Interpreting the service map

After you have drawn the map, the next step is interpreting the service process. The following issues are simply illustrative of those you may wish to address.

- Customer expectations: What can be said, in general, about the level of service customers *desire* and the level of service customers find *acceptable*? How is management planning to address this gap?
- Customer role: How involved is the customer in the production and delivery of the service? How would you characterize the nature of that involvement?
- Employee role (particularly frontline): What skills/competencies are needed (required) versus what skills/competencies do employees actually have? How is management planning to address the gap – e.g. with training, better employee selection practices, improve/simplify the service process (perhaps through technology)? How would you characterize the quality of the work environment? Consider such issues as training, pay, supervision, physical environment, etc. as explanatory variables.
- Procedures: Are they standardized or customized?
- Technology: How significant a role does it play in the process? What impact does it have on customers? On employees?
- Organizational culture: Consider the phrase 'This is the way we do things around here' by asking 'Is there a better way to deliver the service?' Where are the areas of organizational resistance to innovative service delivery ideas?

Summary

In sum, first you will be attempting to explain 'What is involved in delivering this service – i.e. What is the *actual* service process?' Then you will attempt to explain *why* the service system operates the way it does. Finally, you will offer your judgement regarding how effectively the prevailing modus operandi meets customer requirements. You may choose to offer suggestions as to how the service process might be modified to bring it into better alignment with customer requirements.

References

1. Maister, D. H. and Lovelock, C. H. (1982) 'Managing facilitator services', *Sloan Management Review*, Summer, 19–31.
2. Schmenner, R. W. (1986) 'How can service businesses survive and prosper?' *Sloan Management Review*, Spring, 21–32.
3. Thompson, J. D. (1967) *Organisations in Action*, McGraw-Hill, New York.
4. Wolstenholme, S. M. (1988) 'The consultant customer – a new use for the customer in service operations,' *Proceedings of the Operations Management Association Annual International Conference*, University of Warwick, pp. 192–203.
5. Chase R. B. and Tansik, D. A. (1983) 'The customer contact model for organisation design,' *Management Science*, **29**(9), September, 1037–1050.
6. Chase R. B. and Hayes R. H. (1991) 'Beefing up operations in service firms', *Sloan Management Review* (Fall).
7. Chase, R. B. (1981) 'The customer contact approach to services: theoretical bases and practical extensions', *Operations Research* **29**(4), 698–705.
8. Larsson, R. and Bowen, D. E. (1989) 'Organisation and customer managing design and coordination of services', *Academy of Management Review*, **14**(2), 213–233.
9. Shostack, G. L. (1984) 'Designing services that deliver', *Harvard Business Review* January–February, 133–139.
10. Quoted in Coleman, L. G. (1989) 'Blueprint gets foundation for better service and customer satisfaction', *Marketing News*, **23**(26), 18 December, 24.
11. Heskett, J. L., Sasser, W. and Hart, C. W. L. (1990) *Service Breakthroughs*, Free Press, New York.
12. Kingmann-Brundage, J. (1989) 'Blueprinting for the bottom line', *Proceedings of AMA Annual Services Marketing Conference*.
13. Levitt, T. (1972) 'Production-line approach to service', *Harvard Business Review*, September–October, 41–52.

Chapter 4

The service setting

Introduction

The setting and surroundings in which a service is delivered can be vital. It shapes expectations since it is the first tangible clue that the consumer is given about potential service delivery.

The control by the designer of corporate elements that form interior spaces can impact on the success of that delivery in a variety of ways. It can influence the client's or customer's perception of the particular service sector and can enhance the function, appropriateness and ambience of the activity.

It is important to regard design in terms of the possibilities it has to offer marketing. Every situation is unique and a 'painting by numbers' approach to design is inappropriate.

The service setting framework

On viewing and subsequently entering a bank, hotel, restaurant, or solicitor's office, customers will have reflected consciously or subconsciously on some or all of the following:

- What does the exterior say about what is on offer inside?
- Does it communicate, clearly, anything about the nature of the service?
- What does the interior communicate in terms of atmosphere?
- What mood/feeling is evoked?
- How is one expected to behave?

Many service providers have not given elaborate consideration to how the design of the service setting may affect consumer feelings and responses.

Unfortunately, there are no ten commandments which would determine how a service setting should or should not be designed. From the customers' viewpoint it is still very much a matter of taste coupled with perceptions of what is appropriate. Nevertheless, just as companies want to know how and why customers respond to packaging, price, product, advertising, service organizations should develop understanding of customer responses to layout, furnishings, colour, light etc. Research should focus on overall impressions and feelings (Table 4.1) followed by an investigation of specific environmental ones.

The atmospheres displayed in Table 4.1 generate an expected response. The wider questions are:

- Does the environmental design always bring about the appropriate response?
- What is meant by 'elegance, professionalism, welcoming etc.'?
- What aspects of the environment convey such atmospheres?
- How should a solicitor's office, hairdresser, hospital, advertising agency, social security office appear?
- Are there limits (in a cultural rather than physical sense) on design options for particular services?
- If there are limits, how severe should they be?

Specific environmental cues should be subjected to user evaluation. Research must reveal:

- What is important/unimportant
- What is liked/disliked
- How various aspects are rated on a scale of excellent through to poor.

User's attitudes and perceptions can be gathered by open-ended discussion and/or measurement of scales. The following list is a sample of the kind of topics that could be covered:

Table 4.1 Atmosphere and feelings

Environmental atmosphere generated	Reaction in terms of customer feelings
Elegance	Status
Professionalism	Trust, security
Welcoming	Happiness, enjoyment
Sombre	Depressed, gloomy
Forbidding	Anxious
Warmth	Comfort
Lively	Inviting

- How adequate is the space? Does it lead to overcrowding and is this desirable or stressful?
- What is the effect of the layout on safety?
- How appropriate is the layout for the activity involved?
- Is the temperature comfortable or uncomfortable?
- Is the noise unobtrusive or uncomfortable?
- Is the lighting adequate?

The primary objective would be the determination of relationships between environmental conditions and behavioural outcomes.

Drawing on developments in decision making in which customers were responding to more than simply the tangible product or service, Kotler[1] proposed that atmospherics be regarded as an important marketing tool. He suggests that, 'In many areas of marketing in the future, marketing planners will use spatial aesthetics as consciously and skilfully as they now use price, advertising, personal selling, public relations and other tools of marketing'. He maintains the atmosphere of a place affects purchase behaviour in three ways:

1 As an attention-creating medium – use of colours, noise etc. to make it stand out.
2 As a message-creating medium – communicating with the intended audience, level of concern for customers etc.
3 As an affect-creating medium – use of colours, sounds etc. to create or heighten an appetite for certain goods, services or experiences.

Kotler concludes with an example of antique retailing. It would seem that there is more to atmospherics than meets the eye!

> Many antique dealers also make use of 'organizational chaos' as an atmospheric principle for selling their wares. The buyer enters the store and sees a few nice pieces and a considerable amount of junk. The nice pieces are randomly scattered in different parts of the store. The dealer gives the impression, through his prices and his talk, that he doesn't really know values. The buyer therefore browses quite systematically, hoping to spot an undiscovered Old Master hidden among the dusty canvasses of third rate artists. He ends up buying something that he regards as a value. Little does he know that the whole atmosphere has been arranged to create a sense of hidden treasures.

Supermarkets, of course, have known for some time, that consumption behaviour can be manipulated by the judicious use of lighting, space etc.

What this means is that when planning the design of a service setting, service providers should have in mind a framework that will assist debate over the impact of the physical surroundings.[2] They should consider this design in terms of the three headings in Figure 4.1.

Environmental stimuli

- Ambience – temperature, air quality, noise, music, odour
- Space – layout, equipment, furnishings
- Signs, symbols, artefacts – e.g. style of decor, personal objects displayed.

Beliefs and feelings

- Cognitive – beliefs
- Emotional – mood, likes/dislikes, attitudes
- Physiological – pain, comfort, ease of movement

Responses

- Approach – willingness to stay, explore, interact and subsequently return
- Avoid – avoid interactions, a wish to get out and not return.

It may be that users of a service are largely indifferent to the physical surroundings – 'it is just what we expected'. It is the times when expectations are not met that require attention. Consumers may see the setting as an extravagance reflected in an 'inflated' price. Alternatively, it may be seen as so impoverished as to cast doubt on the quality of service. Even the credibility and competence of the employees may be called into

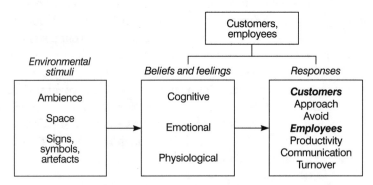

Figure 4.1 A service-setting framework for understanding behaviour and relationships. Adapted from Bitner (1992)[2]

question. Such matters as these should not be left unanswered as customers and employees need to feel comfortable and secure in the knowledge that the physical surroundings are appropriate for the service on offer.

Elements of the service setting

Spatial considerations/planning

Most design training centres around historical precedent and ideas sourcing from either nature and/or mathematics. Precedent has meant that the most common source of creativity has come from a vast visual dictionary that has evolved from concepts being tested and re-tested until principles are established. Symmetry, proportion, rhythm, texture, colour, and other fundamentals can be considered, combined and developed to present the viewer or user with an intellectual, emotional response that is perceived as visual quality. This quality can be manipulated or controlled by the designer to create environments that elicit desired responses from the subject (in our case the service user/ client or customer).

Space planning

In an ideal world, the interior designer works alongside the architect from the initial planning concept stage – by doing so, coordination of the arrangement of all of the interior elements with the architectural features is assured. A large proportion of the sites that the interior designer encounters, however, do not offer this luxury – most jobs are concerned with refurbishment of spaces and buildings originally designed for other purposes. Certain 'rules' do make up the fundamental approach to the planning process.

Generally speaking, the planning exercise with most interiors falls into five categories:

1 The identification of the problem (the brief)
2 The synthesis of the solution
3 The design development
4 The solution
5 The testing of the efficiency of the solution.

The identification of the problem will fall into several subsections. For example:

- What are the functional requirements?
- How will the users circulate?
- What does the client wish to feel like?
- What does he or she wish to see?
- What does he or she want others to see?
- What is going on in adjoining spaces?
- What are the safety and legislative requirements?
- Are exterior spaces involved?
- What kind of lighting, heating and other services are required?
- What is the desired 'mood' or character of the space(s)?
- What is the likely budget?
- How long must the scheme last before refurbishment?
- Are future developments, growth or flexibility prerequisites?

The synthesis or sketch designs of the planning process can take several forms. The most common is to formulate a graphic or schematic model which enables the designer to rank the requirements. Usually this process begins without regard to the physical constraints of the particular site and designers can indicate space relationships and traffic throughput on a purely functional level and can test their ideas against the model formed in the brief.

The development phase occurs when the designer transcribes findings from this schematic visual into the constraints of the actual space. The fitting of furniture and equipment into the space, establishing correct circulation routes, working out all the complex requirements to enable the drafting of a floor plan and associated working drawings and details.

The solution begins to take shape when all of the other phases are in place. It lasts from the time of client approval to the opening ceremony of the successfully completed building.

The final phase is the testing and modifying of the solution when the user or client can be interrogated and suggestions for improvement taken on board. This is as important a phase as any of the other four described. A list of priorities can be formulated without being dogmatic in terms of 'generalized rules'.

Circulation is of primary importance – traffic levels and direction of the user – but also of allowing sufficient space around objects, equipment and furniture to enable them to be used efficiently and safely. Unobstructed approaches to doorways, corridors, and escape routes are obvious considerations. The designer above all hopes to create interest and a particular ambience to the space which is appropriate to its function. A sense of scale, balance of proportion and interaction between adjoining space is important. Simplicity in planning is invariably successful and can lay the foundation for all of the other elements which make up the service setting.

Furniture/equipment/furnishings

Furniture can host people, or it can form a barrier between people. It can host equipment such as computers, cables and cash registers. Furniture can protect precious or delicate objects. It can project or display. Furniture can be welcoming or austere and can have a great deal to say about the status of the owner or user.

Places, tools, furniture and decoration are interdependent elements of our lives. They contribute to our quality of life by dint of functionality and aesthetic enrichment. They can be designed, controlled, and become tools to further the designer's intentions.

Furniture and equipment become of architectural proportions when one considers the cost of subdividing rented space. Often modern refurbishments have a 'designed-in' longevity – two years, five years, ten years. The cost of partitioning and its accompanying rigidity soon provides good reasons for considering the functions of walls and doors being replaced with free-standing furniture elements. Most of the established thinking to do with the subdivision of space is fast becoming outdated with the proliferation of office and business automation. Wide, open spaces are no longer required. The need to keep people in proximity is redundant as office information now flows down cables. In a modern building with a life expectancy of, say, thirty to forty years, the initial capital cost is only 10 per cent of the complete cost. Ninety per cent will be devoted to staff costs associated with maintaining a working environment and the machines and technology necessary for the purpose.

In general terms there is incredible freedom of choice available to the occupier of a commercial interior – artificial environmental qualities (light, ventilation, heating etc.) are controllable. Heights and inclinations of chairs and worktops are variable, furniture and equipment can be 'high tec' or soft and domestic in nature. The only reason for producing ranges in different materials or colours is to allow for personal or corporate choice – a marketing strategy!

Technological development has wrought overwhelming change to the service setting; the office-based service industry means that the office can now be a club, it can be a factory, a series of cosy meeting places, a streetscape or a marketplace. This choice will, hopefully, reflect some of the functions of the particular service. Other changes wrought by the shrinking of class differentials are the loss of importance of status – a bank is now a money shop and one expects to meet a bank manager on equal terms: not so 15 years ago! Financial whizkids are more dependent on the microchips and mobile phone than the old school tie!

Perceptions of equipment are also changing. The typewriter keyboard was invented in the 1860s – this meant the standardization of letters –

obvious but nonetheless staggering. The mechanical keyboard is now
electronic and pressure requirements are now infinitesimal in comparison
to the earlier typewriters but operator posture and ergonomics have
changed to accommodate the new requirements. Operators rarely view
paper, displays are on VDUs. Five or ten years ago an operator in the
service sector would probably search for documents in a filing system,
make notes, write letters and memos, use the telephone, exchange words
with colleagues and be constantly on the move. Now as a link in the
technology-based environment, eye contact might only be between
customer/client or VDU and the service operator. The office now is still a
'shelter' to its occupants but is also a 'display window' to the clients and
customers of that particular service sector. The demonstration of the
efficiency of the now visible 'working parts' of the organization is a
tangible sales promotion tool. The idea of 'front office' as the only area
visible to the client is long gone. The customer has also experienced the
impact of technological change. Most people have drawn money from a
'hole in the wall', spoken to an answerphone or received a computer print-
out on some occasion.

Lighting

This is often a key element in the design of the service setting. The design
and specification of lighting schemes is a specialized activity and is
developed by a process similar to that described in the previous section on
furniture.

When considering lighting design for a service setting the following
factors must be taken into account: daylighting, colour, the nature of the
activity to be performed in the space/s, the service provider's perception
of the task, levels of vision, and finally ambience, the desired mood.

1 Daylighting and the way in which it is controlled influence heat, glare,
  penetration, visibility, and the perception of colour – most schemes take
  account of the orientation of the building to the sun, its changes daily and
  seasonally, as well as poor daylighting conditions and darkness.
2 The direction and strength of daylight affect the perception of colour.
3 The particular activities to be undertaken in the space under consideration
  must be clearly defined; accuracy, speed, safety, recognition etc.
4 What does the organization really want from the space? Is it to sell visual
  satisfaction or is it to sell hamburgers? Is it to indicate the conservative
  solidity of the world of financial services or is it to reassure people about to
  board an aeroplane?
5 The level of vision required can depend upon the nature of the task. It can
  also depend upon the age of the client or customer. If the task requires
  detailed work from the customer or service provider then strong light is

required. If the background setting is well lit then even greater intensity of light will be required for the detailed work as the eyes become accustomed to the relative lessening of the contrast.

6 In many situations the achievement of the desired mood or ambience of the space is paramount. A church or library would generally exude a peaceful calm whereas a fast-food diner or modern music store would wish to create a youthful, exciting, gregarious atmosphere.

On a scientific level, the perception of colour and lighting is governed by a vast array of data such as the depth of penetration of daylight, glare or the reflectance value of the surface that light is falling on and the psychology of colour contrasts. Other constraints on the design of lighting systems have to do with variables such as energy conservation, heat gain and ease of maintenance programmes.

On the designer's level, there is the additional burden of wanting to create magic. The creative use of light can bring an interior to life – the interaction of light and shadow can sculpt, can expand scale, can highlight, can wall wash, can silhouette, can attract the curious, can sparkle and can move merchandise.

Colour

Colour has a language of its own. Much like music, it can evoke moods and emotions – excitement, happiness, serenity, sadness. We daily refer to 'feeling blue', 'seeing red', 'being green with envy', 'in the pink' etc. The symbolic nature of colour has for centuries fulfilled a role in religion, magic, heraldry, communication, and ritual, as well as being a major player in creative processes.

The 'fashion' element of colour use is a subject in its own right but suffice to say that as with most fashions, its use can be traced in cycles. Ancient classical architecture of the Greek and Italian Empires used brilliant, bold colours. This was followed by muted, earth colours. Renaissance Italy revived boldness and we can compare the affluent 1960s in the West with the sombreness of the 1980s.

Colour composes three elements:

1 Hue – the name of the colour, e.g. red, blue, yellow.
2 Value – the lightness or darkness of a colour.
3 Chroma – the intensity of strength or purity of colour.

There are numerous theories about the way in which colour works. It is not sufficient, however, to consider colour without an understanding of the effects of light, the discrimination of relative colours – that is, the different appearance of one colour or hue which is in the proximity of another hue, the spatial and the emotional effects of colour.

It is always dangerous to pragmatize when discussing a notion such as colour and any statements that might appear as 'rules' should only be read as examples in the context of suggestions for the particular service settings discussed.

The effect of light

If lighting values in an interior have not been well thought out, any creative application of colour will be in vain. Well-designed lighting, however, enhances the choice of colour. Low lighting levels with warm colours provide a friendly, intimate environment that evokes an atmosphere of relaxation and rest. Soft lighting with warm colours enhances and flatters the complexion. Warm colours (pinks, oranges, reds and yellows) generally 'work' with low levels of illumination. The converse is true in that blues and greens generally 'don't work' in low lighting situations and complexions appear pallid and unflattering. These same colours applied under high levels of illumination, however, can create good working environments and under 'white light' make for a more natural appearance. Consider fruit and vegetable displays in supermarkets – strong, white light against 'artificial grass'.

The colour white, like its opposite, black can be one of hundreds with different chroma values but the same white sample viewed in bright sunshine will appear as grey if taken into a dimly lit environment.

Colour in relation to other colours

Colour can only be measured in relation to other colours and while an adult with normal vision can distinguish probably two thousand colours, this experience is, at best, highly subjective. Colour can never be isolated and the resultant experience modifies the perception. Look at a strong red sample for about a minute and then focus on a white surface – the resultant green vision is the after-image of a colour's opposite or complement. A colour always has to be considered in relation to its neighbour in any successful lighting design. In simplistic terms one can say that colour schemes that are largely monochromatic (different values of the same hue) are the safest solution. Next best in terms of little risk are schemes which rely on using colours that are adjacent in the spectrum and therefore have one hue in common. The riskiest and therefore sometimes the most rewarding or interesting schemes are those based on complementary colours or those of high contrast. This almost elementary appeal perhaps stems from experiences and memories we had as children. Nature, of course, employs exotic schemes in the plant world and colours of courtship or warning in animals, fish, birds and insects.

A further problem in relation to controlling colour in the service setting is that the units are required to be balanced so that adjacent rooms have some relationship or harmony. Generally speaking, large spaces are better balanced by using a scheme of soft, low-intensity colour with strong, vibrant hues reserved for accent or highlight value. Again as a general rule, background colours are selected and developed first for the large planar areas (floor/ceiling/walls) with 'accessories' (equipment, furniture, curtains, pictures) figuring as stress or accent points.

Optical and emotional values of colour

Warmth and coolness are easily distinguished by colour choice so that red, orange, yellow and their family are warm; green, blue, violet and their family are cool. A finer division can occur at junctions in the spectrum so that red-violet and yellow-green can occupy both camps or form a bridge between warm-cool.

Red indicates danger, excitement, stop etc. – the pulse rate and blood pressure of a viewer increase when shown the colour. Conversely, green indicates peacefulness, safety, go etc., likewise for blue. Perceived sizes of areas of colour vary with the selection of hue – warm colours appear to advance towards the viewer, cool colours to retract or recede. Colour choice can therefore be used to modify the perceived size and shape of areas.

It will come as no surprise to the reader to learn that these colour theories can be, and are, used as a functional tool in the design of interiors. Colour is utilized to improve efficiency in the workplace, colour can help people to relax, colour can help lower accident rates, aid convalescence, help market merchandise or create an appetite where food is served. Specifics will be discussed under the five colours selected.

In their book based on the television series *The Colour Eye*, Cumming and Porter[3] give some valuable insights into colour psychology. For example:

Red – the colour of fire and passion, suggesting activity, energy, joy. It is used by interior designers to increase comfort levels in unheated spaces and is also regarded (along with pink) as good for restaurants, especially the fast-food variety. One study showed that red-stimulated diners tend to eat more quickly and move on for the next person.

Orange – although researchers have claimed that an orange environment improves social behaviour, cheers the spirit and lessens hostility and irritability, it is seldom used by professional designers.

Yellow – conflicting evidence here which, on the one hand, suggests its ideal stimulative effect where concentration is required. However, if used too strongly those in its environment are likely to get 'stressed up'.

Green – symbolizes the natural world and is widely believed to be a calming hue. Ideal for areas where relaxation is required and along with blue is found to enhance our appetite; thus good for dining areas.

Blue – symbolizes authority and implies truth, prudence and wisdom – ideal for banks and building societies. It is considered as having a calming effect which makes it ideally suited for hospital cardiac units.

Purple – regarded as disturbing and psychologically 'difficult'. In a Swedish study it was the most disliked colour in terms of environmental settings.

Signage

Graphically transmitted messages or signage are fundamental to communication in all areas of the service sector. The visual appearance, the placing, the physical construction, the colour, lighting and choice of typeface are all important and interdependent.

'Letters are signs for sounds' is a well-known quote and serves as an apt definition of what signs are about. A good sign is one which imparts information as simply and directly as possible. As with colour and spatial considerations, letter forms can evoke visual and emotional responses.

Signs, unlike print, are read quickly and therefore the choice of weight of the letter form is paramount. It should seek to provide maximum clarity and contrast from the sign's surroundings.

Signs can be of some importance in many service settings. The 'you are here' map (YAH) is designed to answer the questions, 'Where am I?' and 'How do I get from here to there?'. The trouble with many of these maps apart from not being particularly well designed is that they are not always aligned with the territory. The difficulty seems to be with the fact that YAH maps are usually placed vertically on a wall. 'If', as stated by Levine, Marchon and Hanley,[4] 'the direction which is in front of you is up, on the vertical map, the map and the terrain are aligned and the map will be relatively easy to use. If, on the other hand, the direction in front of you is down on the map, they are contraligned, the map will be relatively difficult to use'. Contralignment and alignment can be demonstrated quite simply (Figure 4.2).

Figure 4.2 Placement and misplacement of the YAH maps. *Source*: Levine, Marchon and Hanley (1984)[4]

Three service settings

Financial services

The public interface with financial services especially in banking and other high street institutions has undergone radical change in the last generation. We have witnessed the metamorphosis from elegant, dark, expensive and foreboding interiors to the 'fun money shop' era of the past decade to the current trend of serious design, professional service and interaction between people.

During the 1980s, the yuppie mentality was all. High street banks and building societies resembled retail establishments and nightclubs in contrast to the Victorian approach of previous decades. Neon light, distressed surface finishes and dreamy uplighting housed high-tech machines that obviated the need for personal contact. Banks and the like became 'take-away' or 'fast money' outlets resembling the franchised fast-food chains that proliferate in every shopping mall or provincial high street. There is no doubt that the money business itself has undergone radical change.

Building societies initiated the change by offering attractive interiors. The banks have had to follow to continue to compete successfully.

In general terms, layouts tend not to vary and follow a common design. Entrances have become lobbies that house self-service cash dispensers (and other routine transactions – deposits, statement provision etc.). These are often fitted in fairly sturdy surroundings that recognize the out-of-banking-hours activities and the need for anti-theft, anti-vandal and in some cases anti-weather protection. The reception area is found behind this area and this first point of customer–staff interface is afforded adventurous frontline reception desking that is generally modern and colourful. The transition for the customer is marked by a change in floor covering from marble or tile or hard surface to soft surface such as carpeting of a warm hue. Wall surfaces likewise will blend from a stone cladding or laminate surface to a textile base or wallpaper and lighting will change from security conscious task lighting to uplit pools that are warmer and more 'domestic' in context. Beyond the reception point is the area design for financial consultations where bandit-proof glass screening and counter tops are being replaced with informal, low-level, comfortable and discrete consulting areas. The customer will feel that he is being afforded status and personal attention. Much of the brutality of design approach has disappeared to be superseded by a thoughtful more gentle approach where the customer is allowed to feel less threatened.

Interestingly, one area of comparison with the fast-food industry remains. Behind the area designated for personal consultations, the working area of the institution often remains as open-plan and clearly visible personnel movements reflect the exposed working kitchen seen in McDonald's and Burger King establishments.

The financial service sector is also responding to the rapidity of change by generally reviewing interior design policy every five years or thereabouts and recognizes that the 'service setting' is an increasingly important asset to its marketing strategy.

Fast-food restaurants

Born in the USA out of the hot-dog stand or lunch-wagon genre, the fast-food chains and franchises have spread throughout the world. Previously the menu revolved around 'burgers and fries'. The quick-service restaurant industry has changed out of all recognition since the early part of the 1980s. The 'yuppy youth' culture demanded healthy food, salads, baked potatoes, pulses and pastas, fresh fruit and vegetables. The menu says it all. The interior design reflects the menu and what it says is 'quick turnover'.

The successful design is the one which attracts the customers in to the restaurant, organizes their traffic flow, creates just enough (and no more) comfort, arranges seating configurations that are economic and then hustles the customer out!

Fast-food outlets have produced a lot of innovative designs. Successful schemes (financially rewarding *and* aesthetically pleasing) invariably combine slick and lively ambience with often whimsical, youthful, colourful surroundings enhanced with a good portion of pop music or musak.

Wall and floor surfaces are invariably hard – usually tile or laminate for durability, ease of maintenance and cleaning. Soft base colours always serve to contrast with a dramatic splash of colour red or green. All interior materials are simple and appear inexpensive. Seats are just too short and just too close to the next table to encourage customers not to linger. An emphasis is often on serve yourself and dispose of the debris yourself in self-consciously signposted receptacles. The kitchen is the focal point, always busy, clean in appearance and in some instances forming a stage or 'altar' in the case of pizza ovens.

Lighting is brutally harsh and no attempt is made to pool light over individual tables as this would create an intimate ambience and invite the diners to dally too long. Graphics are over-sized, unmistakable and again centre around blown-up versions of the menu. In this industry, success or failure may depend on the ability of the service setting to stimulate a speedy throughput of customers.

Hotels

Hotels have also undergone a tumultuous change in recent periods. The total design package employed in the creation of a hotel is awe-inspiring. The architect and designer today must be capable of creating a village within four walls. Landscaping, construction and fitting of offices, lobbies, themed restaurants, coffee shops, guest rooms, suites, conference centres, gymnasiums, swimming pools, casinos, lifts, foyers, rest rooms, shopping malls, bars, bathrooms and all associated services must present a cohesive theme that identifies the corporate strategy of the operator or franchisee.

The entrance to a hotel must invite the client in. It should appear and feel gracious and extravagant yet afford some weather protection. Resort hotels that double as conference centres are different to urban hotels that are one-night stops for business people or vacationers. Whatever the location, the space must be designed with flexibility to cater for a multitude of users.

First impressions last! The reception area which greets the guest is in itself a multifunctional space – lobby, reception/welcoming/check-in/out facilities, baggage handling, and lift entrances. Staircases all have to be blended to welcome rather than overwhem the guest. If too sumptuous guests may baulk at what they think the room rates might be.

Signposting is important, making it easy for guests to find the entrance from the car park and then the check-in. Graphics can help but nothing works as well as careful attention to the detailed arrangement of the functions listed. Sculpting a huge space that is multifunctional can be useful. Generally conceived as atrium spaces, the lobby has to double as 'my club' to guests, a place to meet friends, colleagues or business associates, somewhere to read the financial papers, somewhere to hail a taxi from etc. This space is the key which indicates the status and standing of the particular hotel or group. It signifies what is happening behind the front of house facade.

Spatial excitement is important, sparkling lighting, judicious use of planting and water, large vistas broken down into intimate club-like private spaces. Comfortable 'classic' armchairs and sofas, rich materials like stone, leather and glass all bound together in muted autumnal colour groupings. People respond to small spaces they can commandeer – no one will sit on a large sofa that is isolated in the middle of an area.

Lifts and their foyer areas are important in the marketing strategy. People have to congregate and wait. The designer has to recognize that people will fidget, lean on walls, smoke, deposit luggage etc. and the surface qualities and their maintenance will reflect this wear. Mirrors work well in this instance. People generally are not bored if they can contemplate their own reflections. They also provide the opportunity to observe fellow travellers with discretion.

Coffee shops differ from fast-food type outlets in that they offer a different pace and can usually be operated by a skeleton staff (often 24 hours). It is likely that floor surfaces will be in a soft fibre which can be easily cleaned. Lighting will be very controllable to enable staff to ring the changes reflecting time of day or night. Unlike the main restaurants, however, the ambience cannot be too elegant or sumptuous but will rather reflect its purpose and offer a feeling of cleanliness and purposefulness. Bright colours and sharp forms help, and the treatment of graphics, menu, dishes and table settings reinforces a strong visual identity.

Guest rooms form the very *raison d'être* of the hotel and take on a domestic scale in contrast to the public areas of the hotel. Sizes are determined by economics. Lighting can be employed to pool discrete areas of the room or wash uncluttered walls. The use of vertical furniture as opposed to our usual norm of horizontal can make good use of limited space.

Some hotels group rooms on colour themes so that individual preferences can be catered for – this can present problems if, for example, the guest wants a blue room and they have all been let. If, however, there is only one scheme repeated through the hotel, the guest is rarely disappointed since he has no choice. A single palette of colour reduces costs and facilitates easy refurbishment or replacement. A hotel is always a transitory place and strong or bold schemes rarely achieve success since the guest usually wants to relax or feel at home as soon as possible and does not want to spend (even unconscious) time adapting to foreign surroundings.

Hotels are invariably filled with corridors. The design must aim to make the guest feel more at home; foreshorten the vista, break up the long, narrow spaces by changes in ceiling form or height, texture or colour of floorcoverings, and lighting intensity. The designer can treat the corridor as a gallery and position stimulating pictures or other graphics at strategic points.

The designs reconcile all of the varied guests' expectations, function, glamour, excitement, comfort and service.

Summary

Where a service takes place is now receiving the attention it deserves. Designers are being called upon by organizations to create an environment that will support and reflect the service being offered.

Atmospheres must be engendered that will stimulate appropriate customer feelings and reactions. To achieve this the designer applies his knowledge and skills in respect of space idealization, lighting, colour and so on.

There are no ten commandments which state that different service activities should be designed in particular ways. It will be for the customer, in the final analysis, to decide whether the design has any meaning and impact on what is being received.

The three 'case studies' emphasize the point that there is no exclusive design for a certain service. However, there will be clues from the selection of colours, lighting and the layout of space etc. as to the nature of the activity in operation.

References

1. Kotler, P. (1973) 'Atmospherics as a marketing tool', *Journal of Retailing*, **49**(4), 48–64.
2. Bitner, M. J. (1992) 'Servicescapes: the impact of physical surroundings on customers and employees', *Journal of Marketing*, **56**, April, 57–71.
3. Cumming, R. and Porter, T. (1990) *The Colour Eye*, BBC Books, London.
4. Levine, M., Marchon, I. and Hanley, G. (1984) 'The placement and misplacement of you-are-here maps', *Environment and Behaviour*, **16**(2) 139–157.

Chapter 5

Service quality

Introduction

It is widely acknowledged that efforts to define and measure the quality of products have proved more successful than the definition and measurement of service quality. The characteristics of services have made the determination of what constitutes quality more difficult and hence its measurement less than comprehensive. To increase our understanding and to enable practical steps to be taken, two things need to be attained:

- Specification of the determinants of service quality
- Measurable quality standards.

Achievement in these two areas will vary depending on whether the focus is:

- A low-contact or a high-contact service, e.g. fast-food outlet versus an education course
- Process or output.

Determining the process and output quality of a fast-food restaurant is arguably more straightforward than an education course.

Whatever the service, it is useful to bear in mind the following questions when it comes to quality:

- What is the service supposed to do?
- What does the service actually do?

Quality then refers to the extent to which a service is what it claims to be and does what it claims to do. It must not be confused with grade. For example, the quality of a library cannot be judged in an abstract way by, say, counting the number of Shakespeare volumes possessed and subtracting the number of light romances. Instead the prime aspect of quality is whether the library provides people with what they want – it is a good library if it does and a bad library if it does not.[1]

One eminent spokesman in the quality business over many years is Philip Crosby. In an update[2] of his most famous book *Quality is Free* he berates the army of bandwagoneers for having made a good living out of quality by reducing a profound idea to a set of box-ticking exercises such as ISO 9000 or the criteria for entry for quality awards. These, he claims, just encourage the notion that quality is about techniques and systems. 'But techniques and systems don't accomplish anything by themselves', claims Crosby. 'Management has to do that'. Management's preference for dealing with money rather than people (customers and employees) goes some way to explaining their obsession with 'ritualistic stuff' like ISO 9000 and TQM – 'trivializing quality management' as he describes it. For Crosby 'quality is conformance to requirements, and reliability is conformance to requirements over time'.

The impact of service quality

Quality needs to be understood and managed throughout a service organization. Four areas in particular may serve as an arena within which the question of quality can be addressed (Figure 5.1).

Service encounter – the customer interacts with animate (the service employees) and inanimate objects (the physical evidence, e.g. an information sign).

- How knowledgeable and courteous is the service employee?
- How effective is the sign in terms of visibility, information provided, postioning?
- How can the customer contribute to the quality of the encounter?
- What contribution do script theory and role theory make?

Figure 5.1 The impact of quality

Service design – the customer goes through a process to obtain a service.

- How well designed is the process?
- Is there a blueprint/flowchart of the process?
- To what extent is there flexibility in the system?
- Does the process require customization or standardization?

Service productivity – there is a relationship between the quantity and quality of goods or services produced and the quality of resources used to produce them.

- What are the possible relationships between changes in quality and changes in quantity? If quantity increases (number of patients seen by a general practitioner), what effect could that have on the quality of service?
- What role should the customer play in the productivity equation?

Service organization and culture – the culture of an organization and the way it is organized can affect the quality of service.

- How do the various organizational cultures (power, role, achievement and support) act as a key to understanding the kind of service produced?
- What characteristics/features of an organization enable it to respond positively to customer needs and deliver a quality service?

Another way to consider quality and its impact throughout an organization is to put the customer at the centre of the process and highlight the number of encounters, or 'moments of truth' he or she may have with the organization. Consider the case of a student in an educational institution (Figure 5.2). Expectations of both the educational

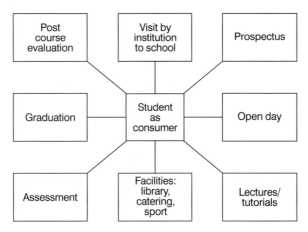

Figure 5.2 Student contact with service

institution and potential student can be determined at the beginning. We can then compare these expectations with the perceptions of students and staff during and at the end of the course.

This kind of exercise can be undertaken with any service organization. The benefit of doing so is that it disciplines the service provider to think of how all aspects of the organization contribute to service quality. The customer can be asked how important each part of the service is and how well the organization performs on each aspect.

A model of service quality

To enhance knowledge of service quality and encourage investigation of the key issues, a model has been developed[3] (Figure 5.3). Its key features are:

- The identification of key attributes of service quality from a management and consumer perspective
- Highlighting the gaps between consumers and service providers with particular reference to perceptions and expectations
- Understanding the implications for service management of closing the gaps.

The most important insight obtained from the research on the service quality model was that:

> A set of key discrepancies or gaps exist regarding executive perceptions of service quality and the tasks associated with service delivery to consumers. These gaps can be major hurdles in attempting to deliver a service which consumers would perceive as being of high quality.

The following is a brief account of the gaps:

Gap 1 – it states that many service organizations just do not understand what customers expect and what really matters to them. This gap can only be bridged through customer research.

Gap 2 – even where customer expectations are understood, management experiences difficulty in translating that understanding into service quality specifications. This exists because:

- Management may believe that customer expectations are unreasonable or unrealistic

Figure 5.3 Service quality model. *Source*: Parasuraman, Zeithaml and Berry (1985)[3]

● Management may believe that the degree of variability inherent in service defies standardization
● There is an absence of wholehearted management commitment to service quality.

Gap 3 – even when formal standards or specifications for maintaining service quality are in existence, the delivery of a quality service is by no means certain. This is caused by poor, inadequately deployed resources in terms of people, systems and technology.

Gap 4 – advertising and other forms of communication by a service organization can affect consumer expectations. The danger is that promises made are not kept. Many service organizations use the brochure or prospectus (some very glossy) for communicating with potential customers. It should be a statement of what the customer will receive, not an attractive set of promises that cannot be delivered.

Gap 5 – this gap represents the key challenge. To ensure good quality the provider must meet or exceed customer expectations. Perceived service quality is the result of the consumer's comparison of expected service with perceived service delivery.

What to measure

Service quality is viewed as a multidimensional concept. Consumers assess and evaluate a number of factors or dimensions. Clearly the question of what to measure will vary from one service to another, but a list of dimensions by which consumers judge quality has been developed.[4] The appropriateness of these dimensions has been tested in a variety of service industries. Consequently they appear applicable to most services. The dimensions are:

Reliability – the ability to perform the promised service dependably and accurately. It is regarded as the most important determinant of perceptions of service quality. This dimension is particularly crucial for services such as railways, buses, banks, building societies, insurance companies, delivery services and trade services, e.g. plumbers, carpet fitters, car repair.

Responsiveness – the willingness to help customers and to provide prompt service. This dimension is particularly prevalent where customers have requests, questions, complaints and problems.

Assurance – the employees' knowledge and courtesy, and the ability of the service to inspire trust and confidence. This dimension may be of particular concern for customers of health, financial and legal services.

Empathy – the caring, individualized attention the service provides its customers. Small service companies are better placed for treating customers as individuals than their larger invariably standardized counterparts. However, relationship marketing is designed to offer a more individualistic approach for customers of large organizations!

Tangibles – the appearance of physical facilities, equipment, personnel and communication materials. All of these are used in varying degrees to project an image that will find favour with consumers. Tangibles will be of particular significance where the customer's physical presence at a service facility is necessary for consumption to occur e.g. hair salon, hotel, night club.

To apply these factors to a particular service organization will require definition in specific and behavioural terms. For example, what does

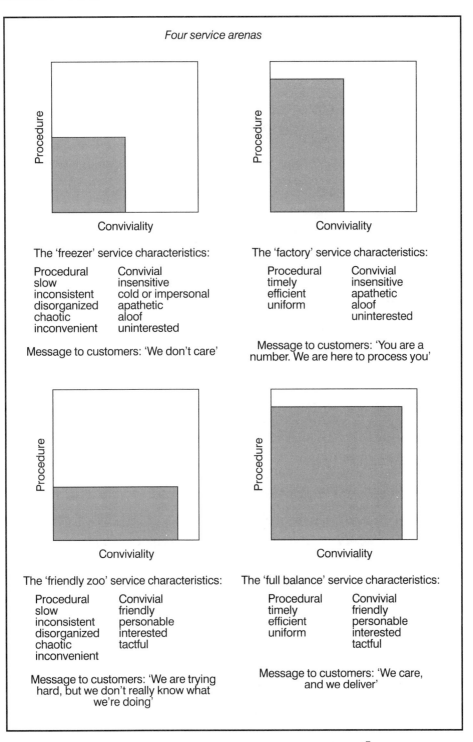

Figure 5.4 Four arenas of service quality. *Source*: Martin (1986)[7]

reliability mean in Service A as distinct from Service B? How does an organization show responsiveness? How does assurance differ between Service A and Service B? What can an organization do specifically to demonstrate empathy?

For the five determinants of service quality already mentioned, a multiple-item scale called SERVQUAL has been developed.[5] It aims to measure customer expectations and perceptions and the gaps as described in the service quality model. Measurement is done through a Likert scale in which respondents are required to indicate their strength of agreement/ disagreement to statements about the delivery of service quality (see Chapter 12). On a more general level it has been argued that service organizations should be subject to a quality audit as well as the legally required financial audit. Generally accepted service principles (GASP)[6] would provide service organizations with explanations of upward and downward trends in quality, just as companies explain good and bad trends in terms of sales and profits. It would be an index of customer satisfaction, measuring all the activities and attributes that affect customer satisfaction. The findings of a service quality audit may be portrayed as in Figure 5.4 and it might prove quite revealing to ask your customers 'Of the four, which one best reflects your perception of us?'

Causes of service quality problems

Several reasons have been put forward as explanations of poor service quality.[8]

Inseparability of production and consumption and labour intensity

The provision of service, as distinct from the manufacture of goods, occurs in the presence of customers. Inevitably as with any human encounter, problems do arise. The service employee may exhibit poor presentational skills, conduct himself improperly and dress inappropriately. All of these and others may influence the customer's perception of service quality. The intensive involvement of humans in service delivery will always have the potential to pose problems for quality.

Inadequate services to intermediate or internal customers

The frontline employee is by definition at the 'sharp end' of the service delivery system. To execute the service effectively, the employee requires proper support from further back in the organization (Figure 5.5)

Figure 5.5 The importance of employee support in the execution of effective service

The support will emanate from the main management functions (operations, marketing and human resource) and involve:

1 Equipment e.g. tools, materials, uniforms
2 Skills training
3 Information e.g. of a new service launch's operating procedures.

Communication gaps

Good communication is the life-blood of a healthy organization, and its contacts with customers. However, it is a problem of some magnitude and manifests itself in the following ways:

1 Failure to deliver promises made
2 Failure to keep a customer informed
3 Failure to communicate in a manner the customer can understand
4 Failure to listen.

Viewing customers as statistics

For a service organization there are often compelling reasons for offering a standardized service, not least of which are the efficiencies to be gained from treating a large number of customers in a standardized manner. For the customer, this approach to service delivery is often welcomed. By contrast, customization of the service seeks to recognize the particular needs of individual customers. Service organizations should be sensitive to how their customers feel about how they are treated. A remark made by a student perhaps exemplifies the issue. He said 'In my two years at college, not once did a lecturer recognize me by name'.

Short-run view of the business

Organizations in general, and particularly in the UK, take a short-run view of the business when it comes to performance evaluation. Management are frequently required to meet targets on a yearly basis. The obsession inevitably becomes one of cost reduction and productivity increases to meet a profit target. This is understandable but detrimental to building a quality service in the longer term.

How to improve service quality

Improving service quality is certainly not a simple, straightforward exercise. It will have implications for the whole culture of the organization. Some ideas put forward are worthy of consideration.[8]

Identifying primary quality determinants

Knowing what determines quality is, of course, crucial. However, consumers and producers of services do not necessarily perceive service quality on common dimensions and even when they do hold common dimensions, they evaluate them differently.

Managing customer expectations

To attract custom, organizations are often tempted to raise customer expectations. Companies make promises to consumers on aspects of their business that they think the customer will value in order to give the organization a competitive advantage. However care must be exercised in making promises to customers. For example, consider the following sample taken from the *Yellow Pages Directory*:

> 'Nobody does it better'
> 'The very best of care'
> 'Immediate delivery from stock'
> 'On time – every time'
> 'You can't beat our service'

They are both difficult to measure and raise consumer expectations unrealistically. As a rule it is better to exceed customer expectations than to let the customer down.

Managing evidence

The 'evidence' from the viewpoint of a service organization includes many things and consumers look to these as an indicator of what the service might be like (pre-service expectation) and what, in fact, the service was like after using it (post-service evaluation).

Physical and human evidence play a significant part in image formation. Retailers are interested in several aspects relating to architecture and design for promoting an image. Similarly, atmosphere influences image. The term 'atmospherics' has been coined to define the conscious design of space to influence buyers. The atmosphere influences the buyers' expectations and perceptions of the service. For example lawyers' offices and banks are designed to communicate confidence.

Various factors such as colours, music, furnishing, space etc. can evoke a variety of feelings about the service organization, e.g. friendliness, austerity, sobriety, authority, rationality, stability, flexibility. One author stresses that it will be the physical aspects of a service that will allow us to make sense of it and we expect the physical signs to be in tune with the nature of the service. Incongruity can make us uncertain and uncomfortable.

Educating consumers about the service

Helping the customer to understand the service would appear to be a *sine qua non* for dispensing a quality service. However, for many services, e.g. garage repair business, professional services, the challenge can be a daunting one and one that perhaps they are not willing to confront. Equally, the willingness of the customer 'to be educated' requires evaluation along with their capacity to assimilate the nature of the service being delivered.

Developing a quality culture

Quality is not delivered in a vacuum but through an organization with all its imperfections. Commitment to quality must pervade the whole organization. A number of institutional factors can either help or hinder the provision of quality service. They are:[9]

1 Human – job descriptions, selection, training, rewards, career path.
2 Organization/structure – integration/coordination of functions and reporting structure.
3 Measurement – complaint and customer satisfaction tracking and performance evaluation.
4 Systems support – technical, computers, databases.
5 Services – value added, range and quality, standards of performance, satisfying needs and expectations.
6 Programmes – complaint management, sales/promotional tools, management tools.

7 Communication (internal) – policies and procedures, feedback within the organization.
8 Communication (external) – consumer education, creation of expectations, image.

A useful tool for identifying the causes of poor service quality is the fishbone diagram. All that is required is the identification of a poor output and then work backwards in order to attribute the cause(s). It is versatile in that it can be applied to a range of situations. When several such analyses are conducted, a distribution of the causes can be plotted on a Pareto histogram (see 'Tools of quality').

Automating quality

The variability in quality service emanating from human inadequacy can be avoided through automation. Before such a decision is made, research needs to establish which parts of the service require the human touch and which require automation. The danger is that automation takes over for reasons other than automation.

Following up the service

Organizations need to continuously monitor their performance by contacting customers to determine their view of the service delivered.

More recently, organizations have been asked to consider five imperatives for improving service quality.[10]

1 Define a clear service role and standard for service employees and communicate and reinforce these standards.
2 Compete for talent – allocate people to jobs according to ability and aptitude and give them more flexibility and control to do the job. The problem with this is that many service jobs are by nature narrow in scope and perceived as 'dead end'.
3 Emphasize service teams – getting people to work as a team is an attractive proposition and potentially very effective for delivering quality. However, entrenched attitudes (negative) to work and strong personalities can quite easily prevent the development of a team spirit. The action (or inaction) of management is crucial here. Good employees need to see management doing something about the members of the team who are simply not pulling their weight.
4 Go for reliability – at the heart of excellent service is reliability and it is argued that nothing less than 100 per cent reliability is acceptable:

Think for a moment about what it would mean in our daily lives if people got things right only 99 per cent of the time: at least 200,000 wrong prescriptions would be processed every year; there would be nine misspelled words on every page of a magazine; we'd all have unsafe drinking water; there would be no telephone service for fifteen minutes every day.[10]

Reliability has been defined as the 'ability to perform the promised service dependably and accurately'.[11]

● When an organization says it will call you back within fifteen minutes, does it do so?
● Is your bank statement free of errors? Is your plumbing repaired correctly the first time?

Service organizations should strive towards achieving 100 per cent reliability. However, the existence of certain conditions often impede the service organization in pursuit of that goal, e.g. lack of resources, unpredictable swings in demand levels.

5 Be great at problem resolution – service organizations cannot avoid things going wrong for a customer but it is their reaction to this that is critical. Their response can make things better or very much worse. Customers need to feel that actions are being taken to try to resolve the problem. For large service organizations client dissatisfaction of attempts at problem resolution is a real issue.

Customers are categorized and treated by the application of general, abstract rules, without regard for individual needs and situations. The depersonalized behaviour is considered functional because it prevents emotional involvement with the customers' problems and tends to promote consistency in behaviour throughout the organization. Also, the careful and thorough establishment of rules by the organization makes it possible to delegate substantial authority to people far down in the organization structure. In effect, complex problems can be routinely handled by a person with relatively little training or commonplace ability.

Tools of quality

A commitment to quality is enhanced through the use of a range of tools designed for monitoring its delivery and acceptability. The following discussion outlines the most frequently mentioned tools.

Flowchart

Flowcharting is perhaps the simplest yet the most helpful in terms of overall service process improvement. The easiest and best way to understand a process is to draw a picture of it – that's basically what flowcharting is. It presents information that allows management to analyse the way a service is being delivered. As the format, in terms of the picture, becomes more elaborate, reference is made to a service blueprint or service map (see Chapter 3).

Cause and effect diagram

'Quality begins with education and ends with education'. These words, attributed to the late Kaoru Ishikawa sum up a principal philosophy of quality. To improve processes, one must continuously strive to obtain more information about those processes and their output. One unique and valuable tool for accomplishing this goal is the cause and effect diagram. The diagram's purpose is to relate cause and effect. It is also known as the Ishikawa diagram and the fishbone diagram because it resembles the skeleton of a fish.

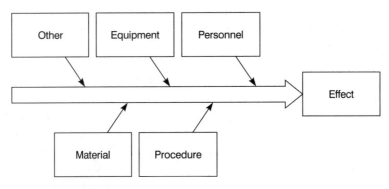

Figure 5.6 Cause and effect diagram

All that is required is the identification of an effect and then work backwards in order to attribute the cause(s). The diagram (Figure 5.6) helps managers to focus on a specific problem faced in a quality management context, e.g. late deliveries and to identify the factors contributing to that problem. The versatility of the cause and effect diagram means the words in each box will vary depending on the situation. Consider the case of a service/distribution business that has determined five areas as the main potential causes of dissatisfied customers (Figure 5.7).

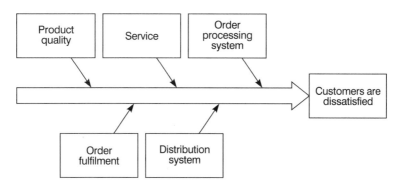

Figure 5.7 The main cause headings. *Source*: Sarazen (1990)[12]

After these areas were determined, the next step was to brainstorm all the possible causes of problems in each of the major cause categories. These ideas are captured and applied to the diagram as subcauses. Figure 5.8 shows the completed portion of the diagram for one of the main causes: service. The company identified reliability issues, carrier issues (e.g. a trucking company), poor communications, and lack of, or poor training.

The next level of causes was identified by asking the question 'What would cause a problem in these areas?' In the case of the poor communications, the company focused on functions and jobs – sales people, field representatives and managers – as potential causes. It can be seen that lack of knowledge of the customer can cause managers to communicate poorly. Subsequently it can be seen that inexperience and

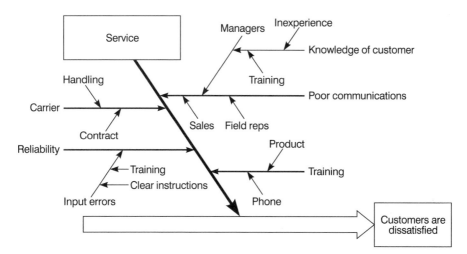

Figure 5.8 A detailed look at the main cause. *Source*: Sarazen (1990)[12]

training can be two key contributors to a manager's lack of customer knowledge. Thus, there are six levels of causes in this example.

Three points should be borne in mind in respect of a cause and effect analysis:

- Where difficulties are experienced in creating a diagram for a specific situation, use should be made of the generic diagram (Figure 5.6).
- All employees with an involvement in the problem should be party to identifying the causes and suggesting solutions.
- The objective of cause and effect analysis is to determine which of the causal factors are major influences on results. To illustrate this we need a Pareto chart.

Pareto chart

The Pareto principle is named after Vilfredo Pareto, a nineteenth-century Italian economist who found that a large share of the wealth was owned by relatively few people. It came to be known as the 80/20 rule which suggests that 80 per cent of any problem or phenomenon is often due to 20 per cent of the possible causes. Therefore, around 80 per cent of most companies' sales are produced by about 20 per cent of its products. Similarly, in a service context, 80 per cent of service failures may be accounted for by only 20 per cent of causes.

A study done for a pizza parlour experiencing problems with its home delivery service revealed possible causes of failure and their contribution in not meeting target response times (Table 5.1). A Pareto chart (Figure 5.9) can be constructed from the survey. It shows three factors (d, f and e) which together account for 70 per cent of the causes.

Table 5.1 Causal factors with a Pareto distribution

Causes	% contribution to failure in meeting target response times
(a) Giving order to kitchen	3
(b) Shortage of drivers	8
(c) Slowness in preparation of pizzas	3
(d) Drivers unfamiliar with faster route	30
(e) Breakdowns in delivery vehicles	15
(f) Traffic congestion	25
(g) Weather conditions	6
(h) Slowness in boxing cooked pizzas	3
(i) Extent of catchment area	7
	100

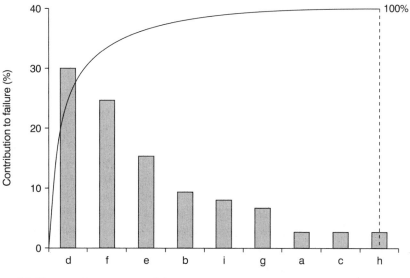

Figure 5.9 Pareto chart – causal factors

Histogram

A histogram can also be used to illustrate variations. It is a distribution showing the frequency of occurrences between the high and low range of data. Figure 5.10 shows two histograms illustrating times taken by two organizations to perform a particular service. From the histograms it is clear that the variation of company A's service process is smaller than B's.

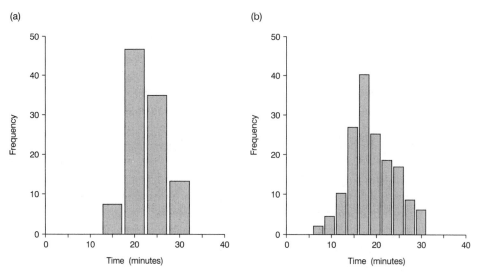

Figure 5.10 Time taken by two organizations to perform a particular service

The question is why the quality of A's service performance should be much better than B's. Possible reasons are better equipment, better trained employees and more effective procedures.

Control charts

Variation is a fact of life. In our personal life we are often surprised when the mail does not arrive at the same time every day, complain when the weather forecast is inaccurate and become frustrated when our train does not leave or arrive on time.

All processes vary to some extent, e.g. a machine will never give precisely the same result each time it is used: materials will vary a little, operator performance will differ marginally, the environment in which the process takes place will vary. Variations which derive from these common causes can never be entirely eliminated (although they can be reduced). Common cause variation occurs in processes which are essentially stable. A stable process such as order processing time displays a random pattern and its future behaviour is predictable.

How much common cause variation occurs will depend on the circumstances. However, the question that needs to be asked is 'Is this variation in the process performance acceptable? The answer will lead to the determination of what is often called a tolerance or specification range. In other words, an upper and lower control limit will be set within which performance will be allowed to vary and be deemed acceptable. The control chart displays this performance over time against specific quality criteria.

Not all variation in processes is the result of common causes. Something may be wrong with the process which is assignable to a particular and 'preventable' cause. The causes of such variation are called assignable or special causes. It will appear on the control chart as a point outside the upper or lower control limits. Whereas common cause variation focuses on improving the system, special cause variation requires a problem-solving approach of finding the cause and developing solutions to prevent its recurrence.

The upper and lower limits on the control chart usually represent three types of value:

- **Measurable data**, e.g. time spent in a service or time spent waiting for service, order processing time
- **Percentages**, e.g. the percentage of orders delivered late or the percentage of customers complaining
- **Counting data**, e.g. the number of mistakes in an order, number of complaints

Each of the above types of value is represented on the vertical Y axis and the horizontal X axis represents a period of time, e.g. a week, month, year. An example of a control chart for stability testing of customer complaints is shown in Figure 5.11.

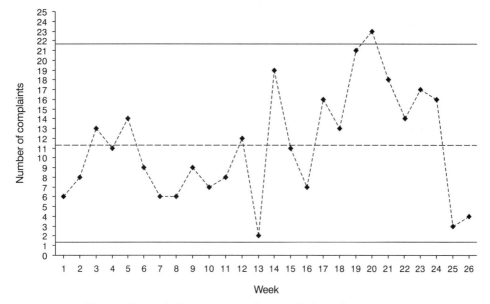

Figure 5.11 Testing for stability: statistical control chart for customer complaints, July–December. *Source*: Cravens (1988)[13]

The figure indicates that the process is out of control. First, the number of complaints for week 20 is outside the upper control limit. Second, eight observations beginning in week 17 on the top side of the central time indicate a statistically significant non-random shift in the process average. The control chart upper and lower limits are established by calculating above and below the grand mean.

Determining whether or not the process is stable is an essential step in the quality improvement process. Attempting to correct an unstable process provides no assurance that corrective action will improve the process because of the possible counter effects of the variables causing the process to be out of control. In the control chart of Figure 5.11 it was noted that the customer complaint process was out of control. The control chart in Figure 5.12 covers the six month period after correction of the causes of the out-of-control process.

The process is now under control, and the average number of complaints has been reduced from 11.3 (Figure 5.11) to 5.7 (Figure 5.12). Also note that the variability of the process has been reduced. This can be

Figure 5.12 Customer complaints: process under control, January–June. *Source:* Cravens (1988)[13]

seen by comparing the upper and lower control limits for Figures 5.11 and 5.12. Before control of the process was accomplished the span between the upper and lower limits was 21; after control the span was reduced to 13.

It should be remembered that careful consideration needs to be given to the presentation of key performance indicators to ensure that the results are easily interpreted and not misleading. For example, look once again at Figure 5.11. Although it appears that the number of complaints has increased over the period analysed, the information must be taken in context. The graph would have been a much more useful performance indicator if the number of complaints had been presented in relation to the number of customers taken on over the period. Without an understanding of the customer numbers, we are not in a position to determine whether the rise in customer complaints, as represented in the graph, is a worrying trend or not.

Scatter diagrams

In many situations we may come across two sets of data which seem related. These relationships can be non-mathematically evaluated by using a scatter diagram, the *Y* axis is usually reserved for the characteristic

No. of service failures

Figure 5.13 Scatter diagram: strong positive relationship

we would like to predict (the dependent variable) and the X axis for the variable that we are using to make the prediction (the independent variable). Figure 5.13 does seem to show a clear relationship between number of service failures and number of complaints.

It could be argued that one would reasonably expect there to be quite a strong relationship between number of service failures and number of complaints, though not always so. Figure 5.14 shows a situation where evidence of a strong relationship is not quite so clear-cut.

Factors other than length of service may be better predictors of productivity levels, e.g. willingness to work, financial incentives, competency, etc.

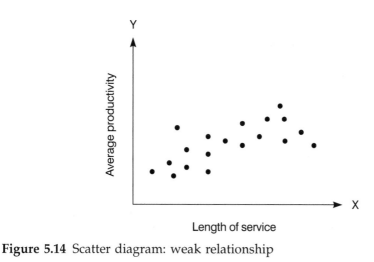

Figure 5.14 Scatter diagram: weak relationship

Tallies or check sheets

A tally or check sheet is perhaps the most commonly used method for collecting and compiling data. A computer will normally do the counting. When working by hand the task can be eased by using the 'five-bar' technique.

Method
- List the possible categories.
- Work through the column of data systematically, putting a stroke next to the appropriate category.
- Every fifth mark should go diagonally across the previous four, as on a gate, to make counting the marks at the end very easy.

Table 5.2 illustrates a tally or check sheet recording the incidence of complaints by subject.

Table 5.2 Tally/check sheet

Subject of complaint	Number of complaints	Total
Delivery times	JHT JHT JHT JHT II	22
Installation	JHT JHT I	11
Company personnel	JHT III	8
Product	JHT JHT	10
		51

Once you have your tally, look at it to see what it tells you. Consider:

- Whether the counts are what you expected
- Which are the most frequently occurring categories
- Whether looking at percentages would be a good idea

Percentage tallies

Table 5.3 Percentage tallies

Subject of complaint	Count	Percentage
Delivery times	22	43 (22/51 × 100)
Installation	11	21
Company personnel	8	16
Product	10	20
	51	100

Cost of quality

The cost of quality can be defined as the total of all resources spent by an organization to assure that quality standards are met on a consistent basis.[14] Quality costs are grouped into two broad categories with two types in each:

1 *Costs of maintaining good quality*
   (a) **Prevention costs** – the costs incurred to prevent errors from occurring. These are said to include the time and effort spent in recruiting, training and reviewing performance of employees along with determining customer requirements and establishing quality standards. Of the types of quality costs, prevention costs are viewed as of central importance but they have been regarded as double counting because prevention is a normal aspect of any manager's responsibility.
   (b) **Appraisal costs** – costs incurred from inspection, testing and auditing aimed at identifying non-conforming aspects before a service or product is delivered.

   Prevention and appraisal costs are incurred because poor quality of conformance can exist.
2 *Costs of poor service quality*
   (a) **Internal failures** – these are errors and defects that are caught before they reach the customer.
   (b) **External failures** – these are problems identified by the customer and the cost may include any refunds or additional services provided at no cost to the customer.

   Failure costs are incurred because poor quality of conformance does exist.

Cost of quality should be continuously monitored through making use of, amongst other things, the tools of quality. Above all organizations should perform a cost of quality audit which is designed to identify:[14]

- The circumstances, events, activities, and problems that occur within the organization that fall within the categories already mentioned.
- The frequency with which these circumstances occur.
- The resources (time, materials, money) devoted to these circumstances and events.

Of course, it has to be remembered that cost of quality was originally developed for a manufacturing context. Transferring it to the service sector is not devoid of problems. However, there are still many aspects of service that can be subjected to a cost of quality analysis. This is particularly true the more standardized the service is as the operating conditions are similar to a manufacturing facility.

As to what can be done, the following example illustrates cost of quality in a service environment. A large hotel where the average rate is £80 and length of stay is two days undertook a cost and performance review of its front-desk operation. Specifically, the focus was on transactions at the front desk, primarily registration and checking-out procedures. The information was obtained from employee observations. A range of errors was considered in terms of their occurrence and cost (Table 5.4).

Table 5.4 Cost of quality calculation. Adopted from Luchars and Hinkin (1996)[15]

Error type	Hourly wage	Time spent fixing error (hours)	Error occurrence per day	Cost over the year (£) (365 days)
1 When guests check out extra charges on the bill are incorrect	£6	0.085	70	13 030
2 Specific information about a reservation has not been entered into the computer	£6	0.15	25	8 212
3 The reservation for an arriving guest cannot be found in the computer	£6	0.12	15	3 942
4 Guest registers and is not given the requested room type	£6	0.2	3	1 314
5 The guest is checking out and the receptionist cannot find the registration card	£6	0.165	3	1 084

The table reveals that errors 4 and 5 individually are relatively minor. Errors 1 and 2 together comprise nearly 80 per cent of the year's cost and therefore merit close attention. A Pareto chart (Figure 5.15) can be constructed from the data. These errors are largely external failures as they have not been caught before they reach the customer. External failures can be reworked as is the case in manufacturing industry. For example, a customer can demand warranty repairs on a faulty car. Services are not so amenable to rework as evidenced by a faulty ATM or a bad haircut. Where rework is not possible, some form of compensation may be given.

The appraisal costs of inspection and testing are of fundamental importance in manufacturing. Services can equally be inspected and tested prior to consumption. However, the service as experienced by the customer cannot obviously be pre-tested or inspected. Customers, themselves, may

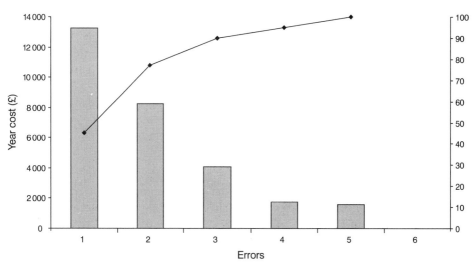

Figure 5.15 Pareto chart: error/cost analysis

actually share responsibility for the quality and hence the cost of service. Where a service is one of high contact, customer involvement and uncertainty can impact on cost of quality (see Chapter 1).

Business excellence model

In early 1992, the UK Quality Award (UKQA) Committee was established 'to consider and report . . . on the feasibility of developing a new prestige award for British business'. The proposals were to be in a form suitable for self-assessment, in harmony with the European Quality Award (EQA), launched by the European Foundation for Quality Management (EFQM) in 1992, and incorporate the lessons learnt from the Malcolm Baldridge National Quality Award (MBNQA). The EQA model had been developed from the MBNQA, with the active involvement of UK organizations: to have developed an alternative model for the UKQA could have undermined the worldwide TQM development process. The EQA model with its emphasis on self-assessment and improvement planning was therefore accepted by the committee.[16] However, the European award process was not seen as a catalyst to inspire nationally focused businesses, small and medium-sized UK organizations, regional or locally based UK businesses, or the public and voluntary sectors, and therefore there was a need for a new UKQA. This model is now known as a Business Excellence Model, and experience of using the model in a wide range of commercial organizations has shown that it is widely applicable both as a means of assessment and as the basis for planning improvements. The model is based on the premise that customer satisfaction, people (employee) satisfaction and impact on society are achieved through leadership driving policy and strategy, people management, resources and processes, leading ultimately to excellence in business results (Figure 5.16).

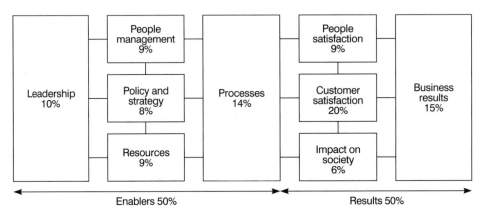

Figure 5.16 The Business Excellence Model. *Source*: British Quality Foundation, London, 1995

Each of the nine elements of the model is a criterion used to assess an organization's progress towards excellence. The percentages shown are those used for the purposes of the UK and European Quality Awards. Both the model and the relative weightings were developed following a wide consultation exercise across Europe, and they are annually reviewed for continuing relevance, criterion and subcriterion definition/deletion/ expansion and relative importance. The model is split on an equal basis between the

- **Enabler** criteria, concerned with **how** an organization approaches its business in each of the areas described by the criteria and subcriteria.
- **Results** criteria covering **what** an organization has achieved and is achieving.

The model criteria

- **Leadership.** This criterion relates to the behaviour of all managers in as much as how the executive team and all other managers inspire, drive and reflect total quality as the organization's fundamental process for continuous improvement.
- **Policy and strategy.** This criterion reviews the organization's mission, values, vision and strategic direction. **How** the organization's policy and

strategy reflect the concept and principles of total quality are used in the formulation, deployment, review and improvement of policy and strategy.

- **People management**. This criterion studies the management of the organization's people and **how** the organization releases the full potential of its people to improve its business and/or service continuously.
- **Resources**. This criterion refers to the management, utilization and preservation of resources and **how** the organization's resources are effectively deployed in support of policy and strategy.
- **Processes**. This criterion analyses the management of all value-adding activities within the organization, **how** processes are identified, reviewed and revised to ensure continuous improvement of the organization's business and/or service.
- **Customer satisfaction**. Examines **what** the organization is achieving in relation to the satisfaction of its external customers.
- **People satisfaction**. Investigates **what** the organization is achieving in relation to the satisfaction of its people.
- **Impact on society**. Probes **what** the organization is achieving in satisfying the needs and expectations of the community at large.
- **Business results**. Reviews **what** the organization is achieving in relation to its planned business and/or service objectives and in satisfying the needs and expectations of everyone with an interest in the organization.

A full exposition of the model can be found in the *Guides to Self-assessment* published by the British Quality Foundation (1995).

Summary

Customers desire a quality service but few can agree on a definition. It expresses itself in the service encounter, service design, service productivity and throughout the organization and culture. A model of service quality has been developed to increase our understanding. It states that gaps exist between the service provider and the customer over expectations and perceptions of quality. The message for management is one of managing customer expectations as well as ensuring that what is promised in respect of quality is actually delivered.

Apart from the contribution of the model, a good place to start is isolating the causes of poor quality. This will then serve as a basis for taking action to improve it. Improvements will be more detectable if steps are taken to set standards and measure performance against these standards.

Monitoring the delivery and acceptability of service quality is now regarded as very important and a range of tools is available for that purpose.

Equally, organizations are increasingly concerned about the cost of delivering quality. For services this kind of exercise offers up a challenge.

The importance attached to the delivery of quality in all kinds of organizations and activities has given rise to a number of awards, in particular the European Quality Award.

References

1. *Measuring Up* (1986) Public Libraries Paper 3. National Consumer Council, London.
2. Crosby, P. (1996) *Quality is still free*. McGraw-Hill, New York.
3. Parasuraman, A., Zeithaml, V. A. and Berry, L. L. (1985) 'A conceptual model of service quality and its implications for future research', *Journal of Marketing*, **49**, Fall, 41–50.
4. Zeithaml, V. A., Parasuraman, A. and Berry, L. L. (1990) *Delivering Service Quality*, Free Press, New York.
5. Ibid.
6. Liswood, L. (1989) *Serving Them Right*, Harper & Row, New York.
7. Martin, W. B. (1986) 'Defining what quality service is for you', *The Cornell HRA Quarterly*, February, 32–38.
8. Berry, L. L., Zeithaml, V. A. and Parasuraman, A. (1985) 'Quality counts in services, too', *Business Horizons*, May–June, 44–52.
9. Goodman, J. A., Malech, A. R., Bargatze, G. F. and Ledbetter, C. (1988) 'Converting a desire for quality service into actions with measurable impact', *Journal of Retail Banking*, **X**(4), 14–22.
10. Berry, L. L., Zeithaml, V. A. and Parasuraman, A. (1990) 'Five imperatives for improving service quality', *Sloan Management Review*, Summer, 29–38.
11. Ibid.
12. Sarazen, T. S. (1990) *Quality Progress*, July.
13. Cravens, D. W. (1988) 'Marketing's role in product and service quality', *Industrial Marketing Management*, **17**.
14. Bohan, G. P. and Horney, W. F. (1991) 'Pinpointing the real cost of quality in a service company', *National Productivity Review*, Summer.
15. Luchars, J. Y. and Hinkin, T. R. (1996) *Cornell Hotel and Restaurant Administration Quarterly*, February.
16. Henderson/Quality Award Committee (1992) *Report on the Feasibility of a New UK Total Quality Award*, DTI.

Chapter 6

The service encounter

Introduction

Interaction between customer and organization lies at the heart of service delivery. The interaction may take many forms, from a brief encounter with a directions sign to a protracted encounter with a service employee. Whatever the nature and type of contact, each represents a moment of truth for the customer. According to Shostack,[1] 'Controlling and enhancing the encounter is a critically important task that no service organisation can afford to leave to chance'.

Types of encounters

Shostack describes three types of service encounters:

1 The remote encounter – where customers interact with a service, or part of it, through the mail, e.g. financial services, mail order. The remote encounter may also occur via a machine, e.g. the ATM. Leaflets, brochures and forms sent by mail need to be designed with the consumer in mind. Machines need to function and be user friendly. This type of encounter should be the easiest to control as it is based on some form of physical object, be it printed material or a computer terminal. Quality should be assured as they can be tested, modified and made uniform.
2 The indirect personal encounter – where customers interact with a service by telephone. There is potentially more scope for variability entering the service delivery. This can be avoided by requiring the employee to work to a script, but problems may still arise if the customer's enquiry/complaint requires reference to other parts of the organization only to find their support is not forthcoming.

3 The direct personal encounter – where customers interact face to face with the service provider. Customers now have the opportunity of visualizing the providers of the service. Judgements about service quality may be made from the appearance and demeanour of the service provider. The increasing use of uniforms, now referred to as corporate clothing, and the development of interpersonal skills training are recognition of the impact direct personal encounters may have on customer satisfaction.

In addition to these three types of encounter, there is a host of other encounter points that may influence the customer's view of the service. For example:

- The front entrance to an organization
- The car park
- The organization's vehicles
- The interior of a building – type of furnishings, plants (real or plastic)
- Signs
- Brochures/leaflets

The above list is simply illustrative but indicates that service organizations contain a wealth of encounter points (not only human). It is at these points that impressions are formed which are subsequently converted into feelings, beliefs and perhaps lasting images.

In certain service situations (some observers may say the numbers are increasing) the customer has a choice between a personal and impersonal encounter. Langeard et al.[2] sought to measure customers' willingness to participate in the process of producing a service. By developing scenarios for a range of services (bank, petrol station, hotel, airport, restaurant, outlet selling travellers cheques) respondents were asked to indicate which type of encounter they preferred. An example of a scenario used is given below.

The bank scenario

It is 10.00 am and you wish to withdraw £50 from your account. You have a card which would enable you to use an automatic teller machine or you could go to a human teller with your cheque book. So your choices are:

Either use the automatic teller *or* use the human teller

There are equally short lines of people waiting to use the machine and at the teller window.

Respondents varied widely in their willingness to use the more participative of the two service alternatives presented in each scenario.

Willingness to participate varied according to demographic characteristics and a number of influencing factors:

- Total amount of time required
- Customer control of the situation
- Amount of effort required by customer
- Customer need to depend on others
- Efficiency of doing it
- Amount of human contact involved
- Risk of something going wrong

This study would seem to raise the following issues:

- Greater participation by the customer in producing the service can lead to gains in productivity
- Service organization reaction to an increasing desire by consumers to becoming involved in production and delivery
- The extent of consumer involvement across service types and activities

Framework for analysing service encounters

Service encounters have been described as comprising phases and elements:[3]

Phases – The delivery of any type of service normally follows a fairly standardized set of steps. These phases begin with the customer's initial contact with the organization and end with any follow-up that is performed. Each phase of the encounter has certain customer require-ments and expectations associated with it, and it may demand varying skills from employers or a specialized infrastructure in the organization examining these phases separately allows the firm to better address their unique characteristics (see below for outline of each phase).

Elements – There are essentially three elements (waiting time, personal interactions, and expectation and perceptions) and they occur in all of the sequential phases cited below. (For discussion of these elements see Chapters 1, 6, 8, 11 and 12.)

Phases

Not all the following phases occur in every service encounter but they do serve as a valuable guide.

Access – e.g. by telephone, fax, computer, personal visits. To make a good first impression services must be easily accessible. Freephone numbers, helplines, visible signs, parking availability, encourage ease of access.

Check-in – customer provides some personal details together with reason for contacting the service organization. A key consideration here is making the customer feel welcome. Service personnel must be knowledgeable enough to know whether a customer's needs can be met, and how best to route them through the service process.

Diagnosis – organizations must listen carefully to the details of the customer's requirements and thereby demonstrate an understanding of what the customer wants and expects.

Service delivery – this is the heart of the encounter with the other phases supporting it. Issues of quality will abound during this phase.

Check-out/disengagement – the last impression can be as important as the first. Anything a service can do at the point of departure that makes the customer feel good is to be commended. It may be as simple as encouraging feedback from customers or providing a manual containing additional advice and information.

Follow-up – service organizations are increasingly making contact with customers after service consumption to determine levels of satisfaction/dissatisfaction.

Obviously there is a host of factors that may contribute to the nature of any given service encounter. However, it is possible to organize these into four broad categories.

● Service employees – their attitudes, personality, competence, appearance
● Service setting – lighting, decor, use of space, temperature, seating, comfort, furnishings, equipment, noise level.

(The above two are referred to again in Section 6.4.)

● Service customers – the expectations and experience they bring with them
● The service process – the manner in which the service is delivered in terms of the number of steps involved in its performance and/or the nature of organization–customer interaction, e.g. how complex is the service, is it standardized or customized?

Service encounter as theatre

The writings of Erving Goffman, particularly *The Presentation of Self in Everyday Life*,[4] have prompted service encounters to be portrayed as performances as in the theatre. Customers and service personnel are cast in the role of actors where every line, gesture, etc. is rigidly specified in the sacred script. In playing a role the genuine identity of the actors is never revealed, hidden behind a mask donned to hide real feelings. The theatre analogy is not totally apt (e.g. masks slip, scripts get abandoned) but it does assist understanding of the service encounter.

Of fundamental importance in delivering a credible performance is the issue of impression management. To convey the right impression use is made of certain expressive equipment collectively termed the front. It comprises two aspects:

Personal front – insignia of office or rank, clothing, sex, age and racial characteristics, size and looks, posture, speech patterns, facial expressions, bodily gestures.

The setting – furniture, decor, physical layout and other background items which supply the scenery and stage props.

How appropriate then are the fronts used in conveying a particular service? What do they say about the particular service? For example, care must be exercised in deciding whether a pin-striped suit is simply a statement of how a businessman should look or a fundamental projection of an air of competence. Is the service encounter and perception of quality enhanced if the car mechanic is covered in oil? The fronts then may convey impressions, rather than any revelations, about abilities, skills, attitudes and demeanours. What is important during the service encounter is maintenance of expressive control by service personnel. Unmeant gestures, indiscretion, faux pas, creating a scene, may jeopardize performance credibility. There should be consistency between the fronts. The appearance of the props, what people look like, say and do must combine to form a package of what the service aims to be. Otherwise, during the encounter, customers may feel confused by contrasting signals. The lawyer sitting in a pink boiler suit in his elegant office would be an extreme but nevertheless vivid reminder of the need to achieve consistency.

Role

Consistent with the theatre metaphor, employees and customers are role players in the service encounter. Each participant is expected to act and behave in a way that is appropriate for the particular service. Situations can, of course, vary, from one of mindlessness[5] to engrossment[6] extending all the way to ecstasy and bewitchment that might characterize situations where a consumer becomes totally engrossed in a service.[7] What this essentially means is that role behaviour will take its cue depending on where the situation lies on a service encounter continuum:

passive ⟵——————————————⟶ active
automatic ⟵——————————————⟶ unpredictable
routine ⟵——————————————⟶ non-routine
standardized ⟵——————————————⟶ personalized

Role enactment will, therefore, vary from the exchange of a few pleasantries (i.e. a smile, friendly greeting with a bank teller, waiter) to one of deep, personal and emotional involvement.

The latter is more difficult to specify as most service encounters, it is argued, rest on the left-side of the continuum. Service encounters may be classified by the degree of psychological involvement and mechanisms required for creating the appropriate level of involvement. Psychological involvement is defined as 'the degree of psychological closeness, with the service provider, as experienced by the customer during the service delivery process. It can range from a customer experiencing the service employee as polite but essentially indifferent towards him/her as a person (resulting in a low degree of psychological closeness), to medium levels of involvement in which customers experience the service employee as sympathetic, to high levels of involvement in which customers experience service employees as concerned, caring and sympathetic towards them.[8] Organization-designed 'rites of integration' are mechanisms for achieving the appropriate degree of involvement. By applying these rites in various ways (language, gestures, ritualized behaviour, physical setting, symbols, displayed emotion) the service encounter is clarified in terms of role behaviour.

There is an assumption, however, that different levels of psychological involvement are associated with certain types of encounters. Many professional services are proposed as high in involvement. However, much as the customer may wish high psychological involvement, (say, with a doctor, lawyer, lecturer), his or her experience may be the opposite. Therefore, a distinction must be drawn between what should be and what is, for those services high in psychological involvement.

Equally, some have argued that treating customers as individuals will not be well received and will probably not pay. There is no evidence to support this proposition. Encounters with bank tellers, waiters, bar staff, taxi-drivers, hotel porters etc. will, in the main, be low in psychological involvement but concerned, caring sympathetic employee behaviour cannot be excluded, particularly when things go wrong.

Power and commitment are important factors in role relationships. Power is defined in terms of how much the consumer perceives he possesses relative to the service provider. Therefore, a relationship is categorized as 'low power' when the consumer believes he has less of it than the provider. Commitment involves intentions with regard to continuing or maintaining a relationship and identification with the role defined by the relationship. Combining the amount of power and commitment, has produced the following classification.[9]

High power, high commitment	– hair stylists, health club, neighbourhood grocery and pharmacy services.
High power, low commitment	– airline cabin service, individual bank tellers, waiters, hotel clerks, bus drivers.
Low power, high commitment	– university education, religion, counselling services, lawyers retained for a trial.
Low power, low commitment	– police services, funeral directors, professional tax preparers, lawyers engaged for brief consultation.

Although one could argue over the examples, every service encounter will have a mix of power and commitment. Depending on where an organization perceives itself to be, appropriate communication strategies can be devised to encourage and retain consumer loyalty, together with procedures for handling complaints. On commitment, the implication for role behaviour is one of willingness to cooperate and participate. On power, consumers may either exercise it to complain or feel frustrated by the lack of it. Although sources of power should enter the discussion one can derive some insight into how consumer power may be reduced or enhanced. For example, military-style uniforms may be an attempt at reduction of consumer power and police officers stopping to chat as they walk the beat, an exercise in enhancement of consumer power.[9]

Whatever the strategies and views on role in the service encounter, organizations should develop some kind of framework within which the issue of role can be discussed and understood. Figure 6.1 is simply an illustration of how one may proceed.

The customer has been defined as a 'partial employee[10] in the service delivery process. This means that services must determine whether customers or employees are the principal performers. For many services, customers will act as 'co-producers' with employees. In some cases, namely the automatic teller machine, the customer becomes the sole producer.

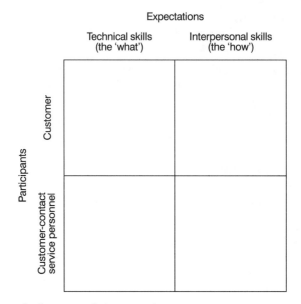

Figure 6.1 The role framework in a service encounter

Allocation of production and delivery between customer and employee will be reflected in responsibility for technical and interpersonal skills. They can be summarized as follows:

Employee technical skills – application of knowledge and equipment in providing solutions.

Customer technical skills – provision of information and labour.

Interpersonal skills – for employee and customer it means how they are going to behave, e.g. caring, assertive, domineering.

Effective performance will depend on how well the participants acquire and put into practice the appropriate skills. In addition, it is important to remember that delivering a quality service may require role undertakings before and after the actual encounter as well as during it. Education is a good example of this. Preparation before a lecture together with how the participants manage what they have learnt after it can contribute enormously to effectiveness in role performances during delivery.

Basically, the organization must ask itself:

● What are the customers and employees expected to do?
● How are they expected to do it?

Answers to these questions form the essence of role determination.

Script

A script is regarded as 'a predetermined, stereotyped sequence of actions, that defines a well-known situation'.[11] People experience hundreds of stereotypic situations with routine activities, e.g. riding a bus, visiting a dentist, eating in a restaurant. Script theory has been proposed as evidence of how we use specific knowledge to interpret and participate in events we have been through many times. Scripts basically tell the customer what his or her role should be, the sequence of events and what other people are likely to do. Customer satisfaction will largely depend on whether the service received conforms to the script. Parts of a script are illustrated in Table 6.1.

The restaurant script is one to which most people can relate. It is perceived as against causal chain in which each action results in conditions that enable the next to occur. Any script will consist of a set of activities that has conventional roles, props, event-sequences, standard entering conditions and standard outcomes. The script approach is highly relevant as it depicts service delivery as a process. For each step in the process performance can be monitored and set against organization specifications and customer expectations.

Script generation

The importance of customer scripts is that they represent customer's knowledge of what to do for effective participation in the service production. People can be asked to describe what goes on in detail during a variety of service situations. From these descriptions an understanding of the level of agreement there is between consumer and organization on the nature of the characters, props, actions, the order in which they occur can be obtained.

As part of an investigation of cognitive process, a group of under-graduates were asked to write scripts about common activities[12] (Table 6.2). They were given the following instructions (the lecture script will serve as an example).

> Write a list of actions describing what people generally do
> when they go to a lecture in a course. We are interested in
> the common actions of a routine lecture stereotype. Start the
> list with arriving at the lecture and end it with leaving after the
> lecture. Include about 20 actions or events and put them in
> order in which they would occur.

Not surprisingly there was a large measure of agreement in the actions mentioned and the order in which they occur. This was because the

Table 6.1 Theoretical restaurant script (adapted from Schank and Abelson, 1977)[11]

Name:	Restaurant		
Props:	Tables	Roles:	Customer
	Menu		Waitress
	Food		Cook
	Bill		Cashier
	Money		Owner
	Tip		
Entry		Results:	Customer has
Conditions:	Customer has		less money
	money		Owner has
			more money
			Customer is
			not hungry
			Customer is satisfied/dissatisfied

Scene 1:	Entering
	Customer enters restaurant
	Customer looks for table
	Customer decides where to sit
	Customer goes to table
	Customer sits down
Scene 2:	Ordering
	Customer picks up menu
	Customer looks at menu
	Customer decides on food
	Customer signals waitress
	Waitress comes to table
	Customer orders food
	Waitress goes to cook
	Waitress gives food order to cook
	Cook prepares food
Scene 3:	Eating
	Cook gives food to waitress
	Waitress brings food to customer
	Customer eats food
Scene 4:	Exiting
	Waitress writes bill
	Waitress goes over to customer
	Waitress gives bill to customer
	Customer gives tip to waitress
	Customer goes to cashier
	Customer gives money to cashier
	Customer leaves restaurant

situations were largely routine and familiar. Nevertheless, for the proper conduct and management of the service encounter, people (i.e. customers and service employees) need to agree on the essentials of the script.

Description of scripts may be less predictable and result in less agreement if the following qualifications are added:

- Inputs vary – a service situation as experienced by different customer types e.g. socioeconomic groups.
- Processes vary – from simple to complex, standardized to customized.
- What should happen versus what does happen.

A couple of examples will illustrate part of this expanded view. Owners starting up small businesses could be asked to generate scripts following an application for a bank loan. Two scenarios would be researched. For example, start with 'Decide to apply for a bank loan' and end with either 'being granted a loan' or 'not being granted a loan'. This would provide an interesting contrast between the actions and events that lead to success and those that end in failure. Or, people could be asked to describe a visit to the doctor. In this case a distinction could be drawn between a patient experiencing a degree of discomfort, the origin of which is not very clear (at least to the patient and perhaps even to the doctor), versus a straightforward ailment. Comparisons could be made between what patients expected to happen in the course of the consultation and what actually did happen.

Opportunities are therefore available to extend script generation and establish the extent of agreement on the part of respondents.

Scripts for service jobs

Due to the very nature of their job, customer contact personnel in the service sector are subject to a great deal of attention and scrutiny. To achieve efficiency and effectiveness in employee performance, management must devote time and effort to developing proper job descriptions. Scripting is an important aspect of specifying how the job should be done. Tansik and Smith[13] proposed a model that specifies the dimensions of scripts and how these may be applied in a variety of service settings. The dimensions are:

- Script intensity – extent to which a script specifically determines the employee's actions and words. Low intensity will allow ad-libbing, high intensity will not.
- Script complexity – extent to which at some point in the script there is a need and opportunity to abandon the script and go to another one, to

Table 6.2 Empirical script norms at three agreement levels

Going to a restaurant	Attending a lecture	Getting up	Grocery shopping	Visiting a doctor
Open door	ENTER ROOM	*Wake up*	ENTER STORE	*Enter office*
Enter	*Look for friends*	Turn off alarm	GET CART	CHECK IN WITH RECEPTIONIST
Give reservation name	FIND SEAT	Lie in bed	Take out list	SIT DOWN
Wait to be seated	SIT DOWN	Stretch	Look at list	Wait
Go to table	Settle belongings	GET UP	Go to first aisle	Look at other people
BE SEATED	TAKE OUT NOTEBOOK	Make bed	*Go up and down aisles*	READ MAGAZINE
Order drinks	*Look at other students*	Go to bathroom	PICK OUT ITEMS	*Name called*
Put napkins on lap	*Talk*	Use toilet	Compare prices	Follow nurse
LOOK AT MENU	Look at professor	*Take shower*	Put items in cart	*Enter exam room*
Discuss menu	LISTEN TO PROFESSOR	Wash face	Get meat	Undress
ORDER MEAL	TAKE NOTES	Shave	Look for items forgotten	*Sit on table*
Talk	CHECK TIME	DRESS	Talk to other shoppers	Talk to nurse
Drink water	Ask questions	Go to kitchen	Go to checkout counters	NURSE TESTS
Eat salad or soup	Change position in seat	Fix breakfast	*Find fastest line*	Wait
Meal arrives	Daydream	EAT BREAKFAST	WAIT IN LINE	Doctor enters
EAT FOOD	Look at other students	BRUSH TEETH	*Put food on belt*	Doctor greets
Finish meal	Take more notes	Read paper	Read magazines	Talk to doctor about problem
Order dessert	Close notebook	*Comb hair*	WATCH CASHIER RING UP	Doctor asks questions
Eat dessert	Gather belongings	Get books	PAY CASHIER	DOCTOR EXAMINES
Ask for bill	Stand up	Look in mirror	Watch bag boy	Get dressed
Bill arrives	Talk	Get coat	Cart bags out	Get medicine
PAY BILL	LEAVE	LEAVE HOUSE	Load bags into car	Make another appointment
Leave tip			LEAVE STORE	LEAVE OFFICE
Get coats				
LEAVE				

Items in all capital letters were mentioned by the most subjects, items in italics by fewer subjects, and items in text type by the fewest subjects Source: Bower, Black and Turner (1979)[12]

simply continue the script or to enter some subprogramme within the existing script.

- Number of scripts – how many must be learned to do the job.
- Percentage of time in scripts – what percentage of time is spent in scripts.
- Percentage of duties in scripts – what percentage of tasks or duties are scripted.

They apply the dimensions to three service settings in which the customer-induced uncertainty (CIU) ranges from low to high (Table 6.3).

Table 6.3 A scripting model based on customer-induced uncertainty

| | Customer-induced uncertainty | | |
	Low	*Medium*	*High*
Number of scripts in a job	Low	Medium	High
Percentage of job duties scripted	High	Medium	Low
Percentage of work time in scripts	High	Medium	Low
Script complexity	Low	Medium	High
Script intensity	High	Medium	Low

Source: Tansik and Smith (1991)[13]

Customer-induced uncertainty (CIU) simply reflects the amount and nature of involvement in the service delivery process. It is quite clear that a low CIU almost equates to a standardized format of service delivery where:

- Few scripts are used
- Scripts are very precise
- Much of the job is scripted

Fast-food retailing is a typical example.
On the other hand, in a situation of high CIU, scripts:

- Are numerous
- Are complex and allow for variation
- Are not applied in all situations and at all times

This situation is not the exclusive preserve of the professional services as may be thought. For example, the surgeon in theatre must follow a tightly prescribed script in the event of a patient having a heart attack, whereas the fast-food employee may find the standard scripts available to be of little value when dealing with an unruly customer.

The critical incident technique

Organizations need to know what customers expect from the service experience. In particular they need to study what goes on during the encounter with service personnel to see if it lives up to customers' expectations. A method particularly suited to achieving that objective is the critical incident technique which has been described as a set of procedures for collecting direct observations of human behaviour in such a way as to facilitate their potential usefulness in solving problems and developing broad psychological principles.[14]

Flanagan[14] described and applied the technique in an industrial setting. By collecting statements from the participants in an encounter it seeks to determine incidents (behaviours, actions) that are especially helpful or inadequate. It is particularly valuable for evaluating employee/customer interactions but can be equally revealing when applied within an organization. For example the following questions can reveal effective or ineffective behaviours of a supervisor. Employees, and even management, could be asked to:

- Think of a time when your supervisor did something that you felt should be encouraged as it seemed in your opinion an example of good supervision
- Think of a time when the supervisor did something that you thought was not up to par

What may be interesting is the degree of agreement/disagreement between management and employees as to what constitutes effective and ineffective behaviour by the supervisor.

Applications of the critical incident technique to the service encounter

Communication problems

Having a technically sound operational system is insufficient for delivering service quality and providing customer satisfaction. Positive service encounters require effective oral communication skills on the part of the employees. This is particularly so in the case of high contact service organizations like hotels, airlines, restaurants, colleges etc.

The aim must be to identify, with the aid of the critical incident technique, employee behaviours that are regarded as either effective or ineffective in exchanges with customers. There is an endless amount and variety of customer behaviours that may prove difficult to manage. For example.[15]

- Unreasonable demands
- Demands against company policy
- Unacceptable treatment of employees
- Drunkenness

It may often be the case that customer expectations or demands exceed the organization's and its employees' willingness and/or ability to meet them. In knowing how to handle these demands employees should have a knowledge of customer expectations and how they are formed. Organizations often equip their employees with scripts which specify a range of responses to be used in a given situation. There are inherent dangers with this approach as the customer perceives the organization to be impersonal and inflexible. To overcome this, employees should be encouraged to expand their repertoire of possible responses.

Organizations need to train employees to be competent communicators. There is a large body of research from which communication strategies can be developed. However, there are a number of fundamental principles that every employee should adhere to when confronted with a difficult situation:

- Remain calm – an irate customer can be equated to a pressure cooker so the lid needs to be taken off gently
- Let the customer vent his or her anger – don't interrupt, laugh etc.
- Listen with understanding – this diffuses anger and demonstrates concern. Apologize to the customer for being inconvenienced and state that you are there to help. It is vital to show a sincere interest and willingness to help. The customer's first impression of the employee is all important in gaining cooperation
- Restate what the customer is saying, in summary form. This tells the customer that you have listened and understood what has been said
- Don't blame others or make excuses. Instead, take the responsibility and initiative to do whatever you can to solve the problem as quickly as possible
- Find out what the customer wants. If that cannot be met, state why and propose your own solution. The customer may also be asked what he or she would consider a fair alternative
- Once a solution is agreed, act quickly. If agreement cannot be reached, refer the customer to someone else able to resolve the problem.

In all the dealings with the customer it is important to be courteous and considerate and respect the feelings of the customer.

Satisfactory and unsatisfactory encounters

In addition to asking employees for examples of interactions with customers that were difficult and uncomfortable, the views of customers are invaluable for revealing the specific events and employee behaviours that make for a satisfactory or dissatisfactory encounter. Critical incidents (events and behaviour) are uncovered by asking consumers the following:

- Think of a time when, as a customer, you had a particularly satisfying (dissatisfying) interaction with an employee of (service specified).
- When did the incident happen?
- What specific circumstances led up to this situation?
- Exactly what did the employees say or do?
- What resulted that made you feel the interaction was satisfying (dissatisfying)?

Responses to questions such as these can shed enormous light on the performance of the entire service delivery system. It can reveal specific customer perceptions of how well (or badly) employees responded, failures in the service delivery system and customer needs and requests. It can provide surprises, e.g. excellent service as a consequence of unexpected and unrequested employee behaviour. In addition to individual expressions of satisfaction or dissatisfaction with a particular event or behaviour customers may intimate their overall feelings, for example.[16]

> Everything went right – 'a sincere and professional team effort, accommodating, polite but not pushy, warm atmosphere, courteous, efficient and professional, no waiting, best service ever received, everything was perfect'.

> Everything went wrong – 'inefficient, unprepared, slow, not accommodating nor attentive, no assistance, unprofessional, bad decor/atmosphere'.

Customer satisfaction or dissatisfaction will depend to a large extent on whether, and how, employees apply their ability, willingness and ingenuity. Implicit in all of this is the recurring theme of how well prepared, motivated and rewarded the employees are. Personality may explain acts of extreme helpfulness. However, employee response must be planned on a much firmer footing. The service organization bears a heavy responsibility for ensuring that employees are well resourced to act in a positive manner.

Encounters of more than human proportions

High-contact service organizations are particularly exposed in terms of the number of potential encounter points. A good example is a college library. Given the pressure on staff resources, management could look at ways in which the consumers (students) could play a more prominent role in the production and delivery of the service. To do this questions would need to be asked of existing student experiences. One such study[17] used the critical incident technique for highlighting the problems students encounter when trying to use the library. The results yielded a wide range of problems and comment ranging from use of the catalogue, location of books and library layout. In addition, students expressed feelings of anxiety, a reluctance to ask for help and a lack of information. Some of the comments made by the students indicate the amount of work to be done before the library could be regarded as user friendly:

> 'The first time I came in the library I hadn't got a clue about anything. You just sort of get in there and it's so big and you just sit there and say "Oh no!".'

> 'You don't really know what's available . . . it's only if you find out from someone else that it's there, it's not publicized, you haven't got signs.'

> '. . . and then the computer kept flashing up at me and I couldn't get rid of it . . . I was getting a bit panicky . . . and in the end I just left it.'

These few examples typify the difficulties/problems that consumers can experience in trying to make full and proper use of a service. The solution is not always to get the consumer to design the system. There may often be procedures and systems that have to be put into practice without any consultation with the consumer. However, it is the responsibility of the service provider to ensure that the potential users are equipped with information skills etc. to use the service effectively.

Another service with similar challenges is hospitals. They have the added problem of serving people (patients and visitors) who may be vulnerable and who are experiencing stress of some kind. The following complaints[18] are clear evidence of unsatisfactory encounters amounting to failure on the part of hospitals to deliver a quality service:

- Waiting for ages in out-patients without any explanation or apology
- Waiting a long time for admission to hospital
- Not understanding what the doctor is saying

- Important test results not being there when they see the consultant
- Not knowing what the options are or who to ask
- Doctors who have no time to listen and ignore what they say
- Being treated like a child and patronized
- Feeling that they are seen as a medical condition, not as a whole person
- Operations being cancelled at the last minute
- Transport home being hours late.

Typical service behaviours

Generally speaking, people's behaviour can be categorized as aggressive, submissive or assertive. The service encounter will be enhanced by assertiveness but devalued or impoverished by aggressiveness or submissiveness. Employees in service organizations are usually trained and encouraged to be assertive but submissiveness may occur. On the other hand, customers are prone to adopting an aggressive stance in the event of service failure. The three types of people's behaviour have been characterized as follows:

Submissive people

- Allow themselves to be dominated
- Withhold opinions and feelings
- Are indecisive
- Apologize constantly
- Have poor eye contact and posture

Assertive people

- State their wants and needs directly
- Give opinions and feelings
- Are decisive
- Confront issues
- Have good eye contact and open posture

Aggressive people

- Interrupt
- Conceal information and opinions
- Dominate and are poor listeners
- Are loud, blaming and sarcastic
- Have intense and glaring eye contact and dominant posture

The importance of body language

Communicating effectively means sending the right signals. For many people, the message they are sending is not necessarily the one that is received. Body language is an area in which things can go wrong. Body language accounts for about 70 per cent of what we communicate, tone of voice about 20 per cent and the actual words about 10 per cent.

Whereas control is often exercised in selecting the words we use, body language is often left to 'fend for itself'. What comes out is the unedited version of what we really feel. Although body language is a study in its own right, the following areas offer a summary of what is involved.

1 **Posture** is concerned with body positions and movement. A number of elements are commonly used to express the various positions:

lean:	forwards	arms:	open
	backwards		closed
	sideways		on hips
head:	lowered	legs:	stretched
	raised		open
	tilted sideways		crossed

Combinations of the above are said to indicate a range of attitudes and emotions, e.g. dominance, fear, relaxation, interest, boredom etc. In general, it has been said that 'people who feel comfortable with a situation and with themselves raise their head and look openly at you. They may lean back slightly indicating they are relaxed or lean forward to indicate attentiveness. People who are on the attack or who feel aggressive generally adopt a "full frontal" stance with head, shoulders, hips and feet all pointing at you. They will probably raise themselves up and lean forward in a dominating manner. Those who are feeling defensive will probably "close-up" physically, making themselves smaller; hands and arms may protect their mouth or abdomen; legs may be crossed tightly. People feeling superior and arrogant may cross their legs openly (ankle of one leg resting on the knee of the other) and lean back with their hands clasped at the back of their head'.[19]

2 **Gestures** involve bodily actions by the head, hands or other parts of the body. Gestural styles are partly a product of many factors, e.g. culture, occupation, age, sex and so on. They can reflect an emotional state, e.g. anxiety (fidgeting) or a general style of behaviour, e.g. aggression (clenched fist). The hands, in particular, can be used in endless ways to communicate countless messages.

3 **Face** is the most important non-verbal channel. It is particularly important for expressing emotions and attitudes to other people. There is general agreement as to the range of emotional expressions. They are happiness,

surprise, fear, sadness, anger, disgust/contempt. These emotions find expression through a communication of eye, eyebrows, lips, and mouth movement. Some emotions are found in certain parts of the face, e.g. raised eyebrows and an open smile indicating pleasure. Care must be exercised, however, when judging another person's emotional state from his or her face.

4 **Gaze** is important in interpersonal behaviour. Although a non-verbal signal it is essentially a means of perceiving the expression of others. It can be measured in terms of how much time is spent looking at another person or looking at each other. It can be in the form of a brief glance or extended eye contact. It is often referred to as 'staring', looking 'intently', looking 'daggers' or 'looking right through' another person. There are cultural rules about gaze, e.g. 'don't stare' and don't look at certain parts of the body. How much of it there is can be an indication, in certain situations, of attentiveness. Those who indulge it more are said to be better interactors, more persuasive, influential, credible and so on. But again, care must be exercised. It does play an important role in establishing relations between people. For example, a teacher uses the amount of gaze as an indication of whether or not pupils are listening.

5 **Tone of voice** is an important part of communication. It is not only what we say but how we say it, e.g. are the words delivered in a loud or soft manner, quickly or slowly? Is the delivery monotonous or varied? The way a communication is delivered can give rise to a variety of reactions ranging from interest and excitement through to downright boredom.

6 **Proximity** is concerned with spatial behaviour. How close we are to other people will depend on such things as cultural norms (e.g. Arabs tend to stand close) and the type of social situation. In some cases, like a crowded train we have no choice. But in others there are rules of engagement in so far as how far apart we should be. It is generally recognized that there are four main space ranges:

Intimate: 15–48 cm (6–18 inches)

Personal distances: 0.45–1.2 m (1.5–4 feet), closer than which discomfort is often experienced

Social distance: 1.2–3.5 m (4–12 feet), used for formal business purposes

Public distance: over 3.5 m (12 feet) and up to 7.6 m (25 feet) or more. This is the distance kept from important public figures.

To use body language effectively, according to Terry Gillen,[19] we have first, to ensure that it is positive. He groups some aspects of body language into positive and negative, the latter being further subdivided into submissive/inferior and aggressive/superior.

Positive

Smile
Interested expression
Moderate eye contact
Sufficient volume, varied pace and pitch of voice
Open posture
Hands, arms support what is being said

Negative

Submissive/inferior	*Aggressive/superior*
Wobbly voice	Hard voice
Slow speech	Rapid speech
Worried expression	Extremes of expression
Evasive looks down	Excessive eye contact
Defensive arms/legs	Dominant posture
Mouth covered with hand	Finger wagging/jabbing
Excessive distance	Invasions of person space

Gillen then combines the 'how' of interaction with what is said to illustrate the possibilities (Figure 6.2). The main point about this is that effectiveness in communication stems from actions and words that are in tune with each other.

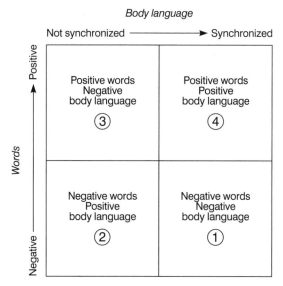

Figure 6.2 Synchronizing verbal and non-verbal communication. *Source*: Gillent (1990)[19]

Summary

The service encounter can take a variety of forms, ranging from a cursory glance at a sign to a protracted personal interaction. The nature and degree of customer involvement is an important issue in the service encounter.

Of all the types of encounter the interpersonal contact, particularly face to face, is the most challenging. The nature of the interaction and the final outcome will be explained by reference to a number of factors.

Encounters occur during a number of phases of the service process. Within each phase particular elements need to be understood and managed. Performances during the encounter are likened to those witnessed on stage in the theatre. The service provider and customers are, in effect, actors who have been assigned a role with an appropriate script.

Analysis can be undertaken of role behaviour and script generation. The critical incident technique is a valuable tool for determining what the parties to an encounter expect and what constitutes a satisfying or dissatisfying experience. It can assist the organization trying to ensure that the experience, and subsequent memory, is one of satisfaction at the very least. Any encounter represents a moment of truth in which lasting impressions may be created.

References

1. Shostack, G. L. (1985) 'Planning the service encounter'. In *The Service Encounter* (Czepiel, J. A., Solomon, M. R., Suprenant, C. F., eds), Lexington Books, D. C. Heath and Company, Lexington, MA.
2. Langeard, E., Bateson, J. E. G., Lovelock, C. H., Eiglier, (1981) 'Marketing of services: new insights from consumers and managers', *Marketing Science Institute, Report*, Number 81–104. Cambridge, MA.
3. Bitra, N. G. (1993) 'A framework for analysing the quality of the customer interface', *European Management Journal* **11**(4).
4. Goffman, E. (1972) *The Presentation of Self in Everyday Life*, Penguin, London.
5. Langer, E. (1978) 'Rethinking the role of thought in social interaction'. In *New Directions in Attribution Research* (Harvey, J., Ickes, W. and Kidd, R. eds), Erlbaum, Hillsdale, NJ.
6. Goffman, E. (1961) *Encounters: Two Studies in the Sociology of Interaction*, Bobbs-Merrill, Indianapolis.
7. Solomon, M. R., Suprenant, C., Czepiel, J. A. and Gutman, E. G. (1985) 'A role theory perspective on dyadic interactions: the service encounter', *Journal of Marketing*, **49**, Winter, 99–111.

8. Siehl, C. and Bowen, D. E. (1991) 'The role of rites of integration in service delivery', *International Journal of Service Industry Management*, **2**(1), 15–34.
9. Goodwin, C. (1989) *Using Consumers' Roles to Classify Service Excellence: marketing's impact on performance*, Eighth Annual Services Marketing Conference, American Marketing Association.
10. Mills, P. K. and Morris, J. H. (1986) 'Clients as "partial" employees of service organisations: role development in client participation,' *Academy of Management Review*, **11**(4), 726–735.
11. Schank, R. C. and Abelson, R. P. (1977) *Scripts, Plans. Goals and Understanding*, Erlbaum, Hillsdale, NJ.
12. Bower, G. H., Black, J. B. and Turner, T. J. (1979) 'Scripts in memory for text', *Cognitive Psychology*, **11** 177–220.
13. Tansik, D. A. and Smith, W. L. (1991) 'Dimensions of job scripting in services organisations', *International Journal of Service Industry Management*, **2**(1), 35–49.
14. Flanagan, J. C. (1954) 'The critical incident technique', *Psychological Bulletin*, **51**(4), July 327–358.
15. Nyquist, J. D., Bitner, M. J. and Booms, B. H. (1985) 'Identifying communication difficulties in the service encounter: a critical incident approach'. In *The Service Encounter* (Czepiel, J. A., Solomon, M. R., Suprenant, C. F., eds), Lexington Books. D. C. Heath and Company, Lexington, MA.
16. Bitner, M. J., Booms, B. H. and Terteault, M. S. (1990) 'The service encounter: diagnosing favourable and unfavourable incidents', *Journal of Marketing*, **54**, January, 71–84.
17. Andrews, J. (1991) 'An exploration of students' library use problems', *Library Review*, **40**(1), 5–14.
18. *Framework for Action: The National Health Service in Scotland* (1991) HMSO, London.
19. Gillen, T. (1990) *Training Workshops for Customer Care*, Gower, Aldershot.

Chapter 7

Service employees

Introduction

People who deliver the service are of key importance to both the customers they serve and the employer they represent. To the customer they are in fact part of the product. Their ability and willingness to satisfy, their manner and appearance, all play a part in determining how satisfied the customer is with the service encounter. To the employer, those delivering the service can make or break the organization. On the one hand, they may be the only way that a service brand differentiates itself. On the other hand, they can also be the reason why people do not come back.

In many organizations everything that the frontline employees do is stage managed. They have little discretion or flexibility in the way they offer the service, rather they are restricted to implementing a strict set of rules and procedures. This leaves the jobs deskilled and the workers demotivated.[1] In other organizations frontline employees can be given too much flexibility and responsibility without the commensurate training or rewards.[2]

Frontline personnel

Not every frontline employee plays an equally important role in the delivery of service. Lovelock[3] suggests that the two most significant variables in this respect are the degree to which the service offering is customized and the extent to which customer contact staff exercise judgement in meeting an individual customer's needs (Figure 7.1). In box 1 where the service is standardized and frontline employees are not empowered to exercise their judgement, frontline staff play a relatively

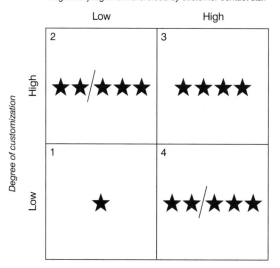

Figure 7.1 The importance of frontline staff. * = not very important, **** = very important. Adapted from Lovelock (1996)[3]

minor role in the service experience, e.g. a ticket cashier at the cinema. On the other hand, frontline employees are very important to service operations in box 4. These services are characterized by a high degree of customization and customer contact staff exercising their judgement in the desire to fulfil customer expectations, e.g. a marriage guidance councillor. Boxes 2 and 3 will fall somewhere in the middle. The degree of importance attached to frontline employees in these situations will depend on the specific service being offered.

Frontline personnel are not a homogeneous group. The hotel chambermaid and the plastic surgeon are both frontline employees in that they both deal directly with customers. Some of the skills that are required are common to both jobs. These core skills have become common requirements of all frontline staff regardless of the specific service that they provide (Figure 7.2).

In addition to these essentials, most industries also require some supplementary skills. Frontline staff will only provide a quality service if they possess all the qualities required, both core and supplementary. Historically, those who provided services that required a lot of technical ability got away without the core skills. If a doctor was rude, or kept patients waiting, no one complained. No one accused him of providing a poor service. His position allowed him to behave in this manner. Now, though, even those in the professional services are expected to possess core service skills.

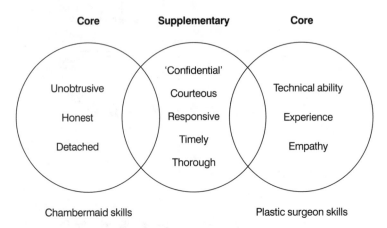

Figure 7.2 Core/supplementary skills

Frontline staff act as another element of communication. They help portray the desired image of the company. If the intended image is one of sophistication then do not employ people who chew gum and bite their nails. If it is important that customers empathize with staff then ensure that service personnel are segmented by their personalities so that they meet the customers' requirements. In a department store the total pool of shop assistants should be segmented so that for example, those serving in the children's department are patient and fun-loving, while those serving in the china department are careful and light of foot.

Customer and staff care

'Customer care' is often discussed in relation to the service sector. The concept came to prominence in the 1980s through the highly publicized customer care campaigns of companies such as British Airways and British Telecom. Today, we often hear of companies deploying 'customer care' programmes, but what does it all mean?[4]

The concept has been defined as 'a fundamental approach to standards of quality service. It covers every aspect of a company's operations, from the design of the product or service to how it is packaged, delivered and serviced. Even the accompanying instructions, so often forgotten by the customer-care conscious Japanese, are part of the process'.[5] This definition talks of a process for delivering quality service, and is therefore more substantial and far-reaching in scope, than the smile and charm school approach that has given the concept of customer care a bad name.

In effect this approach to business is merely a restatement of Levitt's proposition that 'the customer is king'. Taking this analogy a stage further, those who provide for the king's needs are his 'servants'. Satisfying him is of paramount importance, not only to the selfish king, but also to those who wish to remain in the kingdom.

Whether or not the customer regards himself as a king, he has come to expect 'care' from the service provider. Management have long recognized the importance of frontline employees in the provision of this care. They are the key to success during what Jan Carlzon calls the 'moments of truth'.[6] However, what organizations often fail to recognize is the importance of 'staff care'. Customers are far more likely to receive good service if the staff delivering the service are happy in their work. Employers who treat their staff like kings are far more likely to have a motivated and committed workforce who are interested and willing to deliver a quality service. In organizations where the employees have a good opinion of the human resources policy, customers also have a good opinion of the service that they receive.[7] Management cannot expect to deliver customer satisfaction if it has little regard for the satisfaction of its own internal customers – the employees.

Staff dissatisfaction

One suspects that if you asked service customers the question. 'Are you treated like a king?', that at best you would get some hysterical laughter and at worst you would be physically abused. For many consumers in this country there is certainly still a long way to go before the transition from 'organization is king' to 'customer is king' is complete.

The customer dissatisfaction that arises is often laid at the feet of the frontline employees in the service organization. While at times this is unjust, we can probably all recount instances where the blame lies almost entirely with them.

Scratch the surface of most of these situations, and you will find in most cases the employees are also unhappy with the organization. Why should they attempt to make customers happy when they are not happy themselves?

In transactional analysis these individuals have adopted what Harris,[8] describes as an 'I'm not OK' position. The organization has made them feel 'Not OK', and they take it out on the customers – 'You will not be OK either'.

If the service providers are to improve the interaction of these staff with customers, then they have to make them feel, 'I'm OK, the organization's OK, you're OK, and I'd like to help you'.

But before the organization can remove the dissatisfaction, it has to be understood. So what makes employees dissatisfied with their jobs?

Many factors have been found to contribute to this problem.[9] These are:

- Role ambiguity
- Role conflict
- Role overload
- Employee/job mismatch
- Performance measured on quantity not quality
- Lack of empowerment
- Lack of a common purpose
- Lack of management commitment

Role ambiguity

Employees do not understand what management or customers expect of them (see Chapter 2). This situation is improved with role clarity; clearly communicate what individuals must do, and tell them how they are doing. However, telling the individual what you want him or her to do is not enough. It is the employer's responsibility to give the employee the ability to perform the job. This can be achieved by training, leaving him or her a competent and confident performer.

Role conflict

Two or more incompatible sets of pressures impact on the employee's behaviour. This is more likely to arise in situations where the employee is in what Boas Shamir describes as a subordinate service role.[10] In these situations the provider of the service has no more expertise or ability to deliver the service than the ordinary man in the street. The majority of service encounters that take place in fact do so with the employee in this position. Think of the jobs performed by the receptionist in an hotel, the shop assistant, the waiter, and the bus conductor. We all feel that we could do them, and this makes us more critical of the service that is delivered.

There are four basic sources of role conflict (Figure 7.3).

- Customer siding conflict: employee wants to do more for the customer than the organization allows (provide a child's portion at a reduced price).
- Company siding conflict: employee takes the side of the organization believing that the customer is acting in an unjustified or selfish manner, i.e. refusing to admit late theatregoers during the performance.
- Company combining conflict: the organization expects him to satisfy demanding customers and do lots of paperwork and administration besides.

- Customer combining conflict: separate groups of customers have different requirements for the service, e.g. some customers may regard the main job of their coach tour guide to be one of information provision. Other members of the party may instead believe that this person is there primarily to keep the tour on time.

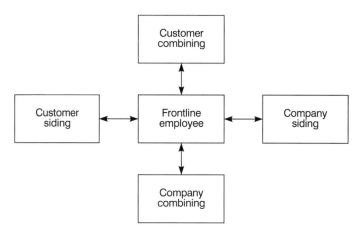

Figure 7.3 Sources of role conflict

So what can the organization do to minimize role conflict?

- Design jobs whose scope is pitched at the abilities of the proficient employee.
- If need be, prioritize the multitude of tasks that the employee is expected to fulfil.
- Define these tasks in terms of customers' expectations.
- Ensure that performance is measured on those tasks which have been given priority. These should be customer-focused tasks.
- Train employees in time management.

Role overload

The name describes the problem! No matter how diligently individuals work they can never do all that is asked of them. They are always behind – causing frustration and dissatisfaction with their performance.

This is most likely to occur where jobs have been badly designed. However, even where the initial job design was excellent, circumstances can change. It may be that the level, or pattern, of demand for the service has changed. If instead of handling equal customer traffic throughout the day, a workforce is faced with periods of relative inactivity followed by periods of intense activity, role overload may result.

Workloads and patterns of demand should be continually monitored and evaluated to reduce the risk of role overload.

Employee/job mismatch

Not every individual performing a frontline service role is an appropriate person for the job. In some cases this is the result of a poor recruitment and selection process. In others, the organization does not really care. It is known that many service companies experiencing high turnover rates among contact staff tend to recruit new staff expediently with little regard for their ability.[11] This is shortsighted, because these individuals probably do not really care much about customer satisfaction. Whatever the job, management should consider the qualities that are necessary to do the job. It should then adopt a selection process that tests for these qualities.

Performance measured on quantity not quality

It can be disheartening for a frontline employee to discover that they work for a company which is more interested in employee efficiency than employee effectiveness. The number of customers that they have dealt with being of more importance than the degree to which these customers were satisfied (see Chapter 10).

Lack of empowerment

Employees who have little flexibility or discretion in the way that they handle customers' demands can find their jobs frustrating. They can be likened to circus animals who slavishly respond to appropriate triggers, with set routines.

Enlightened employers have realized the lack of motivation that normally ensues from such work, and have set about trying to correct this by giving employees more responsibility and authority. This is known as *empowerment*.

We would certainly encourage employers to make the individual's job more rewarding through empowerment. However, in giving this extra responsibility the employer should also be prepared to reward the increased job scope in an appropriate manner, e.g. with a higher salary.

Lack of a common purpose

Frequently the individual employee that greets the customer feels quite isolated in that position. He can believe that he carries out his job without the full backing either of the other employees in the back office or indeed of the company's management.

What is needed is for the company to have a common purpose and for everyone employed in it to pull in the same direction with the intention of achieving the common goal.

One way of doing this is to make customer satisfaction the stated goal, and to make everyone in the company treat the other members of staff that they interact with as if they were customers. They should be encouraged to provide a standard of service to these employees that they would wish to receive themselves.

Lack of management commitment

It is one thing for management to develop a common purpose, and to communicate this mission to all its employees, but it cannot expect this alone to motivate the staff. If employees feel that management say one thing to them and then do another themselves, they are likely to become disenfranchised. As Abraham Lincoln said, 'actions speak louder than words'.[12] So, for example, if part of the stated mission is to improve customer satisfaction, then management should be seen to treat customer complaints seriously.

Role tension

Any of the dissatisfactions discussed above can lead to role tension in the employee. This tension will affect the level of commitment that the individual is willing to make. For an organization to realize the full potential of its employees, it must attempt to build a committed workforce. In a recent study it was found that job tension reduces job satisfaction, which in turn leads to higher rates of absenteeism and turnover.[13]

The greater the tension that employees feel, the less committed to their employers they become. The organization will suffer this lack of commitment, even if it is not to blame for the tension, e.g. discourteous customers can easily make the frontline employee tense.

If such an incident is reported to management, and they take little notice or do not want to get involved, then the level of tension will rise. Management who practise internal marketing are now faced with the conflicting interests of these two groups of customers.

Staff turnover

One way that a dissatisfied employee can deal with his or her dissatisfaction is to leave the organization. There are many companies that accept high rates of turnover as a fact of life in the provision of service. In 1987, counter staff turnover at McDonald's was 150 per cent, and at Burger

King was 250 per cent.[14] Unfortunately, the acceptance of this creates a vicious circle (Figure 7.4).

Management consider that investing in selection and training is a waste of resource. Since employees are likely to leave soon, there is little point in developing their skills. After all, this just makes it easier for them to find another job. An employer who thinks in this way fails to see that lack of investment in selection and training probably contribute to the high rates of turnover in the first place.

Traditional view = training is an overhead and is costly
Enlightened view = training does not cost

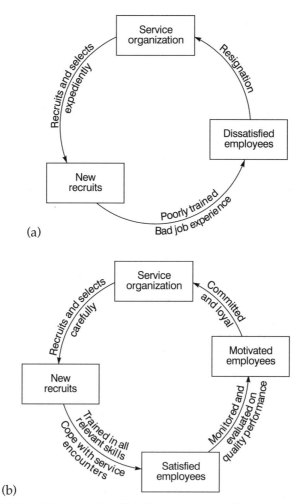

(a)

(b)

Figure 7.4 (a) The vicious cycle of high turnover employment. (b) The virtuous cycle of low turnover employment

Companies should try to avoid high levels of staff turnover for several reasons. In the first place, the management of these companies tends to be less effective. It spends most of its time trying to fire fight the current operation, instead of thinking about the future. For companies listed on the stock market, this can often result in adverse city comment with a consequent fall in the share price, and therefore value of the company. Curtailed expansion will also mean that the good people who have stayed until now begin to look elsewhere.

Companies with high levels of attrition usually provide poor customer service; because employees providing the service will not have been doing so for long, they will often have little training, or understanding of the company's values or product. Their apparent lack of confidence in what they are doing often results in lower sales.

High staff turnover also results in extra costs for the company. It has to spend more on recruitment, administration, and some basic training. Estimates suggest that separation, replacement and training costs are 1.5 to 2.5 times the annual salary for the person who resigns from their job.[15] In addition, there is a cost implication from the productivity losses that are experienced before new staff are up to speed.

However, while high levels of staff turnover should be avoided, the company should not set as its personnel goal, no staff turnover at all. For one thing, an organization that experiences no attrition goes stale.

Fresh blood can bring new thinking and energy to take a company forward. Without this injection the organization can become complacent, and fixed in its view of how things should be done, resisting the challenge of change. Companies whose management has been in place for some time often resist until it is too late. Consider other creatures who once populated this planet, but through a lack of evolution are now extinct.

Another reason why some attrition should be encouraged is that no matter how expert an organization's selection process is, the odd misfit will manage to slip through the net. In these cases it is always better for the company to let the individual go rather than expend precious resources trying to keep him on board in pursuit of a zero staff turnover rate.

So the benefits to the company of building a workforce with low levels of turnover are increased commitment from staff, which in turn leads to increased productivity and better customer service.[16] Organization commitment has been shown to be related to personal variables such as gender, and marital status,[17] i.e. personality traits that the company cannot influence. However, it is primarily related to variables that are under the control of the company. For example, the longer an employee has been with an organization, the more committed to it he will be. Conversely, the more that he experiences tension and dissatisfaction with his career progression, the less committed he becomes.

Building a committed workforce

There are two possible solutions to excess staff turnover. One focuses on the individual employee. The other deals more with the organization's role. These routes are not proposed as either/or options. To secure the benefits of low turnover the company must tackle the issue from both directions. Taken together, the two routes represent what is known as *internal marketing*. The practice of internal marketing means using the traditional tools of marketing-segmentation, NPD, market research, promotion, etc. on potential and current employees (Figure 7.5).

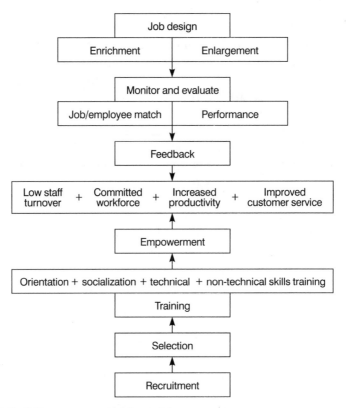

Figure 7.5 Building a committed workforce

The pre-employment relationship: recruitment

In the same way that customers need to build a relationship with the company before the develop loyalty, employees need to form a similar attachment before they become committed. This relationship often begins long before individuals become employees.

Many prospective employees will have been exposed to the external communications of the hiring organization even before they consider working for it (see Chapter 10). They may even be a lapsed or current user of the service. This all plays a part in an individual's decision to work for a particular company.

The company gets another chance to create a favourable impression in its recruitment and selection process. All too often the employer regards this process as a one-sided affair, believing that the onus falls entirely on the applicants to make the company want them. This is a somewhat shortsighted approach.

The company wants the best possible recruits. To ensure that it gets them, the company must be prepared to 'tell and sell'. Recruitment communications should contain the following:

- A clear description of the job specification including job title, reporting structure, and main areas of responsibility.
- A statement of any definite requirements, e.g. academic qualifications, years experience, height (police force).
- Reasons why individuals should consider joining the company.
- A description of the company's culture and mission.

Obviously it is not necessary, or desirable to include all of these in every piece of communication. For example, many of the large accountancy firms produce glossy recruitment brochures that meet the latter two requirements, and neatly perform the telling and selling functions. On the other hand, specific job advertisements placed in the media may choose instead to focus on the first two requirements. By doing so, they may be able to contain advertising costs.

Recruitment communication is most effective when it attracts the right number of the right type of applicants. The company is wasting time if it ends up interviewing applicants who do not meet the company's job specification. Therefore, recruitment communications should seek to tempt appropriate individuals to apply, but at the same time deter unsuitable applicants.

The pre-employment relationship: selection

The importance of selection in the service industry can be summed up in three statements made by Schneider and Schechter.[16]

I The climate and culture of an organization is a function of the people who are employed there.

2 Most service organizations require interdependent employee behaviour, and therefore everyone operating in the system must be performing well. Individual excellence will not compensate for poor performers.
3 The best predictor of future behaviour is past behaviour.

A cornerstone of the selection process is the face-to-face interview. This again is a two-way process. It enables the company to present a picture of what it stands for, and what the job entails. It should also give the applicant the opportunity to elaborate on his or her application.

The power in the relationship at this time tends to lie with the company. It decides on the interview timing, the format, and the techniques and procedures that will be adopted.

To get the best out of this interchange the organization ought to be testing relevant skills. This means that in addition to the obvious technical skill requirements, the organization should have considered what personal qualities are necessary to do the job successfully. Obviously not all service jobs require identical skills. However, William George[18] suggests that interpersonal competence and a service orientation are two basic skills that all service personnel should possess.

In the 1960s and 1970s, role-playing scenarios were used to assess these basic skills. However, many applicants found them relatively easy to manipulate, and the assessment of the scenarios was open to wide variations in interpretation.

In an attempt to overcome these weaknesses, quantitatively based techniques have become fashionable. These are intended to reduce what Woods and McAuley refer to as 'the halo and the devil-horn effect' of the qualitative scenarios.[14] Psychometric testing is one such technique. In many cases, this test takes a similar form to the traditional IQ tests. The applicant answers a series of multiple-choice questions within a tight time frame. Historically, these tests only managed to remove one of the weaknesses of the behaviouralists' approach – the results were not open to the same level of interpretation as before. Individuals are scored using conventional statistical measurement techniques. However, the crudeness of some of the early tests meant that the bright applicants who were aware of the skills that the company was looking for, could see how to answer the questions in such a way that they would achieve high scores on the appropriate skills.

Nowadays, these tests have become much more sophisticated in design. Applicants attempting to manipulate the test become confused and disorientated by the apparent sameness of many of the questions. Table 7.1 contains the output from one individual's psychometric tests. The questions that were asked were designed to capture the 31 personality attributes in the left-hand column. Each of the attributes were scored on a

Table 7.1 Psychometric testing variables

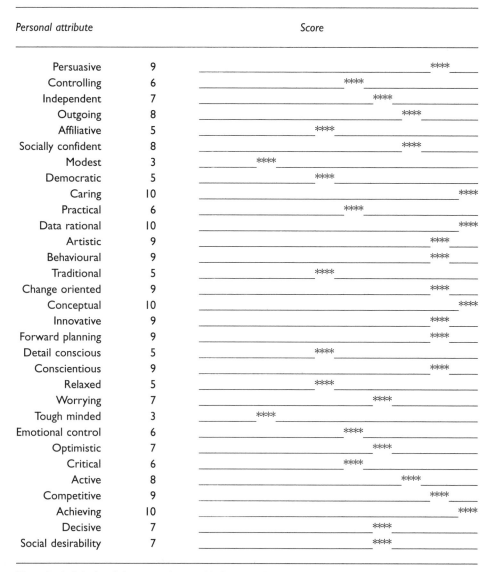

Personal attribute	Score	
Persuasive	9	****
Controlling	6	****
Independent	7	****
Outgoing	8	****
Affiliative	5	****
Socially confident	8	****
Modest	3	****
Democratic	5	****
Caring	10	****
Practical	6	****
Data rational	10	****
Artistic	9	****
Behavioural	9	****
Traditional	5	****
Change oriented	9	****
Conceptual	10	****
Innovative	9	****
Forward planning	9	****
Detail conscious	5	****
Conscientious	9	****
Relaxed	5	****
Worrying	7	****
Tough minded	3	****
Emotional control	6	****
Optimistic	7	****
Critical	6	****
Active	8	****
Competitive	9	****
Achieving	10	****
Decisive	7	****
Social desirability	7	****

This individual displayed the personality suitable for senior level management

ten-point rating scale. So, for example, this individual scored maximum points on the attributes such as Caring, Data rational, Conceptual, and Achieving.

Whatever methods are chosen to assess the applicant's suitability, the company must develop a selection system that meets its needs. What it needs are 'winners at the frontline not just warm bodies'.[11]

Employment: the early days

Hopefully, the outcome of the recruitment and selection process will be new recruits who are *willing* to perform the tasks that are required of them. The willingness which they bring to the company may well have to be strengthened and moulded.

While the new recruit to a supermarket checkout operator's position will probably have some image of what it is like to sit at an EPOS (electronic point of sale) checkout desk, the image that he or she has will be based on his or her own limited experience as a customer. As a customer, the individual may have had a different perspective. They may have expected it to be quite a sociable job. A former checkout operator describing her job on Channel 4 Television said, 'You never see their faces. All you see are their hands. They might just as well be gorillas'.[19]

A company strengthens and moulds the recruit's willingness by training. In addition to shaping their willingness, in many cases the training may also serve the purpose of developing their *ability* to do the job.

Cabin staff recruited to British Airways will not have previous experience of assisting passengers in an emergency landing. They will probably have experience of serving drinks, and should certainly have experience of smiling. The training that they are given will tackle both these 'technical' and 'non-technical' aspects of their job.

Frontline staff are expected to conform to certain role models in the provision of service. This can sometimes mean performing everyday tasks in a slightly different fashion because that is what the company wants. An employee may have to shake hands more vigorously, talk more animatedly, or make more eye contact than they otherwise would, i.e. emotions often have to be 'managed'.[1] Trainers have to work on inhibiting and inducing certain feelings. The overworked nurse is expected to be calm and patient. The swimming pool attendant is not supposed to become irate with the squeals of noisy school children, but instead is supposed to remain detached and vigilant.

Being pleasant to customers is often an intrinsic part of the job. This worked-up warmth is part of many service jobs. The service worker is not encouraged to display their true feelings to the customer. Instead they are expected to do what is known as psychological bowing.[1]

However, employees who are expected to display emotions which they do not feel will eventually suffer from strain and stress if this situation is an enduring one. Therefore, if displayed emotion is required, then the trainer's job is to change the employee's feelings. The recruit has to learn to 'bow from the heart'.[1]

The recipient of this bowing, the customer, is becoming expert in spotting this 'managed heart', and in many cases they have become cynical of the approach. They are fully aware that individuals doing this type of work will be trained by their company to display the appropriate emotion. How many times have you been instructed to 'have a nice day' by a service worker who mouths it mechanically without a thought or care for what they are saying?

Hochschild's concept of emotional labour has been refined by Ashforth and Humphrey.[20] They believe that service providers are expected to comply with required norms of expression through surface or deep acting, and the expression of spontaneous and genuine emotions. Surface acting involves the relatively effortless simulating of an emotion that one does not actually feel. By contrast, deep acting involves trying to psyche oneself into actually feeling the emotion. Finally, service providers may find themselves in the fortunate position where the employee spontaneously experiences the necessary emotion.

Management are then challenged to think of new ways in which the employee can continue to delight the customer. In addition to this, industries tarnished by their smile school approach should certainly aim to hire those individuals who naturally display the kinds of emotions that are required. The less that employees have to be trained to feel these emotions the more spontaneous and therefore convincing they will be to customers.

Of course, different emotions will be relevant to different service industries. Management must consider what the salient emotional expressions are before it begins to train recruits. If the business is debt collection, then frontline employees will be expected to be nasty to debtors. Whereas flight attendants are expected to be pleasant to passengers.[21]

The early days: orientation

Training programmes that seek to orientate and socialize recruits to an organization have been shown to be more effective in building commitment and productivity than those which do not. The quicker this happens after the employee joins a company the better.

In addition to providing new members of staff with the necessary tools for their jobs, enlightened employers will seek to use the training forum as an opportunity to get its recruits fully 'on board'. It does this by practising 'rites of passage',[22] otherwise known as orientation and socialization. All companies will not adopt identical approaches to this process. After all, the purpose of the transition is to shape the recruit in such a way that he or she handles customers effectively. As Rohlen[23] says, 'what is OK to be practised by the US Army, is not quite so relevant for a high street bank'.

Orientation is the process by which the organization helps the new recruit understand the company and its culture. It is particularly important for those service organizations whose frontline employees meet customers at arm's length from any supervision, back up, or control. In these cases it is vital that the employee has been imbued with the company's values. Most orientation programmes ask the recruit to be a receptive, yet passive, audience for this communication. However, since the desired outcome is for recruits to feel enthused about the prospect of working for the company, it is sometimes necessary to work on building receptivity first.

This often involves the recruit in a more active orientation role. If management anticipate that a recruit may be antagonistic to what they have to say, then it should actively try to squeeze this out. One such technique is the practice of EST (Erhart sensory training). This centres around the belief that it is impossible to overlay emotions and behaviour as they pertain to a particular situation (in this case the delivery of service) on those emotions that are already there. People must be taken apart and then built up again. The recruit must be humbled and displaced, in advance of any orchestrated orientation.

During orientation the organization is then free to blow its own trumpet without fear of a slow hand clap. Senior management involvement in this process usually goes down well. But whatever the chosen route for orientation, the programme should seek to leave recruits with an understanding of the purpose and mission of the company. The organization then has more chance of everyone pulling in the same direction.

In addition, any folklore that the company has which demonstrates the culture of the organization should also be communicated. The folklore can be related to a previous employee who made an outstanding contribution to the company's fortunes, or it can be about particular service encounters where the company went to extraordinary lengths to deliver the service.

The contribution that these stories make to orientation is twofold. First, people are more likely to remember the values and goals of the company if they are illuminated with actual situations. Second, these myths and heroes create the impression of a private and elite society that the recruit is privileged to join. Remember, in a service organization, orientation should clearly communicate to recruits the central importance of the customer.

The early days: socialization

Now that the recruit understands the culture and workings of the organization, he or she must be initiated into the workings of its cultural setting. Orientation has told them what to expect in this context, socialization is the process by which they begin to experience it.

Management may build socialization by feeding to recruits the thought that a lot will be expected of them as employees of the company. If the employee does not feel that he or she is living up to expectations he or she will begin to feel guilty. In this case the process of socialization has become internalized in the employee, and management no longer has to rely on coercion to ensure motivation.

Another socialization technique is to make recruits publicly acknowledge these rites of passage. In many Communist countries public declarations of commitment were often demanded. It then became more difficult to betray the Party.

Some companies socialize their employees by giving them hands-on dirty work experience. They get management to take part in the service encounter, e.g. McDonald's gets all its new managers to serve customers on the shop floor. Indeed, it asks its advertising agency and all other service agencies that it uses to do the same. The purpose of these role adoptive scenarios is to give these employees and those in supporting roles a greater understanding of the business.

An area of current controversy in the socialization process is the extent to which individuals have to conform to corporate culture. Schein[24] has developed three basic behavioural responses to socialization:

- Rebellion – rejection of all that is expected
- Creative individualism – acceptance of all crucial behavioural norms
- Conformity – acceptance of everything

Of course, the response of most employees will fall somewhere between the first and the second categories, or the second and the third. The first and third categories are generally regarded as socialization failures. The middle category is most desirable, but it is a difficult position for an employee to maintain.

The degree to which management seeks conformity really depends on their specific industry. If, for example, individuality and innovation are important values (as in hairdressing) then the organization should not seek to make these employees conform.

Individuals who are best placed to work in positions that require individuality and innovation, are those who are *intrinsically* motivated.[2] That means that they prefer complexity, novelty, challenge, and the opportunity to master a skill in their employment. Conversely, an individual who is *extrinsically* motivated seeks job simplicity and predictability. Such individuals lack initiative. To perform their job they need to be told what to do, and then require continual supervision while doing it. Jobs of this nature are few and far between. Even jobs that on the surface would appear to suit this type of person, e.g. postman, or a secretary, normally benefit from someone who can use their intelligence. The postman who recognizes that a letter is wrongly addressed and delivers it to the correct address is performing a better service for his customers.

Empowerment

An effective training programme will be one which is designed to give recruits the willingness and ability to serve. This, in turn, will certainly help to develop a committed workforce. However, the workforce are likely to be more committed if the frontline employees are also given *authority* and are therefore empowered to satisfy customers (Figure 7.6).

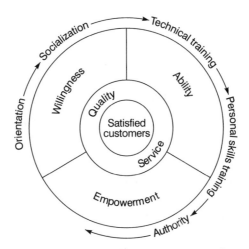

Figure 7.6 Employee development in the customer-satisfaction wheel

Some would suggest that empowerment is merely another business fad, that will soon suffer the fate of many other such trends. However, others believe that the greater decentralization of business decision making that empowerment delivers, will continue to grow on the back of rapidly improving information technology.[25]

Empowerment of employees is easiest when they have few rules to follow i.e. the service delivery process is customized. However, many organizations choose to standardize their operation to help control costs and quality levels.

In some organizations it may even be appropriate to standardize the whole operation. For instance, McDonald's instructs its counter staff on tray assembly – cold drinks first, then hot, and always put the tray within easy reach of the customer.

However, even in organizations where service delivery is almost entirely standardized the empowerment of frontline employees can help. It can, for instance, provide quicker response times to customer complaints. The employee will not have to find a supervisor who can handle the complaint, and then attempt to explain the cause for the dissatisfaction. Instead the employee can make his or her own decision on the spot about the best way to recover the situation.

Quick response times to customer complaints is a restrictive use of the concept of empowerment. In this context, it plays no part in service delivery. Instead it is placed in a purely reactive role within the service recovery arena.

In those industries where service delivery is to some extent customized, there are even greater opportunities for empowerment. Here the employee can be given the flexibility and authority to meet the customers' needs. They are placed in a proactive role where they anticipate problems and correct them during service delivery.

In addition to the extent to which service delivery is customized, research would suggest that empowerment is also most prevalent in companies that have abandoned the traditional top-down, control-orientated management model for a high-involvement or high-performance approach.[26] Such companies are characterized by the extent to which information, knowledge, power and rewards are distributed throughout the organisation. Bowen and Lawler[27] state that empowerment is:

$$\text{Empowerment} = \text{power} \times \text{information} \times \text{knowledge} \times \text{rewards}$$

Since the formula requires individual components to be multiplied together, if any of the four elements is zero, then empowerment will be zero. The equation reminds management to avoid the common error of giving employees more power without the necessary support to exercise that power. They also note that these payoffs from empowerment must be set against the resource implications of increased costs for selection and training, higher labour costs, slower service, and less consistency in service delivery.

The main benefits of empowerment are:

- Quicker response times to customer needs
- Quicker response times to complaints
- Employees feel better about their jobs and themselves
- Employees interact with customers with more warmth and enthusiasm
- Empowered employees can be a good source of ideas for service development
- Great word-of-mouth advertising and customer retention

Empowerment is presumed to deliver the dual benefits of enhanced customer satisfaction, and increased employee commitment. Companies such as Federal Express and GTE have confirmed that service quality and customers' perceptions of the company have improved through empowerment.[28]

Job design

There are two aspects of job design that should be considered in any attempt to empower frontline employees – one is *job enlargement*, the other is *job enrichment*. When people are asked to think of ways that jobs could be enriched they invariably mention things that are really only job enlargements. Enlarging a job means giving the employee more tasks to perform. Herzberg[29] refers to this as 'horizontal job loading', and makes suggestions for ways in which a job may instead be enriched.

However, just as not all employees want to be empowered, they do not all want to be enriched. The chequered history of job-enrichment programmes would suggest that the extent to which employees want their jobs to be enriched, depends on the nature of their motivations.

Other aspects of job design that should be considered by those in the organization entrusted with personnel matters are:

- Job specification
- Training and development
- Working conditions
- Appraisal systems
- Promotion prospects
- Salary and benefits

Maintaining commitment from employees

Encouraging motivation

The previous section examined what the organization should do to help build a committed workforce. To maintain the commitment, the relationship must be carefully nurtured and groomed. Motivation that was built on orientation and socialization programmes during the introductory training may have become quite depleted from everyday bashing at the frontline. So what should the organization do to retain its good staff? And what must it do to keep them committed and motivated?

Organizations can deal with this issue in a variety of ways. Whatever they decide to do, two principles should guide them:

1 Keep the importance of the delivery of quality service and customer satisfaction visible.
2 Top management involvement in the delivery of these goals should also be visible. Not only in terms of what they say, but also in terms of what they do.

A whole variety of techniques designed to foster employee commitment have been proposed.[24] The organization can practise Rites of Renewal which seeks to fine-tune the system using the latest organizational development techniques – quality circles, management by objectives (MBO), team building, to name but a few.

However, there is substantial cynicism about their effectiveness. Many regard them as a series of gimmicks designed to make management feel good about the fact that they are doing something. This game will often act as a smokescreen leaving the real issues undisturbed. Herzberg[29] believes that the only way to motivate employees is to give them challenging work. He lists the following factors as contributing to motivation:

● Achievement
● Recognition for achievement
● The work itself
● Responsibility
● Growth or advancement

All the other techniques are at best offering only short-term motivations.

Loyal employees

Fostering commitment can lead to several economic benefits for the organization. Bain and Company have developed a generic model of the benefits that can be associated with employee loyalty.[30] Their model is the result of a ten-year study across a range of industries. (Figure 7.7).

Loyal employees can create value because recruitment and training costs are reduced. These employees tend to work more efficiently and effectively. Their experience makes them better at finding, recruiting and retaining customers. Finally, long-term employees are often a good source of both customer and employee referrals.

The relative importance of Bain's seven indicators will vary from industry to industry. Indeed, in some industries not all seven will be present.

It has been suggested that an easy first step to improving the loyalty of employees is to conduct an employee/job satisfaction survey.[31] Furthermore, satisfaction, be it that of an employee or a customer, is the result of an individual's perceptions of their experience exceeding their

Figure 7.7 Why long-term employees create value. *Source*: Bain & Co.

expectations of it. Consequently, the measurement of employee job satisfaction can be conducted along similar lines to that of customer satisfaction (see Chapter 12 for further discussion).

The employee's contribution to service delivery should be evaluated in two ways.

1 The employees should be given a voice. This is part of the internal marketing concept – if the organization is treating its staff like customers then it must find out their attitudes towards the current organizational practice.
2 The customer's evaluation of the service that he or she received.

Employees should ideally be evaluated and remunerated in terms of their contribution to customer satisfaction (evaluate effectiveness rather than efficiency). This follows the principle of 'what gets measured gets done'. If employees know that they are being evaluated in terms of customer satisfaction, then they are more likely to be motivated to provide this satisfaction.

Feedback

Performance monitoring and evaluation should be concerned with the achievement of customer satisfaction. Employees who help to create this satisfaction must know how they fared. The results of the evaluation should be fed back to employees.

In doing so, the organization would hope to improve its performance, and thereby to satisfy more customers. The appraisal of employees can be carried out on a regular or irregular basis. The appraisals can be tied to a review of pay, but they need not all be. Employees will, of course, expect to be remunerated for their efforts, and a performance appraisal is a good time for this to be discussed. It will be most appropriate in those circumstances where pay is related to performance. However, the organization would be foolish to encourage employees to believe that their performance will only be discussed when their pay is up for review.

One feedback mechanism that is growing in influence is that which encourages 'service wisdom'.[32] Employees are venerated for successfully handling situations that were not covered in their service manuals or training sessions. The Holiday Inn's 'employee of the month' scheme or American Express's annual Great Performance Award are examples of this. In exceptional cases, the service encounters that gave rise to the award may become part of the company's folklore.

The feedback process should not be entirely one-way from management to employees. Instead it should be a three-way process between the employee's internal/external customers, his subordinates, and management.[32]

Unfortunately this is still only practised by the most enlightened of companies. Most employers still behave as if the employees belong to them. They feel that the employees owe the organization something for being given the privilege of working there, and do not see that they might owe the employees more than their salaries in return for their labour.

Redefining the roles of employee and customer

So far our discussion has focused on frontline staff since they are most visible in the delivery of quality service. However, for the organization to operate effectively *all* employees must be pulling in the same direction. There is little sense in selecting and developing excellent frontline staff if they are not supported by those in the back office. While the customer does not see these employees it does not mean that they play an insignificant part in the delivery of a quality service.

All employees who are in the back office should treat the other members of the organization that they deal with as internal customers. Whether they provide direct support to frontline staff as in the RAC's command

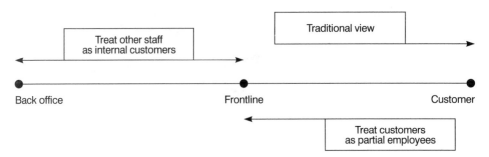

Figure 7.8 Expanding the roles of employee and customer

control room which feeds information to its recovery vehicles, or direct support to other back-office staff, as in the accounts department of an hotel, they should behave towards these individuals in the same way that they would if they were external customers. Everyone in the organization must share the responsibility for delivering customer satisfaction.

The traditional interaction between customer and frontline employee can also be extended (Figure 7.8). Given the inseparability of production and consumption in most service encounters, customers actually become involved in the production of the service. Their behaviour (as well as that of employees) affects the outcome. Service organizations would do well to treat their customers as *partial employees*, adopting the same disciplines that we have discussed in this chapter for dealing with employees. The organization should select its customers, and then train them for the service encounter. This training can be given impersonally, e.g. through the company's external communications. They can be used to inform customers of what is expected of them in the service encounter. This tuition can also be given in person, e.g. the health club manager who takes his or her customers round the club and shows them how to use the facilities.

Summary

The employees who deliver service are of fundamental importance to both the customer that they serve and the employer for whom they work. In many cases, the source of customer dissatisfaction is in fact, the service employee. The employees in turn, deliver less than acceptable service because they are dissatisfied with the way that their employer treats them. There are many factors that can contribute to this dissatisfaction – those related to their role, to their lack of empowerment, or to the way that management run the company.

The existence of these problems leads to a lack of motivation and commitment, and often results in a high turnover rate. Management can do several things which should help to reduce the likelihood of these arising. These include recruiting and selecting appropriate employees who match the job specification, training them in both the technical and non-technical skills necessary for the job, developing relevant orientation and socialization programmes, empowering those at the frontline and compensating them in some way for the extra responsibility, and monitoring and evaluating their performance in terms of the quality of service that they provide not the quantity. The results should be fed back to employees to aid their development and thereby improve the service.

Finally, while the focus of this is the frontline employee, the same principles should also be adopted for all service employees. Those who do not have to face the customer themselves should be encouraged to regard other employees as their customers, treating them in the same way that they would expect customers to be treated.

References

1. Hockschild, A. R. (1983) *The Managed Heart: Commercialisation of Human Feeling*, University of California Press.
2. Keaveney, S. (1988) 'Adding value to services through contact personnel'. In *Add Value to Your Service* (Suprenant, C. ed.), American Marketing Association.
3. Lovelock, C. (1996) *Services Marketing*, Prentice-Hall, Englewood Cliffs, NJ.
4. Mudie, P. (1987) 'Internal marketing: cause for concern', *Quarterly Review of Marketing*, Spring/Summer, 21–24.
5. Clutterbuck, D. (1989) 'Developing customer care training programmes,' *Marketing Intelligence and Planning*, **7**.
6. Carlzon, J. (1989) *Moments of Truth*, Harper & Row, New York.
7. Schneider, B. (1994) 'HRM – A service perspective: towards a customer-focused HRM?', *International Journal of Service Industry Management*, **5**, No. 1, 64–76.
8. Harris, T. (1970) *The Book of Choice*, Jonathan Cape, London.
9. Parasuraman, A., Zeithaml, V. A. and Berry, L. L. (1990) *Delivering Quality Service*, Free Press, New York.
10. Shamir, B. (1980) 'Between service and servility: role conflict in subordinate service roles', *Journal of Human Relations*, **33**(10), 741–756.
11. Schlesinger, L. A. and Heskett, J. L. (1991) Breaking the cycle of failure in services management', *Management Review*, Spring, 17–28.
12. Lincoln, A. (1856) Cited in *Oxford Concise Book of Proverbs*, Oxford University Press, Oxford.

13. Rogers, J. D. *et al.* (1994) 'Increasing job satisfaction of service personnel', *Journal of Services Marketing*, **8**, No. 1, 14–26.
14. Woods, R. H. and Macauley, J. F. (1989) 'RX for turnover: retention programmes that work,' *Cornell Hotel and Restaurant Administration*, May, 79–90.
15. Solomon, J. (1988) 'Companies try measuring cost savings from new types of corporate benefits', *The Wall Street Journal*, 29 December, B1.
16. Schneider, B. and Schechter, D. (1982) Development of a personnel selection system for service job's.
17. Hall, D. T., Schneider, B. and Nygren, H. T. (1970) 'Personal factors in organisational identification', *Administrative Science Quarterly*, **15.**
18. George, W. (1990) 'Internal marketing and organisational behaviour: a partnership in developing customer-conscious employees at every level,' *Journal of Business Research*, **20**, 63–70.
19. Supermarket Cashier (1992) 'Custom-eyes critical eye', Channel Four television series.
20. Ashforth, B. E. and Humphrey, R. W. (1993) 'Emotional labour in service roles: the influence of identity', *Academy of Management Review*, **18**, No. 1, 88–115.
21. Rafaeli, A. and Sutton, R. I. (1990) 'Busy stores and demanding customers', *Academy of Management Journal*, **33**(3), 623–637.
22. Van Gennep, A. (1960) *Rites of Passage*, University of Chicago Press, Chicago. (Originally published by Emile Mourry in Paris, 1909.)
23. Rohlen, T. P. (1973) 'Spiritual education' in a Japanese bank,' *American Anthropologist*, **75**, 1542–1562.
24. Schein, E. H. (1988) 'Organisational socialisation and the profession of management', *Sloan Management Review*, Fall, 53–65.
25. Malone, T. W. (1997) 'Is empowerment just a fad? Control, decision making, and IT', *Sloan Management Review*, Winter, 23–35.
26. Lawler, E. E. *et al.* (1995) *Creating the High Performance Organisation: Impact of Employee Involvement and Total Quality Management*, Jossey-Bass. San Francisco, CA.
27. Bowen, D. E. and Lawler III, E. E. (1995) 'Empowering service employees', *Sloan Management Review*, Summer, pp 73–83.
28. Schlossberg, H. (1991) 'Employee empowerment drives award-winning firms', *Marketing News*, **25**, 19 August, 6–7.
29. Herzberg, F. (1968) 'One more time: how do you motivate employees?', *Harvard Business Review*, January–February, 53–62.
30. Reicheld, F. F. (1996) *The Loyalty Effect*, Harvard Business School Press, Cambridge, MA.
31. Rust *et al.* (1996) 'The satisfaction and retention of frontline employees: a customer satisfaction measurement approach', *International Journal of Service Industry Management*, **7**, No. 5 62–80.
32. Bell, C. R. and Zemke, R. (1988) 'Do service procedures tie employees hands?' *Personnel Journal*, September, 77–83.

Chapter 8

Managing demand and supply

Introduction

In service marketing the matching of capacity and demand is particularly difficult because the perishable nature of services means that they cannot be stored. The extent to which service organizations are challenged on this issue depends on demand fluctuations and the extent to which supply is constrained.

Many services are also characterized by quite large demand fluctuations over short periods. City-centre sandwich shops are significantly busier at lunchtimes than in the late afternoon. In addition to this, the customer participates in the creation of the service and customers in themselves vary. Some customers complete forms quickly, some slowly, some are brusque, some are chatty. This creates variability in capacity.

Although it may be difficult for many service organizations to match supply and demand, it is not an issue that they can safely ignore. For one thing whenever demand is well below capacity then costs are added to each unit of sale. Profitability will be eroded and the service may even become uncompetitive. Many services carry relatively high fixed costs – the customer in effect rents the facilities. An airline, for instance, has to maintain its aircraft to a legal standard no matter how few customers are flying.

When demand and capacity are out of balance the service itself can take on a different form. This can be true when a business is running over its optimal capacity – ask customers desperately trying to catch a waiter's eye in a packed restaurant how they feel about the service! Or it can occur where the business runs under capacity – what's the point of sitting all night alone in a singles bar? There is a difference between the *optimum* capacity and the *maximum* capacity. As Heskett, Sasser, and Hart[1] note, the optimum capacity for an airline ranges from 65 per cent to 75 per cent. Above 75 per cent the service deteriorates as rushed cabin staff deal abruptly with customers. They reckon that below about 40 per cent capacity the service will also deteriorate because at such a low level of business, staff can become demoralized. While for most services the optimum capacity level is below the maximum level, in some cases the optimum lies above the maximum. Consider the pop concert or football cup final. No matter how different the two capacity levels are, the service provider has to strike a balance between profitability and customer satisfaction. In this chapter, the strategies we discuss for managing supply and demand, are aiming to satisfy optimum, not maximum, capacity levels.

Strategies for matching supply and demand

To identify appropriate strategies for managing demand and supply, an organization needs a clear understanding of the constraints on its capacity and the underlying demand patterns.

All businesses need to undertake some kind of long-term planning of demand so that they can ensure adequate capacity. If a bank's customer base is growing by 10 per cent each year, then they will presumably be planning to recruit more tellers and open more branches as the years progress. However, we are concerned here with the problem of matching demand and supply over the shorter term.

Table 8.1 The interaction of demand and supply adapted from Lovelock (1983)[2]

Extent to which supply is constrained	Extent to which demand fluctuates	
	Wide	*Narrow*
Peak demand does not generally exceed capacity	Telephone Electricity Gas Water Emergency services	Banking Insurance Legal services Food retailing
Peak demand regularly exceeds capacity	Restaurants Theatres Tour operators Hotels	Services similar to those above but which have insufficient capacity for their base level of business

There are three possible approaches to tackling this problem. First, one can build flexibility into the system by *tailoring* capacity to match demand at any one point. Second, one can attempt to *predict* the fluctuations in demand, and match capacity to these levels. Third, one can attempt to *manage* demand to fit capacity. Thereby operating with a relatively level capacity and tailoring demand to fit. This last has been described by Sasser, Olsen and Wyckoff[3] as the 'chase' strategy.

These approaches are not mutually exclusive – the service marketer often needs to combine elements of all three.

Tailor capacity to meet demand

Capacity can 'chase' variations in demand. If this is the chosen strategy then it is particularly important for the company to understand the components of capacity. One should answer the question – what limits capacity? Common capacity constraints are time, labour, equipment and facilities. It is not until the primary determinant of capacity constraint is understood that the organization can begin to develop a strategy for coping with this issue. In a restaurant capacity might be limited by the number of tables. If tables were then laid out in the foyer then capacity might be limited by the numbers of waiting staff. If more waiters were recruited then space might be limited by kitchen space.

Armistead[4] has summarized the different approaches to varying capacity to meet short-term demand fluctuations as:

- Changing the number and hours of personnel
- Customer participation
- Resource transfer
- Subcontracting
- Share capacity

In addition there is the possibility of:

- Scheduling downtime.

Changing the number and hours of personnel: the flexible workforce

Service is often highly labour intensive. As a result capacity is often limited by personnel. One common approach to overcoming this problem is to use part-time staff. They can be brought in as demand appears. Pools of casual labour are often used, such as schoolchildren in holidays, mothers of school-age children during term time, etc. In future we expect that pensioners will increasingly be used in this capacity.

These temporary staff can be scheduled so that they provide labour as required. This approach is easier to implement successfully where the service is standardized and little skill is required, e.g. a supermarket checkout operator. However, there are problems associated with using part-timers, they are not usually committed to the organization which results in high levels of staff turnover, errors and supervision costs. These in turn lead to a diminution in customer satisfaction.

Another way to solve the problem is to employ full time staff but to build flexibility into their hours so that they work more hours when necessary. This approach can, however, result in high labour costs through overtime payments. It has been predicted that the flexible workforce will continue to grow and in the near future people will be self-employed and 'freelance' for a number of different organizations. They will not be employed as a permanent member of staff.

Customer participation

Wherever the customer participates directly in the creation of the service then some of the strain on capacity is removed. In effect that part of the capacity becomes variable rather than fixed. This applies in many self-service situations – from supermarkets to restaurants, petrol stations and automatic bank teller machines. So the organization has to consider means by which it can increase customer participation. This will lead to an increase in capacity which in turn has the effect of coping with increased demand.

Resource transfer: multi-skilling employees

If staff can perform more than one task in the service operation then labour can be moved to overcome capacity problems. This requires investment in costs to ensure multiskilling – supermarket shelf fillers who can also work at the checkout.

Subcontracting: outsourcing

This approach, in common with customer participation, effectively turns fixed capacity into variable capacity. Many sectors of the services economy have recently deployed this strategy. Trusts in the National Health Service outsource cleaning and catering services, and local councils have done the same with their refuse collection, traffic wardens and bus services. Private sector companies have similarly outsourced those activities not perceived to be core to their service delivery, e.g. payroll administration is performed for many companies by their bank.

Share capacity

Where capacity is expensive and not too specialized then it can be shared. A concert hall's capacity may be shared between rock bands, comedians and classical concert orchestras. Airlines may share baggage handling facilities. Emergency services share the capacity of the 999 switchboard.

Schedule downtime

Periods of low demand may actually be necessary in many service operations. These times can be used by staff for training, or to catch up on paperwork. In fact if adequate time for these activities is built in to the schedule, and these activities are timed to coincide with periods of low demand, then in effect capacity has been reduced to match demand.

One of the problems associated with an energetic pursuit of demand to fill up troughs is that downtime activities can be forgotten. Eventually this leads to inadequately trained staff with a mountain of half-completed paperwork.

Predicting demand

The previous strategy focused on building flexibility into the amount that the organization could supply in order to meet fluctuations in demand. Another approach is to begin by attempting to explain the reasons for fluctuations in demand and to use this as a basis for predicting future demand. If demand can be predicted with some accuracy, then the extent to which capacity variability needs to be built into the system is reduced.

Management should seek answers to the following questions:

To what extent does demand change cyclically? And if so, what is the duration of the cycle?
Hourly (university canteen use)
Daily (morning/evening rush-hour use of roads)
Weekly (weekend demand for babysitters)
Monthly (tax advisors)
Or even longer (election advisors)

What is it that causes these cyclical variations? Are they connected with
The economic cycle?
Patterns of consumer behaviour?
Legislative constraints?
The political situation?
The culture and customs of consumers?

Do demand levels appear to change in a non-cyclical/random manner?
If demand appears to behave in this way, it is quite possible that patterns
of demand *do* still exist, but they are the result of unusual or situation-
specific factors. To establish the nature of these factors may require in-
depth analysis of the service process. And a lateral brainstorming session
designed to explore what these other factors might be.

Can demand be disaggregated by market segment to make sense of demand patterns?
Do usage patterns fluctuate according to customer type? Mid-week
evening demand peaks in a supermarket may be caused by homebound
workers. They may have markedly different needs from that of the
daytime shopper. They may, for instance, be buying for their evening meal
rather than for a household for the week. In this situation, an evening '5
items or less' priority checkout would improve service delivery for this
group.

The service marketer should aim to explain as much of the demand
fluctuation as possible. If the majority of demand fluctuation can be
explained then two short-term capacity matching strategies are possible.

1 *Customer selection.* The process of selecting specific customer groups to focus
   on can have large effects on the stability and predictability of demand. First,
   some customers act in a more unpredictable way than others. Decisions can
   be taken to discard customers exhibiting high degrees of randomness and to
   replace them by more 'predictable' customers. For example, a hospital might
   decide to close its casualty ward and concentrate on gynaecology. Second, it
   may be easier to predict the overall demand of a large number of small
   customers than a few large ones. A law practice may find it particularly
   difficult to service three corporate clients all demanding simultaneous instant
   attention. Furthermore, there is more business stability with a larger
   number of smaller clients. Third, whatever the size of any particular
   customer group, one might be able to balance a portfolio of customers so
   that growth in demand from one is matched by decline in demand from
   another, e.g. insurance companies sell policies to cover funeral expenses and
   private health care.

2 *Short-term capacity elasticity.* An underground train may carry 60 passengers standing comfortably – this might be the optimal capacity. However, for short periods during rush hour this might rise to 200 standing passengers. Similarly, staff may cope well with excess demand for short periods by working harder than normal or by postponing paperwork etc. It may pay to examine work practices during these busy periods simply to discover ways to improve efficiency during peak demand. It may also be possible to postpone the delivery of augmented quality during peak demand periods. A stockbroker may pride himself on his personal touch in dealing with his customers. This personal contact is an augmented quality. If he is busy, the specific enquiry may be dealt with effectively by an assistant. The stockbroker can still deliver the augmented service by calling the client back the next day.

Again some short-term capacity stretch can result from involving the customer to a greater extent during peak demand periods. A bank teller may personally complete the deposit slip for a customer when there are no other customers around. However, when the bank is busy the tellers should concentrate on those elements of service that cannot be undertaken by the customers? They should leave the customers to do their own form filling.

This overall approach to coping with short-term demand fluctuations can be summarized as 'predict and stretch'. Predict as much demand variation as possible and incorporate an element of short-term capacity stretch to cope with the rest.

Managing demand to fit capacity

This strategy would be followed by companies with major capacity constraints. It is the approach described by Sasser[5] as the 'level' capacity strategy.

The organization can adopt one of four different strategies for managing demand.

Shaping demand

1. Increase demand ⎱
2. Reduce demand ⎰ To utilize excess capacity during peak periods

Store/inventory demand

3. Reservations system ⎱
4. Queueing system ⎰ Until capacity becomes available

Table 8.2 Constraints on capacity. Adapted from
Zeithaml and Bitner (1996)[6]

Nature of the constraint	Type of service
Time/labour	Advertising Legal Accounting ⎫ Consulting ⎭ services
Equipment	Delivery services Health club Construction
Facilities	Education Hotels Restaurants Hospitals

Shaping demand

The management strategy is to influence demand through changing the:

Product (or nature of the service offered)
Place (or time)
Promotion (communication)
Price

Demand can be shaped either by reducing the peaks or increasing the troughs. The same measure can often simultaneously achieve both. An airline offering discounts on selected off peak flights seeks not only to fill up these seats but also to transfer passengers away from busy flights.

Nature of the service offered

Is the service always appropriate at all times? There are some classic approaches to filling up troughs: the college which markets its facilities as a conference centre out of term time; the hotel that is the haunt of business executives during the week which then offers specialist weekend breaks, e.g. 'Murder Mystery' and 'Musical' weekends; McDonald's burger bars offering breakfast menus, and conversely coffee shops offering dinner menus.

Service changes fall into two categories: radically altering the service (as in the case of the college/conference centre); and adding value during trough periods – free cocktails in a restaurant, free tennis lessons at a hotel. For changes in the nature of the service offered to be implemented successfully, the organization needs to consider if other elements of the marketing mix also need to be adapted.

Place/timing of service delivery

One can change the location and timing of service delivery. Dry-cleaning companies might, for instance, offer to pick up and deliver in the evenings. Car rental companies sometimes open temporary offices in tourist locations during the summer. Many retail services are delivered from mobile units – these range from library services and banks through to grocers.

Promotion (communication)

Communication can be used to manage the peaks and troughs. The demand that an organization is expecting to receive is often communicated to customers. These messages can be explicit – 'Mail early for Christmas' – or implicit. Pricing, for instance, often carries a message about pressures on service capacity. Airlines often have structured price lists where cheaper fares are excluded from certain peak flights. Rail operators give off peak fares discounts. Part of the effectiveness of this is that it signals busy periods. Theatres that advertise availability by informing customers of 'sold-out' performances may encourage customers to book matinees instead.

Signs on the service premises that let customers know of busy periods allows them to shift their demand to quieter periods. At least they have been warned. From research carried out in a banking environment, customers who had been informed of the busy periods, were more satisfied even when they had to wait, than were customers who were not forewarned.[7]

Price

Price can, of course, be an effective way to manage demand. However, in influencing demand there can be other implications. Price itself carries a message. Lower prices in off-peak periods may stimulate demand at that time but put off other customers. It is often assumed that price elasticity is always negatively correlated to demand so that as price increases, demand falls.

This is not always true. A large part of the service product is intangible. Moreover the customer delivers part of the product. As Shapiro[8] says,

'Price can connote quality'. Reducing the price can cheapen the product – and put off customers. This can happen for a number of reasons:

1 Changing prices can lead to uncertainty. Customers can decide not to buy because they believe that by holding off, the price might get cheaper.
2 Lower prices can change the type of purchaser. This can be important in high-contact, shared services like restaurants and theatres. Here the other customers are a significant part of the product mix. If a restaurant lowers price and attracts students then it might put off its regular business clientele (or vice versa!).
3 Price itself can be important because it carries snob appeal. It may be important to some consumers to be able to signal that they paid a lot for a service.
4 The consumer can be part of the product. Reducing the price can sometimes be felt therefore to be cheapening the value of the consumer.

However, in many services the principle of discounting unused capacity is an accepted norm, particularly if discounts are accompanied by restrictions in the service. A 'standby' airline passenger has paid less for his ticket, but has taken the risk of not catching the flight.

Store/inventory demand

The previous demand management strategies have focused on shaping demand. Management can decide instead to store or inventory demand. This can be achieved by creating a reservations system or a queueing system. Queueing is discussed later in this chapter. The reservations system inventories demand; for example, a customer ringing to reserve a table in his/her favourite restaurant, an account holder ringing to make an appointment with his/her bank manager. Pricing can be introduced into the reservations system to incentivize customers; pre-booking travel tickets to gain APEX fares.

The problem with any inventoried demand system that does not require pre-payment is the 'no shows'. Many service companies overcome this by overbooking. This, in turn, can create problems. A system that encourages advance booking and *then* cannot deliver is one that almost always leads to customer dissatisfaction. British Airways recovers such situations by offering the customer a free fully flexible flight to be taken to the same destination at some future time, and a seat on the next plane. In implementing this strategy they select customers for whom they perceive their late arrival will be more than compensated for by the free flight.

Another way to store demand is to develop a queueing system. Time that customers spend waiting can be made productive and enjoyable.

Restaurants may ask customers to wait in a bar. This might in turn be an important revenue source. While waiting in the bar the customers might be able to choose their food, thus cutting down waiting time at the table. All of this enhances the productivity of the scarce resource – table space.

Price

In the drive to manage demand and capacity effectively, price will play a central role. While the pricing of services cannot depart entirely from the well-established framework developed for products, it does merit special attention for the particular issues it raises. Service organizations incur costs, face demand and determine pricing objectives, e.g. profit, revenue, market share just like most other businesses. It is the manner in which these are handled that can make the difference. Even the word 'price' is more associated with products than services where the terminology varies, e.g. rates (car hire, hotels), fare (train, bus, air), interest rate (banks), premium (insurance), rent (flat), tuition fees (education).

Intangibility and perishability raise problems for pricing. For products, there is often tangible evidence in the form of performance, reliability and durability. These concrete outputs can be directly traced back to raw materials used, design configurations, labour, skills and equipment quality (the inputs). Prices can be assigned for each of these inputs along with the subsequent conversion through the value chain to a final product. It is not quite so straightforward for services. As well as intangibility, services suffer from perishability making it difficult to synchronize supply and demand.

Basis for pricing

Although customers do not readily understand the how and why of product pricing, service pricing can leave them bewildered. Take, for example, a plumber charging £60 for a small household job. The householder may be shocked but the plumber would argue it is not simply a matter of job time and detail. He aims to recoup the fixed and variable costs of operating the business (labour, telephones, insurance, petrol, rates, vehicles) and generate a profit. These costs will, of course, be there for product businesses as well. However, as already stated above, at the end of the manufacturing process there is a product in evidence which allows a customer to make a judgement about whether it is worth the price. For services there is no pre-consumption evidence in the form of a product. Covering costs plus a percentage for profit is not an adequate guide for a potential customer of a service anxious about the level of skill/competence likely to be received.

The unit of service consumption for the plumber is time. The costs of doing business plus an amount for profit is divided by the total working hours to give a price per hour. This may result in a more competent plumber charging less because less time is taken for completing the job. An example of how costs plus profit is calculated for determining price is shown in Figure 8.1.

Total drivers' wage costs	£125 000	
Total drivers' hours worked	£45 000	
Cost per driver's hour		£2.77
Total vehicle running costs	£100 000	
Total mileage operated	250 000	
Vehicle operating costs per mile		£0.40
Total other overhead costs	£30 000	
Overhead per mile operated		£0.12
Required return on sales turnover	15%	

For a price quotation based on a 200-mile journey requiring 12 hours of driver's time:

Total price =

200 miles x £0.40	=	£80.00
12 hours x £2.77	=	£33.24
Overheads (based on mileage):		
200 hours x £0.12	=	£24.00
Total	=	£137.24
Add 15% margin	=	£20.59
TOTAL PRICE	=	£157.83

Figure 8.1 The 'cost-plus' method of price setting for a coach operator. *Source*: Palmer (1994)[9]

All the standard criticisms of cost plus pricing apply to services as well as goods. A variant of full-cost pricing used by service organizations is marginal cost pricing. Here the charge is based not on the total unit cost but only on the additional costs incurred through servicing a customer. Perishability means revenue is foregone in the event of an unsold unit of capacity, e.g. a seat, hotel room. Therefore the service provider will obtain some income by selling it just above the marginal cost. However, the desire to maximize capacity utilization is offset by resentment from full-cost customers and bewilderment as to the true value of the service.

In addition to time for the plumber, what of other units of service consumption as a basis for pricing? For hotels the basic unit is a room and the price will vary according to size and type, length of stay and time of year. For car hire the basic unit is the car. The operator will take into account the type of car (perhaps including a depreciation assessment), length of hire and seasonality (some operators charge more during periods of high demand). Hiring a car from an airport is more expensive because of high overhead costs (renting a space at an airport) and the price insensitivity of largely business customers (see 'Price discrimination').

Price discrimination

Price discrimination is the practice of charging different prices according to:

- User group, e.g. adults, pensioners, students
- Place of consumption e.g. seats in a place of entertainment
- Time of consumption – hours of the day, days of the week, months of the year

What explains the difference in prices? It is not really a question of differences in costs. One explanation is that when capacity is limited, the service provider on particular days of the week or hours of the day raises prices to levels that the market will bear. A second explanation is that these prices are a form of price discrimination. For example, business calls have to be made during business hours. As a result, the demand for telephone services by businesses is relatively insensitive to prices. Charging higher prices during the day is profitable because it has little effect on demand. Personal calls by individuals are, on the other hand, more price sensitive and are normally made at the lower rate during the evening and at weekends. Price discrimination is therefore a much-used technique by service organizations for managing demand levels and capacity utilization.

One of the commonest forms of price discrimination is where children are charged a lower price than adults whether on public transport or for public entertainment. Take the case of cinema tickets. In most cinemas children pay less than adults during the day. In the evening, however, many cinemas charge both adults and children the same price.

But why do cinemas charge children less during the day? After all, the child is seeing the same film as the adult and occupying a whole seat. In other words, there is no difference in the service that they are consuming. And why are children charged the higher price in the evenings, given that the seat and the film are the same as during the day?

The answer is related to revenue maximization and the price elasticity of demand. Once a cinema has decided to show a film, the marginal costs of an additional customer are zero. There are no additional staffing, film-hire, electricity or other costs. With marginal costs equal to zero, profits will be maximized where marginal revenue is also equal to zero. In other words where total revenue is maximized.

Consider the case of a cinema with 500 seats.[10] Figures 8.2 and 8.3 show the demand and marginal revenue curves of both adults and children. It is assumed that the elasticity of demand for children's tickets is greater than that for adult tickets. Figure 8.2 shows demand during the late

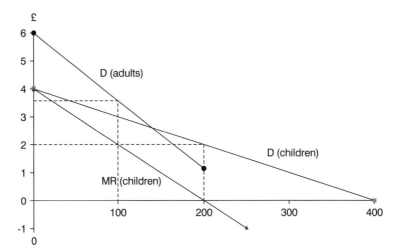

Figure 8.2 Number of tickets (afternoon). *Source*: Sloman (1997)[10]

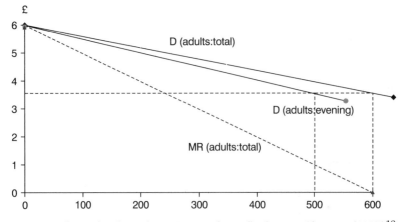

Figure 8.3 Number of tickets (evening and total). *Source*: Sloman (1997)[10]

afternoon (i.e. after school). Here the demand by children is relatively high compared with adults, but the overall demand is low. Figure 8.3 shows demand during the evening. Here there is a higher overall level of demand, especially by adults, many of whom work during the day.

For the afternoon screening (Figure 8.2) revenue is maximized from children by charging them a price of £2, i.e. at the point on the demand curve where MR = 0. At this price 200 child tickets will be sold.

Assuming that the same adult price is charged in both the afternoon and the evening, the total demand for full priced tickets (i.e. for both afternoon and evening screenings) has to be examined in order to ascertain the revenue maximizing price. This will be a price of £3.50 where total MR = 0 (see Figure 8.3). As a result, 100 adult tickets should be sold in the afternoon and 500 in the evening.

But why are reduced-price tickets not available for the children in the evening? In Figure 8.3 the sale of low-priced tickets for children would lead to demand exceeding the 500-seat capacity of the cinema. Each time an adult was turned away because the seat had already been sold to a child the cinema would lose revenue.

Break-even analysis

The perishability characteristic is recognized as a matter of some concern for services. Using price to manage demand is one way of addressing this problem. However, evidence from the passenger transport industry suggests that profitability does not require high levels of capacity utilization. In fact, an average bus needs only around ten passengers on board to break even. It costs just 89 pence to run the average British bus for one kilometre, a figure that has halved in the past years as the industry has consolidated and the large companies have cut staff, wages, fleets and services and investment in new vehicles.[11] Therefore, the lesson, from this industry at least, is that a substantial level of perishability does not mean the service is unprofitable.

Yield management

As well as price another important tool of demand and supply management in service industries is yield management. Basically, it is the process of allocating the right type of capacity to the right kind of customer at the right price in order to maximize revenue or yield.[12] Capacity can be in the form of time, labour, equipment and facilities. Services particularly constrained by capacity include airlines, hotels, restaurants, car repair and entertainment (e.g. theme parks).

For an organization successfully to use yield management the following conditions are necessary:[13]

- A relatively fixed capacity
- Demand can be segmented into partitions such as midweek breaks, weekend demand, business users, those requiring luxury etc.
- Inventory is perishable – if the unit of capacity is not used the revenue is lost
- The service can be sold well in advance
- There can be substantial fluctuations in demand
- Variable costs are much less than fixed costs.

The above attributes represent a challenge for service organizations trying to obtain the best possible financial return from an almost fixed and perishable capacity. It is viewed as a trade-off between the desire for high-capacity utilization and the desire for selling the units of capacity at the maximum price. In practice, difficult choices must be faced:[14]

- Should an hotel accept an advance booking from a tour group of 200 room nights at £80 each when these same room nights might possibly be sold later at short notice to business travellers at the full room rate of £140?
- How many seats on a particular flight or train should an airline/railway sell in advance to tour groups and passengers travelling at discounted rates?
- Should a repair and maintenance shop reserve a certain proportion of productive capacity each day for emergency repair jobs that offer a high contribution margin and the potential to build long-term customer loyalty, or should it simply follow a strategy of making sure that there are sufficient jobs, mostly involving routine maintenance, to keep its employees fully employed?

The basic yield statistic is a straightforward measure. It is expressed as follows:

$$\text{Yield} = \frac{\text{Actual revenue}}{\text{Potential revenue}}$$

Revenue potential is the revenue that could be secured if 100 per cent of capacity is sold at the maximum price possible. In more detail, yield is a function of price and capacity used, namely:

Capacity utilization × price ratio

where

$$\text{Capacity utilization} = \frac{\text{Units of capacity sold}}{\text{Total units of capacity}}$$

and

$$\text{Price ratio} = \frac{\text{Actual price}}{\text{Maximum price}}$$

(*Note:* terminology can vary according to industry, e.g. hotel capacity is occupancy rate, transport capacity is load factor, hotel price is rate, and so on).

If we consider the hotel industry, yield would be found from:

$$\frac{\text{Rooms sold}}{\text{Rooms available for sale}} \times \frac{\text{Rate(price) of rooms sold}}{\text{Rate potential}}$$

For example, a hotel with 280 rooms sells in one night 140 rooms at £80 and a further 70 rooms at the maximum rate of £120. The yield would be:

$$
\begin{aligned}
\text{Yield} &= \frac{140}{280} \times \frac{80}{120} + \frac{70}{280} \times \frac{120}{120} \\
&= 0.5 \times 0.666 + 0.25 \times 1 \\
&= 0.583 \text{ or } 58.3
\end{aligned}
$$

$$
\begin{aligned}
\text{Maximum yield} &= 280 \times £120 \\
&= £33\,600
\end{aligned}
$$

$$
\begin{aligned}
\text{Actual yield} &= £33\,600 \times 58.3\% \\
&= £19\,589 \text{ (or } 19\,600 \text{ to be exact)}
\end{aligned}
$$

While yield will vary over time, different combinations of occupancy and rates could result in the same revenue and yield percentage. In the example above, 100 rooms sold at £70 plus 126 rooms sold at £100 would also give £19 600 in revenue. Figure 8.4 shows how capacity utilization may vary in practice for an hotel.

The question that arises is whether the hotel is satisfied with the capacity utilization given the rates obtained from each customer group. Unlike Figure 8.4 there may be a certain amount of unutilized capacity over the period with inevitable pressure on profitability as all costs must be allocated. To enable yield calculations and assessments to be made, service providers need to classify demand periods and the variations between them. One possible classification can be seen in Figure 8.5 (relevant for transportation and entertainment services).

Reference has previously been made to yield management as a trade-off. In the following example the hotelier needs to analyse the trade-off

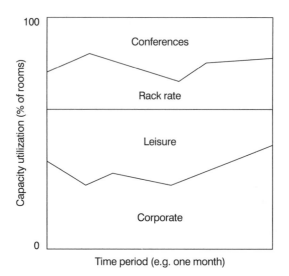

Figure 8.4 Capacity utilization over time

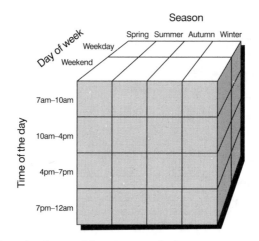

Figure 8.5 Variations in demand by time period

between the value of a prospective group booking and the loss associated with the probable displacement of transient business. Consider the case of an enquiry from a group wanting to book 50 rooms on three days next month.[15] Table 8.3 illustrates the hotels situation before and after the prospective booking.

In this example, booking the prospective group would cause displacement on Wednesday, when the hotel doesn't have enough rooms to accommodate the group. If the 50 rooms displaced by the group were

Table 8.3 Example of displacement. *Source*: Orkin (1988)[15]

	Monday	Tuesday	Wednesday
Rooms in hotel	300	300	300
Rooms committed to groups	150	50	200
Expected transient demand	100	100	100
Availability of rooms to new groups without displacement	50	150	0
Groups under discussion	50	50	50
Primary transient displacement	0	0	50

valued at the seasonal transient average rate of £95, and the prospective group is expected to have an average rate of £70, a simple trade-off can be calculated as follows:

Revenue gain = 150 group room nights (50 × 3 nights) at £70

= £10 500

Revenue loss = 50 transient room nights @ £95

= £4750

But is that the only displacement that will take place? Some portions of transients arriving on Monday and Tuesday would ordinarily stay through Wednesday. If Wednesday is unavailable, these people may go elsewhere, adding to the displacement. Similarly, some of Wednesday's displaced transients would have stayed at the hotel on other days, so even more hidden displacement will occur. (See Table 8.4.)

According to Orkin the advantage of booking the group is still not of the magnitude it seems. Taking the group would incur elements of costs associated with 70 more occupied rooms. Furthermore, a portion of the 80 disappointed transients may be quite pleased with their alternate hotel choice, and their business could be lost forever. Finally, estimates of customer spending on food, drink, etc. must be factored into the equation. Given the complexity of it all, it is not surprising that small hotels have neither the time nor the data to do a full and proper analysis and the large hotels resort to computer models for assistance.

Much has been said of the hotel industry but what of other services use of yield management? Consider an example from the airline industry.[16] Here the focus is on improving the yield of the various routes. To begin with, operational expenses are calculated for each flight and then divided

Table 8.4 Value of lost potential business. *Source:* Orkin (1988)[15]

	Monday	Tuesday	Wednesday	Thursday	Friday
Group under consideration	50	50	50		
Primary displacement	0	0	50		
Total displacement	5	10	50	10	5

Revenue gain: 150 Group room nights @ £70 = £10 500
Revenue loss: 80 Transient room nights @ £95 = £7600

by the number of available seats on that flight. This means each seat has a fixed cost associated with it. To make this figure even more meaningful the cost is then broken down to cost per kilometre. Therefore, each flight has an available seat kilometre (ASK) which is computed by multiplying the number of seats on the aeroplane by the distance of the flight. For example:

Boeing 747 with 400 seats
Flight – London to Johannesburg (10 000 kilometres)
∴ ASK = 4 million (400 × 10 000)

Full cost of flight = £ 210 000
∴ Cost per ASK = 5.25 pence per seat per kilometre
(£210 000 divided by 4 million)

To find out if the yield on revenue of the above flight is good, bad, or indifferent a further calculation is required. The marketing team needs to know the revenue per passenger kilometre (RPK) of each flight. Using the same flight and costs as above the RPK would be worked out as follows:

380 passengers on board
Total revenue is £247 500
Total passenger kilometres = 380 × 10 000

= 3 800 000

Thus RPK = 6.5 pence which gives a yield of 23.8% over the ASK

The conclusion to be drawn is just how marginal airline operations can be. The implication is not one of a daily or even monthly alteration of fares but rather action to improve the mix of seats to suit the flight route.

Queueing: an overview

Queueing or 'waiting in line' is a phenomenon of everyday life for many people. We wait at the bank, on the phone, at the post office, on congested roads, for the lift, and so on. Although reservation systems are in operation, the 'queueing problem' is a fact of life that confronts many service organizations and customers.

However, queueing does have its lighthearted moments by evoking a sense of humour, often perverse, cynical etc., among the participants. The following illustrate the kind of comments 'overheard in the queue':

> German comes up to a queue at Heathrow Airport and asks 'Why are you queueing?'; answer 'We're British'.

> Woman at the front of a bus queue asks the driver of a bus that has just arrived, 'How long will the next bus be?'; reply from the driver, 'Same length as this one, 26 feet'; woman retorts, 'And will it have a monkey like you driving it?'

> Customs officer at airport is immersed in a large book. One person leaves the queue and goes up to the customs officer. On returning he is asked, 'What is he reading?'; answer *War and Peace*.

For consumers, time can be bought, saved, spent and wasted. It is time wasted that is perceived as the major characteristic of queueing. Cultures and groups within any one culture differ in respect of their perception of time.[17] Within the specific area of consumer shopping behaviour there is clear evidence of variations between actual (objective) and perceived (subjective) time.[18] People, when asked, tend to overestimate waiting time. This is particularly so where it is simply a question of waiting. On the other hand, where the passage of time is active (people are involved in or distracted by some activity) there is a tendency to underestimate time duration. There is a clear message here for service organizations if their customers are to avoid a very negative and frustrating experience. The words of a time essayist have a depressing ring about them.[19]

> Waiting is a form of imprisonment. One is doing time – but why? One is being punished not for an offence of one's own but for the inefficiencies of those who impose the wait. Hence the peculiar rage that waits engender, the sense of injustice. Aside from boredom and physical discomfort, the subtler misery of waiting is the knowledge that one's most precious resource, time, a fraction of one's life, is being stolen away, irrecoverably lost.

> . . . Waiting can seem an interval of non-being, the black space
> between events and the outcome of desires. It makes time
> maddeningly elastic, it has a way of seeming to compact
> eternity into a few hours.

Attempts have been made to quantify just how much time is taken up waiting. Although speculative, an example from the USA illustrates the kind of figures involved. The writer[20] states that 'if we estimate that 200 million Americans occupy queues on an average of 30 minutes per day per person, we arrive at roughly 37 billion hours per year spent in standing in line in the United States'. To get some idea of what this actually represents the writer goes on to suggest that, 'since by some estimates the average American watches approximately 4 to 5 hours of television per day, the time spent in queues would appear to be within an order of magnitude of the time spent watching television'. He concludes with the message that, 'as the private sector spends approximately 25 billion dollars a year in television advertising, airing commercials which viewers may choose not to watch, it would seem that 2 to 3 billion dollars spent on marketing products to people in queues would not be inappropriate, considering that these individuals usually have very little in the way of alternatives to divert their attention'. Cleaners of car windscreens at traffic lights and marketers of mobile phones are examples of the exploitation of the 'waiting market'.

Social justice and the disciplines of the queue

Certain queueing situations can promote a fear of social injustice. How often have you experienced a situation in which you have been standing in a queue for some time when suddenly another check-out or processing point is opened. Those at the back of your queue, having just arrived, dash over to the new queue and get served almost immediately. This is the fear of social injustice being realized.

It has long been accepted by those who have studied and written about queues that first come, first served (FCFS) is the socially just queue discipline and first in, first out (FIFO) the socially just system discipline. The type of queueing system will have a decisive effect on whether or not social justice prevails. There are essentially four types of queueing lines:

- Single line – where one queue forms to be processed through a single server, e.g. waitress-free restaurants, cinemas.
- Snake lines – a number of serving points working one line of customers with the first in line approaching the next available server. This is quite common in many service settings, e.g. post office, banks, building societies.

- Express lines – a separate line is made available for those transacting out-of-the-ordinary business, paying by cheque or having a limited number of purchases or items to process.
- Multi-server lines – a number of serving points, each of which serves a separate line. The most obvious example is the supermarket although it is common in many services.

It is this last type, where people jump from one line to another, that promotes feelings of injustice.

Lines are, of course, not necessary under the take-a-number system adopted by some services, e.g. supermarket delicatessen, doctor's surgery, tax office, etc. Here we have a situation of waiting in time without waiting in line.

Managing queues and waiting

People naturally want to spend as little of their time as possible standing in queues and waiting. Given that there will always be 'queues and waits', organizations need to make provision for managing them effectively. There are two ways of looking at this: the statistical perspective discussed earlier where management need to know how many will appear, at what times etc. in order that resources can be deployed to achieve an efficient throughput or the service provider can seek to understand people's expectations and perceptions of waiting with a view to making it more bearable, perhaps even enjoyable. This is the behavioural perspective.

Queueing: a behavioural perspective

A number of behavioural principles or propositions governing queueing and waiting have been proposed[20,21] They can be summarized as follows:

- Uncertainties – there is nothing worse from a customer's point of view than not knowing how long you will have to wait. People must be given an indication of how long they should expect to wait and it should err on the side of caution. For example, it is obviously better to say 'you will be seen in twenty minutes or the take-off will be delayed by thirty minutes' where the wait is anticipated by the service provider to be less in both instances. Promising a wait of less than its actual duration should be avoided at all costs. The worst thing to say would be 'We'll be with you soon' or 'The delay in departure will not be long'. In these cases the risk of customer dissatisfaction is increased because their expectations have been raised.

- The essential characteristic and apparent attractiveness of the appointment system are its complete lack of uncertainty. Unless you arrive early, there is no waiting involved as people expect to be taken at their allotted time. What is not always understood or tolerated is why a service does not adhere to the appointment schedule. A hairdresser will usually keep to the schedule while the local GP may not. The explanation lies in the greater degree of uncertainty and unpredictability surrounding patient needs in the doctor's surgery.
- Explanation – the length of a delay can be given meaning if people are told the reason(s). There are innumerable reasons for delay but the important point is that customers will make a judgment as to whether it is reasonable, acceptable, or justifiable. One might speculate that failure to inform customers is as much to do with avoiding unnecessary ridicule and censure. British Rail's revelation that a particular type of snow or leaves on the line can cause severe disruption was met with incredulity and annoyance that it was seemingly unable to do anything about it. There is nothing more frustrating from the customers' viewpoint than serving points, e.g. in post offices, banks, supermarkets suddenly closing without any explanation, or where service employees are seen to be 'sitting idly by' while the queues get longer. Ideally an explanation of the real cause of the delay should be given, but in the real world organizations may decide to give out either no reasons or ones deemed more acceptable to the customers.
- Anxiety – this feeling can often be the consequence of uncertainty and no explanation. It is the product of thinking, 'I'll never be seen to', which with the advent of appointments and take-a-number systems is less frequent. However, it can be felt when standing far back in a very long queue entering a capacity constrained facility, e.g. a pop concert, a football match. Organizers can eliminate it with the reassurance that 'everyone will get in'.
- Boredom – waiting can be incredibly boring. If organizations can offer some desirable distractions that take customers' minds off the time the response might well be one of 'how time flies'. There has not been a great deal of imagination generated in this area. Successfully filling unoccupied time is a difficult exercise and one in which there is enormous scope for experimentation and development. Quite often customers take it upon themselves to fill in time by befriending each other.
- Pre-process versus in-process – this is partially related to the previous point in that although customers have to wait they want to feel as soon as possible that progress is being made towards the service commencing. The obvious example is being given a menu on sitting down for a restaurant meal. The important point is that customers need to feel they are involved as quickly as possible. Anything the provider can do to fill in the customers' time before the core service begins will achieve that objective.

- Value – in general people value their time so what they are waiting for has to be worth it. What customers define as 'valued' are as numerous as the reasons for delay mentioned earlier. It is not simply a matter of valued being seen as something highly priced. Long waits are endured to obtain an important prescription. People camp out overnight or wait many hours to obtain entry to various forms of entertainment. The wait is very much seen in terms of 'it's worth it.'
- Equity – people correctly feel aggrieved if the FCFS and FIFO systems mentioned earlier are not observed. The take-a-number procedure operated by many services is a good example of FIFO. It works well when all customers' transactions require about the same amount of time, but not where markedly different amounts of time are in evidence. There are instances where FIFO and FCFS would seem to be violated, e.g. an emergency arrival at a hospital, but this is an example where customers accept non-observance of the rule.

  Sometimes what seems to be a breaking of the equity rule is understandable. For example a person waiting in a restaurant for a seat sees a party of four entering and being given a table straight away. The single person may feel a sense of injustice but the restaurant owner cannot be expected perfectly to match his fixed capacity of seating arrangements with the unpredictability of customer demand patterns. Equally a customer in a department store may feel frustration when telephone callers receive priority service. An occurrence such as this can be avoided through the adoption of proper procedures.

The way ahead

It is difficult to envisage a time when queueing and waiting will not exist. What is a real possibility is that in the absence of any affirmative action queues and waits will simply get longer. For many service organizations smoothing out demand over a day, week, year etc. can bring rewards in terms of efficient resource utilization and quality service to customers. However, research will inevitably be required. Robert East and his colleagues in the Consumer Research Unit at Kingston Business School have made a significant contribution.[22] Their research was focused on supermarkets, post offices, banks and building societies. They believe that organizations can do a great deal about managing demand over time.

In one of their research papers, they analyse demand patterns during the course of a day and days of the week in post offices. Using a comprehensive questionnaire, they ask the following:

- Do people dislike congestion and queueing in post offices?
- When do people use post offices?

- Do people have habits about when they use the post office?
- Can they use post offices at different times?
- Do they know when the busy and quiet times are?
- Is there evidence that people avoid peak times if they dislike queueing?
- What factors are associated with dislike of queueing?
- How does the perception of main offices differ from that of sub-offices?

Queueing: a quantitative perspective

The basic, underlying reason for studying and then applying queueing theory is economic. The managers of the bridge that spans the Firth of Forth know that at certain times of day only a trickle of vehicles passes through the toll barriers where the fees are collected; at other times the queues literally stretch for miles. The managers have to ensure that the staff collecting the tolls are used optimally so that the toll booths are manned in the most cost-effective way. On a larger scale, those who run Disney World estimate that on a slack day, 15 000 visitors can be expected while on a busy day the figure is likely to be of the order of 65 000 people. With these numbers to contend with it is imperative that there is a smooth throughput of customers with as few bottlenecks occurring as possible. In both these examples the study of queueing theory has aided the optimizing of the situation.

In this context two basic questions are usually asked of queues and it is the answers to these questions which help managers organize the facilities available. One question is: 'What is the average length of the queue?' ... we want to ensure that the queues are neither too long nor too short for, in either case, the cost effectiveness of the system is in jeopardy. The other question is: 'How long do items have to wait in the queue before they are processed?' Again, we do not want the waiting time to be too long or too short.

There are some basic assumptions that have to be made when dealing with a simple (settled) queue. First, the potential population that is available to use the facility is very large (we often refer to this as an infinitely large population). Second, the probability of all of this infinite population using the facility is exceedingly small. This situation allows the Poisson distribution to be used (n is very large, and P the probability of success is very small). Third, we apply the FIFO (first in, first out) concept ... no baulking (i.e. jumping the queue) is allowed. Fourth, we deal with discrete data and have one queue only, but can have a number of service channels to deal with this queue ... Figure 8.6 sets out this situation.

At this stage we will differentiate between a queue and the system (Figure 8.7).

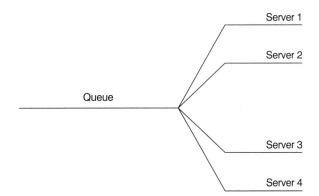

Figure 8.6 Single queue: multiple servers

Figure 8.7 The queueing system

No matter how complicated the queueing model becomes, it all starts by obtaining two basic sets of data; the average arrival rate denoted by λ (the Greek letter lambda); and the average service rate denoted by μ (the Greek letter mu). From these two statistics we derive the traffic intensity denoted by ρ (the Greek letter rho). Traffic intensity can best be thought of as the average utilization of the service facility and has the formula:

$\rho = \lambda/\mu$ (note $\lambda < \mu$, otherwise we can end up with an infinite queue).

Asking the question 'how many . . . ?' we have the two formulae:

$M_q = \rho^2/(1 - \rho)$ and $M_s = \rho/(1 - \rho)$

where M_q is the average number of items in the queue and M_s is the average number of items in the system.

Asking the question 'how long to wait . . . ?' requires the following formulae:

$W_q = \rho/(\mu - \lambda)$ and $W_s = 1/(\mu - \lambda)$

where W_q is the waiting time in the queue and W_s is the waiting time in the system. Another formula that can be useful involves probabilities.

Here we ask the question, 'what is the probability that there are n items in the queue?'; this gives us the facility for calculating the 'idle time' of the servers, this formula is

$$P_n = \rho^n(1 - \rho)$$

Worked example: Customers in a supermarket join a single queue at an average rate of 30 per hour and are served at an average rate of 35 per hour. Find the average:

1 Number of customers waiting to be served;
2 Number of customers in the system;
3 Time spent queueing;
4 Time spent in the system;
5 Also find the probability that the server is idle.

Solutions: $\rho = 0.857$.

1 $(0.857)^2/(1 - 0.857) = 5.14$, i.e. 5 customers
2 $(0.857)/(1 - 0.857) = 5.99$ i.e. 6 customers
3 $(0.857)/(35 - 30) = 0.1714\,\text{h}$, i.e $10.28\,\text{min}$
4 $1/(35 - 30) = 1/5\,\text{h} = 12\,\text{min}$
5 $P_o = (0.857)^0 \, (1 - 0.857) = 0.143$.

It should be self-evident that the size of the queue affects the service rate which, in turn, determines the length of time spent in the queue and the system.

Summary

Service providers face a particular problem when it comes to demand management and capacity utilization. Unlike manufacturing, service organizations cannot stockpile their 'output' in a warehouse and wait for demand to materialize.

Demand for many services can fluctuate in such an unpredictable way that capacity is either unable to cope, or grossly underutilized. Achieving a match between demand and capacity is a difficult goal, but it is an important one for reasons of cost and customer satisfaction.

In this chapter, three different strategic approaches for managing supply and demand have been discussed. First, one can build flexibility into the system by *tailoring* capacity to match demand at any one point. Second, one can attempt to *predict* the fluctuations in demand, and match capacity to these levels. Third, one can attempt to *manage* demand to fit capacity.

Thereby operating with a relatively level capacity and tailoring demand to fit. However, it is not simply a matter of aiming for maximum capacity utilization. A delicate balance may have to be struck between profitability and quality of service. This is known as 'optimum capacity utilization'.

Two other issues that also affect the demand for and supply of services are the pricing of services and yield management. Finally, queueing and waiting are particular features of service. They have a behavioural and a statistical perspective, and both must be understood and managed if customer dissatisfaction is to be avoided.

References

1. Heskett, J. L., Sasser, W. E. and Hart, C. W. L. (1990) *Service Breakthroughs – Changing the Rules of the Game*, Free Press, New York.
2. Lovelock, C. L. (1983) 'Classifying services to gain strategic marketing insights', *Journal of Marketing*, **47**, No. 3, Summer.
3. Sasser, W. E., Olsen, R. P. and Wyckoff, D. D. (1978) *Management of Service Operations*, Allyn & Bacon, Boston, MA.
4. Armistead, C. G. (1988) *Operations Management in Service Industries in the Public Sector*, Wiley, New York.
5. Sasser, W. E. (1976) Match supply and demand in service industries', *Harvard Business Review*, November–December, 133–140.
6. Zeithaml, V. and Bitner, M. J. (1996) *Services Marketing*, McGraw-Hill, New York.
7. Clemmer, E. C. and Schneider, B. (1989) 'Towards understanding and controlling customer dissatisfaction with waiting during peak demand times'. In *Designing a Winning Service Strategy*, (Bitner M. J. and Crosby L. A. eds). American Marketing Association, Chicago.
8. Shapiro, B. P. (1968) 'The psychology of pricing,' *Harvard Business Review*, July–August, 14–44.
9. Palmer, A. (1994) *Principles of Services Marketing*, McGraw-Hill, New York.
10. Sloman, J. (1997) *Economics*, Prentice Hall, Englewood Cliff, NJ.
11. Walters, J. (1998) 'Any more fares please. They're mostly profit', *The Observer*, 26 June.
12. Kimes, S. E. (1989) 'The basics of yield management', *The Cornell HRA Quarterly*, November.
13. Kimes, S. E. (1989) 'Yield management: a tool for capacity-constrained service firms', *Journal of Operations Management*, **8** (4).
14. Lovelock, C. H. (1996) *Services Marketing*, Prentice Hall, Englewood Cliff, NJ.
15. Orkin, E. B. (1988) 'Boosting your bottom line with yield management', *The Cornell HRA Quarterly'*, February.
16. Ingold, A. and Huyton, J. R. (1977) 'Yield management and the airline industry.' In *Yield Management* (Yeoman, C. and Ingold, A. eds). Cassell, London.

17. Hall, E. T. (1959) *The Silent Language*, Doubleday, New York.
18. Hornik, J. (1984) 'Subjective vs objective time measures: a note of the perception of time in consumer behaviour', *Journal of Consumer Research*, **11**, 615–618.
19. Morrow, L. (1984) 'Waiting as a way of life', *Time*, 23 July.
20. Larson, R. C. (1987) 'Perspectives on queues: social justice and the psychology of queueing,' *Operations Research*, **35**(6), November–December, 895–905.
21. Maister, D. H. (1985) 'The psychology of waiting lines'. In *The Service Encounter* (Czepiel, J. A., Solomon, M. R. and Suprenant, C. F. eds), Lexington Books, D. C. Heath and Company, Lexington, MA.
22. East, R., Lomax, W., Willson, G. and Harris, P. (1991) 'Demand over time: patterns of use and preference among post office users', *Occasional Paper Series*, Kingston Business School.

Chapter 9

Service communications

Introduction

Today's environment is fiercely competitive. It is therefore not enough to develop a service for which there is known demand. It is not enough to say that a good service will sell itself. The service must be communicated to the target market in order to generate and develop a loyal customer base. While communications can be planned before the service is ready for consumption they should certainly not be implemented.

The role for communications

Communication can *add* value to the service in the eyes of the consumer. This is one of its key benefits. In many cases this will enable the provider to charge a premium over that of competitors. This is important given that the majority of companies have as their principal objective the maximization of profits. Profit is, of course, related to the difference between costs and revenue which, in turn, are influenced by value added. Advertising is one of the most visible ways through which an organization communicates with its customers. In 1997 service organizations in the UK spent some £3500 million on advertising (Table 9.1). This expenditure has grown significantly in recent years both in absolute terms and also as a share of total advertising in the UK.

Services communication

The key differences between products and services should be taken into account in considering service communication as follows:

Table 9.1 UK service sector advertising
expenditure 1997

Industry	£000
Retailing	1 243 887
Financial services	714 576
Mail order	402 374
Holidays and Travel	361 006
Household stores	263 055
Entertainment	194 008
Government	136 602
Charities	47 014
Business-to-business	45 394
Utilities	32 940
Education	32 325
	3 473 181

Source: ACNeilsen MEAL

- *Simultaneous production and consumption.* The layout, shop facia, and the appearance and manner of the staff are critical communication variables.
- *Intangibility.* Service providers should attempt to reduce the risk to the consumer of buying an intangible product by providing tangible clues about the service offering. These clues come from all aspects of corporate communication.
- *Heterogeneity.* This, too, leads to greater perceived risk. Again communications can help to reduce this factor. It may be appropriate to communicate a service guarantee or promise (Figure 9.1) or to demonstrate how well trained your staff are.
- *Perishability.* Many promotional tools, e.g. advertising, sales promotion, and direct marketing, have a role to play in shaping demand. This is one of the most challenging aspects of service management and arises from the fact that services cannot be inventoried.

Flowing from this there are five key aspects of communication for the service marketer:

- The role of personal selling
- The targeting of employees in external communications
- The management of expectations
- The provision of tangible clues
- Word-of-mouth communications

Figure 9.1 Kwik-Fit advertisement: the communication of a guarantee

Key communication variables

The role of personal selling

Most service delivery involves human encounter. The way in which that encounter develops can determine whether the customer walks away feeling pleased, satisfied, annoyed, or victimized. Although the customer's expectations help determine levels of satisfaction, the encounter itself will invariably play a significant part in determining satisfaction. The person who delivers the service is often actually part of the service itself. He or she is not merely facilitating the exchange of a product that is already fully developed and is waiting to be picked from a shelf. Waiting staff in a restaurant deliver not just food but customer satisfaction.

Research conducted by John Bateson for his book *Managing Services Marketing*[1] concluded that personal selling and image-creating strategies were the communications tools most often used by service organizations. He notes that they must choose their contact personnel carefully and train them to interact effectively with customers.

The role of personal selling is not the same for every service organization. The partner in a large accountancy firm will be performing quite a different personal selling role from that of a checkout operator in a supermarket.

In attempting to mould the interpersonal skills of contact personnel, service managers should ask themselves the following questions:

- Who are the salespeople in the organization?
- What other functions do they fulfil?
- What ought they to be communicating about the service?
- On what dimensions do consumers judge the standard of service delivery?
- What factors shape expectations of each service encounter? Are they related to service complexity? To frequency of use of the service?
- Is it more appropriate for customers to be offered a customized or a standardized response? (Of course, service delivery varies not only among people but also within people. We all have our good and bad days. On a good day customization will probably result in an improved service offering. However, on a bad day, standardized service has a greater chance of achieving satisfied customers.)

If some thought is given to these factors then the communication function of contact personnel has a greater chance of being effective.

Personal selling is often the most important variable in the development of expectations. No matter what the advertising communicates, or what the consumers' friends say, their expectations will be shaped by any personalized communication that they receive from the company. If your hairdresser tells you that the colourant that he has used will last for eight weeks then that is how long you expect it to last. If a department store says that it will deliver the following day then that is what customers expect. Frontline employees have to be trained to understand that it is important to develop *realistic* expectations in consumers however tempting it may be to overpromise.

Employees as a target of communications

The importance of the employee in the delivery of a quality service means that they should not be ignored when it comes to considering who the relevant communication targets are. The most prolific writer in this field, Leonard Berry[2,3] makes this point.

There are certainly internal pieces of communication that can help improve their job performance. The mission statement is a critical tool in this respect. The employee can also benefit from external corporate communications which appear to be aimed at the consumer. There are several reasons for this.

First, many services are delivered through a geographically dispersed network of branches and outlets. Employees have little contact with head office. In this case external communications can help to maintain their commitment to the organization. It can also help remind them of the corporate culture that was imbued during their induction (Figure 9.2).

It may serve as a reminder or a reassurance of what the organization expects of them, or, as Zeithaml states, 'if [the communications] features employees doing their jobs, it communicates to them that they are important'.[4] However, the proposition that these communications are more effective if they use actual employees rather than professional actors could be refuted. An aspirational role model may be more appropriate and effective.

Finally these communications can help to manage customers' expectations and in so doing they can communicate with employees about what to expect from their customers.

Managing expectations

Communicating with the customer about what to expect of the service is very important. If expectations can be managed so that the customer has more realistic expectations of the service delivery then his expectations are more likely to be met. American Express informs its cardholders that 'Membership has its privileges'. Customers then come to look for their privileges.

When you're only No.2, you try harder. Or else.

Avis can't afford to relax.

Little fish have to keep moving all of the time. The big ones never stop picking on them.

Avis knows all about the problems of little fish.

We're only No.2 in rent a cars. We'd be swallowed up if we didn't try harder.

There's no rest for us.

We're always emptying ashtrays. Making sure gas tanks are full before we rent our cars. Seeing that the batteries are full of life. Checking our windshield wipers.

And the cars we rent out can't be anything less than lively new super-torque Fords.

And since we're not the big fish, you won't feel like a sardine when you come to our counter.

We're not jammed with customers.

Figure 9.2 The Avis advertisement communicates management's expectations of employees and shapes customers' expectations of the service

Czepiel, Solomon, and Suprenant[5] note that most problems about customer satisfaction relate to expectations exceeding service delivery. Satisfied customers result from the service experience fulfilling expectations. This is why the management of these expectations is so important. External communication is only one of a number of variables that are influential (Figure 9.3). It is, though, perhaps the most easily controlled.

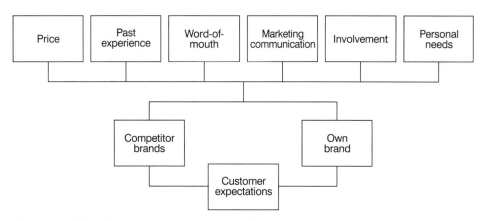

Figure 9.3 Developing customer expectations

Raising expectations through communications can increase the risk of customer dissatisfaction. It may be tempting to overpromise in order to get business through the door. However, the repercussions often outweigh any initial benefit.

Delta Airlines at one time vowed 'we're ready when you are', and Holiday Inns told its customers 'no surprises guaranteed'. Both companies had to revise their communications because they were overpromising. Consumers' expectations were raised and then not fulfilled. They did not expect any delays if they travelled with Delta, nor were they happy when Holiday Inns did indeed produce some surprises.

In the UK, in the 1980s British Rail fell into the same trap by advertising the fact that 'we're getting there', when it was obvious to the commuting public that British Rail were patently *not* getting there. 'The wonder of Woolies' is yet another example from the same era. This advertising led consumers to re-evaluate their expectations of these services. However, it led them to revise them upwards which in turn led to increased levels of dissatisfaction. Organizations began to realize that while this practice may encourage new business it does not encourage repeat business.

External communications that help develop expectations may involve a 'look behind the scenes' approach. This enables organizations to demonstrate all the effort that they go to in order to provide the service. This has been a popular theme with utilities companies.

Another approach is to provide customers with a script or scenario of the likely service encounter. Financial services and airline companies have used this approach in the past. Both strategies work well on television. They use this medium to its full potential allowing characters to develop in live-action situations.

Most literature on this subject actually suggests that the role of communication is to revise consumers' expectations downwards. This arises from the view that consumers set themselves unrealistically high expectations in the first place.

However, a more challenging task for the service marketer is to develop and maintain a quality service that meets or exceeds most consumers' expectations. Product manufacturers that are regarded as being leading-edge companies in terms of delivering quality products such as Motorola and NEC now take as their manufacturing goal six-sigma quality. This is a means of measuring how close production comes to total quality.

Six-sigma quality means that there are only 3.4 defects per million parts produced. Motorola may soon adopt an unheard-of goal 60 defects or less for every billion components it makes. Some Japanese manufacturing companies attempt to go further by manufacturing to zero defects. Toyota have introduced the concept of *poka-yoke* which aims to make the workplace mistake-proof, i.e. to manufacture to total quality.[6] So rather than externally aiming to reduce expectations these organizations instead internally aim to raise quality.

While this is more readily achievable in product marketing, service marketing should not ignore this potential strategy. Indeed, it may be a way of sustaining a competitive advantage. Future developments will certainly see more companies aiming to reduce the gap between expectations and delivery by tackling the issue internally as well as externally.

Tangible clues

The less tangible the generic service, the more powerfully and persistently the judgement of it gets shaped by the packaging. As Levitt states,[7] 'Metaphors and symbols become surrogates for the tangibility that cannot be provided or experienced in advance'.

The consumption of services is often associated with high levels of risk. Much of this risk stems from the intangible nature of services. It is not just the fact that the service cannot be touched in the same way that a product can. It is also that consumers often find it difficult to comprehend what they are being offered. This risk can be reduced by the provision of tangible clues that relate to the service offering. In a restaurant, the use of starched napery will communicate to customers that it is a quality establishment. Similarly, a bellboy on the steps of an hotel says something of its up-market positioning. These tangible clues make the nature of the service more easily understood.

Figure 9.4 Legal and General logo

If any of these signposts are to be used in professional communications then care must be taken to select those that are *relevant* to consumers. They should be built around parts of the service offering that are key motivators for purchase.

Legal and General, the insurance company, practise this to good effect with the use of their multi-coloured umbrella. They offer you protection from life's uncertainties, and with this the prospect of a brighter future. The umbrella as a tangible clue communicates this effectively (Figure 9.4).

Word-of-mouth communication

Personal recommendation is a powerful communication vehicle in the service sector. The importance that consumers attach to word-of-mouth endorsement by their peer group arises from their need to reduce risk from the intangible and variable nature of services. Service marketers must learn to capitalize on this tool. So how should they do this? The following list presents some of the options:

- *Introduce a friend scheme.* Encourage current users to inform others of the good service. (American Express offers current card holders a case of wine if they introduce a friend.)
- *Testimonials.* Use satisfied customers' experiences in advertising.
- *Persuasion of opinion formers.* Use PR to target opinion leaders or early adopters.
- *Promotional items.* Promotional items can provide tangible clues implying 'club' membership. The Open Golf tournament umbrella, or the Wimbledon sweatshirt are examples of this.
- *Feedback.* Incorporate it into the communication of a comprehensive complaints procedure. 'If you're happy with what we do tell them (friends etc.), if you're not tell us.'

Branding services

How are communications developed? In many cases the initial stage of the process is to develop a brand image. Brands have increased in importance in service marketing throughout the 1990s. This trend is expected to continue since:

- There is an increasing proliferation of brands within service sectors. Service markets are becoming more competitive.
- It has been shown to be up to five times cheaper to retain current customers than to attract new ones.[8]
- Service life cycles are becoming shorter. New service development thus assumes a greater importance. The risks of product launches are reduced in the context of umbrella branding.
- The service itself may offer no unique tangible benefit – this can be added by development of brand imagery.

Brand image development

The process should begin with an assessment of the benefits that accrue to users of the service. Preferably these should be unique. With no branding of the service at this stage, these benefits are more likely to be functional in character, i.e. a car hire firm will get you from A to B, an hotel will provide you with a good night's sleep. However in the development of an augmented service, an assessment of the social and psychological benefits that also accrue is necessary.

Market research may well have to be conducted in order to understand the consumer response. The outcome of this stage is an understanding of what consumers regard as the key attributes of the service, i.e. a social benefit to a businessman of hiring a car may be that he will look more professional, or a big time player to the client that he is meeting if he arrives by hire car rather than by public transport. A psychological benefit may be his enhanced feeling of self importance.

A social benefit derived from staying at a prestigious hotel may well be the company that the guest expects to keep. A psychological benefit could be the pampering/indulgence of the whole experience. It is from an understanding of these benefits that communications are built. They should highlight what it is that motivates people to use the service. By attaching your brand name to the most important motivator(s) you begin to give consumers reasons to prefer your brand over that of your competitors, i.e. you begin to build brand preference (Figure 9.5).

Figure 9.5 Developing brand loyalty through communications

An effective communications package should attempt to take consumers swiftly from the position of brand non-recognition to that of brand preference. There is little advantage in consumers knowing of your service if they do not act on this knowledge.

Brand rejection occurs when your communications message is not motivating. It may not be motivating to those who are not target consumers. That is not a problem. What is more worrying is when the rejectors are in your target. Research must be undertaken to establish who are the rejectors. If it is the latter group then they must be further researched to understand the reasons why?

Consumers who are brand indifferent need more motivation. In many cases this arises because the service has not been experienced. Sales promotion techniques aimed at inducing trial should be considered.

Brand insistence/loyalty is every marketer's dream. How do you get there?

- Encourage repeat purchase using sales promotion. This makes consumers familiar with your service which in turn diminishes risk.
- Keep your current customers satisfied by developing and sustaining a unique service advantage. As Dobree and Page[8] state, branding is one key method of addressing the problem of competitive advantage. Branding is often the best way of sustaining a competitive advantage. A competitive advantage built solely on functional benefits is much easier for competitors to copy.
- Introduce penalties so that the cost of changing brands is high. Financial institutions, particularly the building societies, practise this to good effect. If you decide to move to a company that offers a higher rate of interest, then the original lending company will charge you a penalty for doing this. This financial penalty will often mean that there is no longer any pecuniary advantage from making the change. (For further discussion, see the section on relationship marketing in Chapter 11.)

Corporate identity

In many cases it is the organization that a service is bought from rather than a specific brand, i.e. Boots may have attempted to segment their service offering into Cook Shops, Sound and Vision and Baby Shops but

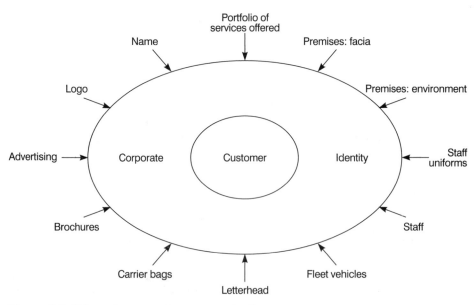

Figure 9.6 External corporate communications

we expect that most people still see themselves as buying from Boots. For this reason the development of a corporate identity becomes very important. It is also important to develop an image that gives the organization a focus since there are many variables working against the projection of a cohesive image. There are many factors which contribute to the building of corporate image.

Figure 9.6 illustrates the main factors. Some of these are discussed in more depth in Chapters 4 and 7. Obviously not all services will use every mechanism; not many solicitors are seen to deploy carrier bags as part of their corporate image, nor will many restaurants run fleet vehicles. Whatever channels are chosen to promote the corporate identity, the task is to create a cohesive image that communicates an appropriate message. To manage this process efficiently and effectively it is important that the identity is carried synergistically across all communications.

Naming the service

What should a service name communicate? The best names communicate the key benefit that the service offers. Creased Lightening for an ironing service, Typerite for a typing service.

If the marketplace is competitive or the key benefit is different for different groups of consumers then the name should attempt to convey creatively the service that is offered, e.g. Branching Out for a florist, or The Potting Shed for a garden centre.

At a third level, it may be that this cannot be done creatively and so the generic service name is incorporated (often alongside the owner's name) e.g. Martin's Removals, or Fraser's Launderette. The three levels of naming are illustrated for a service that unblocks drains.

Drain Kleer	main benefit communicated
Blockbusters	service creatively communicated
P. N. D. Drainage	service generically communicated

All these approaches are superior to those names that give consumers no hints about the service that is offered. They are easier for consumers to remember because the name itself generates a visual image. These images complement the verbal name and leave the consumer with a more fully developed picture of the company.

The human brain finds it easier to store and retrieve words or names when they also have a visual prompt. This was researched by Lutz and Lutz,[9] whose results confirmed that an interactive image facilitates recall of the company or brand name better than a non-interactive image.

The service name can develop verbal interactive imagery. The interaction is between the company name and the service that is provided. We live in an overcommunicated society. We are producing more information and absorbing less of it. So the easier we make it for consumers to remember the company name the more chance we have of being successful.

Product marketing giants have taken this concept a stage further. They have taken to naming new brands in such a way that the core benefit cannot be missed. Unilver launched a new dairy spread in 1991 called 'I Can't Believe It's Not Butter'. Wall's launched a new range of fat-free luxury ice-cream named 'Too Good To Be True'. Does this represent a lack of creativity? Or are these companies trying to make the name itself communicate as much as possible to consumers about the product?

A good example of this approach to brand naming comes from the US toy retailer called 'Toys R Us'. The name itself tells consumers that it is a toy retailer. The 'R' written backwards may be just the way that a child would write it (Figure 9.7).

Figure 9.7 Toys 'R' Us logo

As Berry, Lefkowith, and Clark[10] state, there are four key characteristics that a service name should possess:

- Distinctiveness: identifies supplier and distinguishes from competition
- Relevance: conveys service benefit
- Memorability: understood and recalled with ease
- Flexibility: scope to cover business expansion

Designing the logo

The logo can take this process a stage further. It can help consumers to form a picture of the company by presenting them with visual clues of the service that is on offer (Figure 9.8).

A good logo helps both the company and its customers. It enables the company to have more impact in its desire to imprint a memorable picture on the consumer's mind. This in turn means that consumers do not have to work as hard to create an image for themselves as they did when only presented with a name. This is described as pictorial interaction by Lutz, and Lutz.[9] Remembering the picture also means remembering the company name.

Figure 9.8 Peter Plant cartoon. *Source: Marketing Magazine* (1992)

The corporate identity of British Airways has been reversed three times in the past three decades. In the 1970s the public image of British Airways had been one of a nationalized industry ravaged by strikes and inefficient management practices. The logo that was in place during this period reflected the company image. It was designed at the time of the amalgamation of BEA and BOAC, and in attempting to incorporate design elements from each of those companies the design solution arrived at was a compromise. The logo projected a solid image, yet it lacked any feeling of movement that might be expected of a travel company.

In 1984 British Airways launched a new corporate logo which was intended to reflect the company's new culture. The revised logo represented a significant step forward. BA's new management working towards privatization wanted to convey a much more dynamic image. The logo was expected to assert BA's superiority to staff, customers, and potential investors. The design certainly captures movement, and helped to project the image of a progressive company, driving forward in the travel business.

In 1997 the corporate identity was revised again. This time, the desire was to reflect globalization of the airline. Radical changes in the industry: the emergence of supergroupings; the growth of low-cost niche carriers; and changes in the regulatory environment have all played a part in the redesign of the corporate identity. At the heart of which is the creation of more than fifty world images which appear on everything that bears the British Airways name.

The company's corporate palette of red, white, and blue has been brightened and lightened, more closely drawn from the British union flag than the 1984 scheme. This is intended to reflect the airline's British heritage. The name 'British Airways' has been depicted using a softer, rounder typeface, and a new three-dimensional Speedmarque has evolved from the flat red speedwing symbol of 1984 (Figure 9.9).

Figure 9.9 The evolving corporate logo of British Airways

Yet another way in which a logo can be designed is to take the company name, or the first letters of each word in the company name, and make that the logo. This is referred to as Letter Accentuation. It converts one or more letters in the name to a picture of the service. 'Letter accentuation is not as effective as strict pictorial interaction but does seem to provide a slight improvement over non-interactive presentations.'[10] The Life Association of Scotland is an example of this (Figure 9.10).

Some recent research conducted by the Schechter Group[11] suggested that consumers showed little recognition of logos, even ones like the American Express Centurion which was only recognized by 21 per cent of

Figure 9.10 The Life Association of Scotland logo

US consumers. Perhaps this is because Centurion does not communicate anything that is relevant in the charge card market, or it may be that American Express have suffered from the use of more than one logo. They also use the square pale blue box with the words American Express as a logo. The diffusing of resources and imagery can only serve to weaken the focus of the company logo for consumers.

The uniform

For many service organizations today, the corporate look is incomplete unless all frontline staff are dressed by the company. This can serve three purposes. First, it helps customers to identify those individuals who are in fact employees of the company. To fulfil this signalling function, the uniform must have 'stand-out'. A good example of distinctive corporate clothing is that worn by most of the airlines' steward staff.

These uniforms are also usually good at fulfilling the second objective. That of communicating an appropriate corporate image. In the days of restricted air travel, the 'hostess' would be dressed so that the male passengers (and most of them were men!) spent their airborne time fantasizing about the hostess rather than thinking about the dangers of flying. The girls were there to provide reassurance. Nowadays they are there to be efficient and professional and their uniforms reflect this change in approach. Miniskirts are not best suited for efficiency. As Jean Phillips of the Wensum Corporate Company notes, 'When developing a corporate clothing range for an organisation, not only does one take into account clothing design and company identity, but one equally needs to focus on the working environment. Generally speaking, too many companies lose sight of this major requirement.'[12]

And finally the uniform serves the purpose of suppressing individuality.[13] Idiosyncrasies in behaviour and appearance are much less obvious when an individual is in uniform. In effect uniform clothing promotes uniform behaviour. This happens partly because the employee feels a part of the organization and partly because the customer expects the employee act out the image.

Advertising the service

The advertising of services is often more complicated than for products. In many cases this is due to the intangible nature of the offering. The advertising has to evoke the likely experience of the user, which in turn introduces a second complication. The service can often be unique to each buyer, as is the case for most professional services. The service will be a bundle of attributes that will not all be offered to every buyer at every purchase occasion.

Setting advertising objectives

One approach to the setting of advertising objectives and strategy is to consider the four variables that are used to describe the difference between services and products. In the past, writers have suggested which of the variables they believed to be the most important. Shostack[14] thought that the provision of tangible clues was advertising's biggest task. Urwin[15] believed that presenting an emotional appeal to consumers was the biggest challenge, and Parasuraman, Zeithaml and Berry[16,17] described reliability as the factor most important for the advertising to communicate.

It is our opinion there is no single correct approach. The advertiser should choose the variable that causes consumers most concern in the purchase of his particular service and attempt to overcome their preconceptions (Table 9.2).

Table 9.2 Setting advertising objectives to address service variables

Service variable	Advertising objective
Intangibility	Provision of tangible clues Reduce risk Provide reassurance
Heterogeneity	Customization Reduce risk Provide reassurance
Inseparability	Staff focus: selection, training etc. Customer empathy
Perishability	Use advertising to manage demand (price offers, selling off the page etc.)

For example, in the film industry, the most important variable is likely to be the perishability of the service. Demand for the service normally declines with the length of time that the film has been on the market. The purchase of financial services on the other hand, is often fraught with uncertainty due to the intangible nature of the service.

Another approach to the setting of objectives is to seek answers to the following questions at the beginning of the development process:

- What is it that motivates consumers to use my service?
- What is it credible to communicate to them in this context?
- Can I deliver what I promise?

In other words, in developing the communication the advertiser has to consider 'What, to Whom, How, When, and Where?

Setting the advertising objective answers the first of these questions. It determines what the advertising is intended to communicate. This in turn should feed back into the question of consumer motivations. Ideally, the advertising should have as its objective the communication of the key motivator. This motivator will be different for different services. Note, however, that the same motivator often applies to more than one service.

This is a simplification of the process. What happens if there is more than one key motivator? Take for example a film processing service. Consumers might say that key motivators are responsiveness and effectiveness (Figure 9.11).

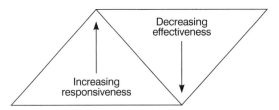

Figure 9.11 Trade-off between key attributes: film processing

However, there is a trade-off here. Doing things faster usually results in more mistakes. Therefore how do the advertisers select which objective to focus on in the advertising?

They begin by considering to whom they are talking. How important are the various motivators to them? One way of establishing this is to ask consumers to build pyramids for each of the relevant motivators. By insisting that the service under investigation must appear in one of the boxes the researcher gains some understanding of the relative level of importance (Figure 9.12).

However, this analysis implies that for any one attribute no two services hold the same levels of importance for consumers. This problem can be overcome by means of multi-attribute analysis (see Chapter 12).

We are assuming here that the service provides every key attribute that the consumer regards as important in their selection of a service brand in that particular market. If it does not, then the company should attempt to develop these if a long-term presence in the market is anticipated.

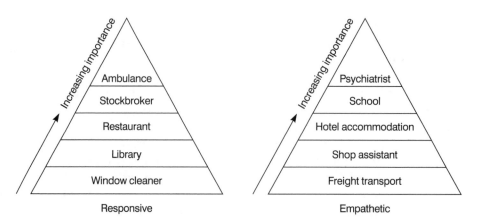

Responsive   Empathetic

Figure 9.12 Building pyramids to understand the importance of motivators

Setting advertising strategy

The next step is to arrive at an advertising strategy. This determines how the objective will be communicated. Setting the objective will not in itself set the strategy. Quite often there are a number of strategic options open to the advertiser. Consider the case of Reed Employment, a large secretarial employment agency that specialises in temporary assignments.

In the late 80s after a period of relatively little advertising, they decided to launch an aggressive advertising campaign. There appeared to be a number of appropriate strategies that Reed could adopt. These were discussed in research amongst some target consumers (Table 9.3).

Table 9.3 The strategic routes tested by Reed Employment

Strategic routes	*Consumer response*
The Reed supertemp. A wonderwoman who thrives on every challenge	Stupid/stereotypic
Most office work is a drudge. With Reed temping you get the perfect job.	Not looking for the perfect job
Reed temping gives you better perks – pay, training etc.	Not the main motivation for temping
The Reed 'consultant'. The office heroine who sorts out everything	It may be the reality, but it sounds hard to believe

The secretaries found a weakness in all of them. However, the same discussions revealed the main motivator: what it was that made these women choose to temp. They did so because of the flexibility that it offered them. Work played a relatively unimportant part in their lives. Other things that they did with their time were more important. Work had to take second place and fit around their other activities. So the flexibility

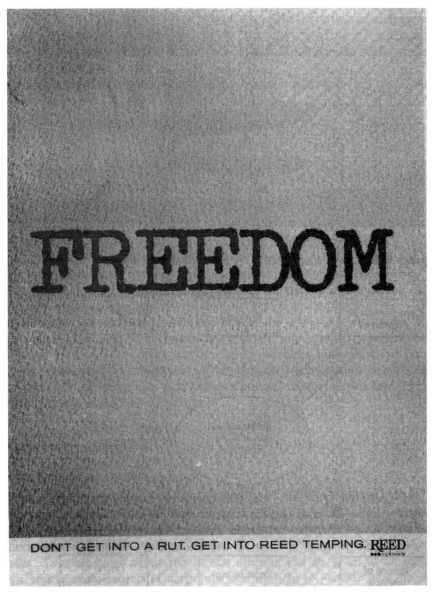

Figure 9.13 Reed Employment: Freedom advertisement

and freedom that temping gave became the strategic route. Although this was a benefit that was not unique to Reed, they made it their property by being the first to brand this generic property (Figure 9.13). The FREEDOM advertisement incorporated the brand name into the single word that said it all for these women (Figure 9.14). This highly successful advertising campaign made a significant impact on Reed Employment's sales.

It is not possible to be prescriptive in the selection of a strategy. The final choice will depend on several factors (Figure 9.15).

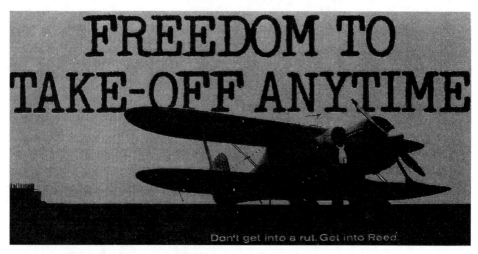

Figure 9.14 Reed Employment: Airplane advertisement

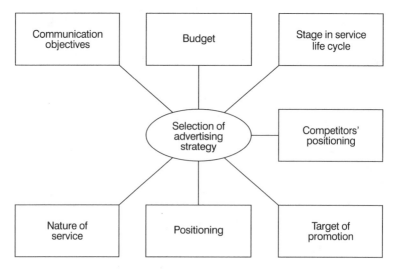

Figure 9.15 Factors affecting selection of advertising strategy

Campaign evaluation

The development of advertising is not a one-off job. After the campaign has run some attempt must be made to assess its effectiveness. Part of this process should be an examination of the continuing relevance of the original objective and strategy. While the most efficient use of advertising monies is often to develop a single-minded campaign that can run and run, e.g. British Airways, the changing nature of the competition and/or consumers can sometimes lead to the need to revise plans. The only way in which this can be determined is by continually monitoring the market.

Advertising professional services

The 1980s witnessed a relaxation in the control and regulation of professional services advertising. It began in 1985 with a test case brought by the opticians.

Research in the USA had shown that the restriction of advertising worked against the interests of consumers because it generally led to higher prices. The absence of advertising left consumers with insufficient information on which to base their brand choice.

The case was decided in the opticians' favour and this led to an Office of Fair Trading Report in 1986 which lifted many of the remaining restrictions on other professional services.

In addition to the methods of promoting services that have already been mentioned, there is another tool that is popular with those in professional services. It is known as a promotional survey.

The organization commissions research into something that it believes will interest their customers. So, for example, an advertising agency might find that its clients would be interested in changing consumer behaviour. The agency will then promote the survey like a new product with headline PR in the trade press, and more detailed coverage in individual presentations. These presentations are then used as soft-selling occasions.

The basic idea is to do something that current and/or potential clients will value. It need not be research. It may just focus on your field of expertise. A law firm could arrange a seminar with prominent legal brains on employment law.

Historically there has been some feeling that the successful professional organization does not need to advertise. To do so reflects adversely on their standing in the industry. This belief may not be as prevalent today as it has been in the past. However, the importance of interpersonal contact and respect means that any form of promotion that brings potential clients face-to-face with the service provider should be encouraged.

The Internet

The Internet was developed in the 1960s by CERN in Switzerland as a communications network that would survive a nuclear attack. During the 1970s, universities around the world adopted the technology for communicating with one another. It was not until the 1980s that the business community began to recognize the potential of the Internet.

Throughout the 1980s and 1990s there has been explosive growth in both the number of consumers accessing the Internet and in the number of organizations with their own web site. Estimates of the number of users by the year 2000 range from 200 million to 1 billion. At the end of 1997 it was estimated that there were 500 000 corporate web sites.

Unlike most other channels that marketing uses to communicate, the Internet presents the opportunity to conduct a two-way dialogue, in real time, 24 hours a day. To date, most people have been visiting web sites for information and entertainment, and corporate sites have been designed to deliver brand propositions and product/service details.

However, increasingly, customers are becoming willing to buy services over the Internet. This has become known as E(electronic)commerce. They are also using the medium for commenting on an organization's performance.

So the World Wide Web presents enormous potential in assisting the deployment of a relationship marketing strategy: it enables customers/ organizations to communicate on a one-to-one basis; it can build brand relationships; act as a channel to market; and provide a customer service function. In doing so, the Internet will make profound changes in consumer, and business-to-business buying behaviour. Service companies such as banks, hotels, and airline companies are already in the process of re-engineering their business to incorporate web technology into their processes.

Summary

In the communication of services there are five key variables that are important to marketers. They are personal selling, word of mouth, targeting employees in external communications, managing expectations through communications, and using communications to provide tangible clues about the service. Tangible clues about the service offering can be given in all sorts of ways. Indeed most aspects of corporate identity help to provide tangible clues. The service personnel, their uniform, the company logo, its advertising etc. all contribute to the impression that the customer has of the company, and therefore help to shape his expectations.

For many companies the development of communications begins with the development of a brand image. Because there is often no discernible difference between brands in the market, the image can become the single differentiating factor. By creating an image of the service that is relevant to the market, the company has the potential to develop a loyal customer base. Customer loyalty is a worthwhile goal. For one thing, it usually results in greater profits.

In most cases advertising will be used to communicate the brand image. The advertising of services presents two unique problems. First, the service experience is not identical for every customer. In fact, in many cases each customer receives a service that no one else ever experiences. Second, the intangible nature of service leaves the advertising with the job of attempting to evoke the likely experience of the user.

References

1. Bateson, J. E. G. (1989) *Managing Services Marketing: Text & Readings*, Dryden Press, New York.
2. George, W. R. and Berry, L. (1981) 'Guidelines for the advertising of services', *Business Horizons*, **24**, 52–56.
3. Berry, L. (1987) 'Big ideas in services marketing', *The Journal of Services Marketing*, Summer, 5–9.
4. Zeithaml, V. A. (1990) 'Communicating with customers about service quality'. In *Service Management Effectiveness*, (Bowen, D. E., Chase, R. B. and Cummings, eds). Jossey-Bass, San Francisco, CA.
5. Czepiel, J. A., Solomon, M. R. and Suprenant, C. F. (1985) *The Service Encounter*, Lexington Books, Lexington, MA.
6. *International Business Week* (1991) 'Questing for the best', 2 December, 18–23.
7. Levitt, T. (1981) 'Marketing products and product intangibles', *Harvard Business Review*, May–June, 94–101.
8. Dobree, J. and Page, A. S. (1991) 'Unleashing the power of service brands in the 1990s', *Management Decision*, **28**(6), 14–28.
9. Lutz, K. A. and Lutz, T. J. (1978) 'Eliciting strategies: review and implications of research'. In *Advances in Consumer Research* (Hunt, H. K. ed.), Association for Consumer Research.
10. Berry, L. L., Lefkowith, E. F. and Clark, T. (1988) 'In services, what's in a name? *Harvard Business Review*, (September–October), 28–30.
11. Bird, D. (1992) 'Image can be damaged by design', *Marketing Magazine*, 6 February.
12. Telephone conversation with Jean Phillips, Managing Director of the Wensum Corporate Company, 1992.

13. Nathan, J. and Nicholas, A. (1972) 'The uniform: a sociological perspective', *American Journal of Sociology,* **77**, 719–30.
14. Shostack, G. L. (1977) 'Breaking free from product marketing', *Journal of Marketing,* April, 73–80.
15. Urwin, S. (1975) 'Customised communications – a concept for service advertising', *Advertising Quarterly,* Summer, 28–30.
16. Parasuraman, A., Zeithaml, V. A. and Berry, L. L. (1988) 'Servqual: a multiple item scale for measuring consumer perceptions of service quality', *Journal of Retailing,* Spring, 12–40.
17. Parasuraman, A., Berry, L. L. and Zeithaml, A. (1991) 'Understanding customer expectations of service', *Sloan Management Review,* Spring, 39–48.

Chapter 10

Performance measurement

Introduction

Organizations need to know how well they are performing not only in an absolute sense but relative to:

- Predetermined standards set out in organizational goals and objectives
- Competitors (if there are any)
- Customer expectations
- Resources deployed (capital, labour, materials, energy, information)

Performance appraisal will inevitably mean undertaking some form of measurement. Questions will be asked about:

- What is being measured
- How it is being measured
- Why it is being measured

Two areas in particular help in addressing the issue of organizational performance. They are productivity and customer retention.

Productivity

Productivity is a measure of relationships between an input and an output namely:

$$\text{Productivity} = \frac{\text{Output}}{\text{Input}}$$

It is a standard measure that has been used by manufacturing industries for a very long time, where, for example:

$$\text{Total productivity} = \frac{\text{Total outputs}}{\text{Sum of all inputs}}$$

The real difficulty lies in aggregating a range of partial measures into a composite measure for the whole organization. In other words, how the organization's total output and the value added are explained by the mix and deployment of resources. As total productivity, therefore, can be difficult to determine and fail to detect specific explanations for poor performance, a number of disaggregate measures are used:

$$P = \frac{\text{Production}}{\text{Machine hours}}$$

$$P = \frac{\text{Production}}{\text{Number of employees}}$$

$$P = \frac{\text{Sales}}{\text{Number of square feet}}$$

$$P = \frac{\text{Passenger miles (railway)}}{\text{Number of guards}}$$

Output is, of course, influenced by a host of factors such as the level of automation, the quality of raw materials, scheduling of labour, layout of operations and customer behaviour. The danger of using only one partial measure of productivity in the form of labour input is that poor performance may wrongly be attributed to unproductive workers. The explanation may quite easily be found in poor materials and equipment, poor layout and awkward customers. Ball, Johnson and Slattery[1] give an example of the range of productivity measure in the hotel industry (Table 10.1).

Nowadays the term performance indicator is often used to describe productivity measures. Given the distinctive characteristics of services, the pursuit of productivity measurement is a challenging one.

It is a topic that generates a great deal of attention. Exhortations are often made about the need to increase efficiency (as distinct from effectiveness) and invariably this is supposed to be achieved by getting more output from the same input or getting the same output from less input. Inevitably, calls are made for more output from less input!

Table 10.1 Example ratios of hotel productivity

	Physical measures	Physical/financial measures combined	Financial measures
Labour measures	$\dfrac{\text{Kitchen meals produced}}{\text{No. kitchen staff}}$ $\dfrac{\text{Housecount}}{\text{Total employee hours}}$ $\dfrac{\text{Restaurant covers}}{\text{Hours worked in restaurant}}$	$\dfrac{\text{Restaurant revenue}}{\text{Hours worked in restaurant}}$ $\dfrac{\text{Total room sales}}{\text{Total reception employees}}$ $\dfrac{\text{Total room sales}}{\text{Chambermaid day}}$	$\dfrac{\text{Banqueting revenue}}{\text{Banqueting payroll}}$ $\dfrac{\text{Hotel revenue}}{\text{Total management salaries}}$ $\dfrac{\text{Total added value}}{\text{Hotel payroll}}$
Energy measures	$\dfrac{\text{Total guest rooms}}{\text{Total kilowatt hours}}$	$\dfrac{\text{No. cooked meals}}{\text{Total cooking costs}}$	$\dfrac{\text{Hotel revenue}}{\text{Total energy cost}}$
Capital measures	$\dfrac{\text{Total hotel customers}}{\text{Square foot of hotel}}$	$\dfrac{\text{No. rooms sold}}{\text{Total capital expenditure}}$	$\dfrac{\text{Net profit after tax}}{\text{Equity capital}}$
Raw material measures	$\dfrac{\text{Chips prepared (lb)}}{\text{Potatoes used (lb)}}$	$\dfrac{\text{No. bar customers}}{\text{Cost of liquor used}}$	$\dfrac{\text{Food revenue}}{\text{Cost of food consumed}}$
Total factor measures	$\dfrac{\text{No. satisfied hotel customers}}{\text{Total no. hotel customers}}$	$\dfrac{\text{Housecount}}{\text{Cost of contributing resources}}$	$\dfrac{\text{Net profit after tax}}{\text{Cost of contributing resources}}$

Source: Ball, Johnson, Slattery (1986)[1]

Labour is a major input in any organization (particularly a service) and the focus for this call for increased productivity has been, and still is, the 'blue-collar' worker. His counterpart, the white-collar worker, has escaped being subjected to productivity measurement. Increasingly, however, the picture is changing. The performance of white-collar workers is being measured, although the term 'performance indicator' seems to take precedence over productivity.

It is generally agreed that it is much easier to measure productivity on an assembly line than a service business where the 'product' is often the customer's intangible experience. Services, themselves, will of course vary in terms of how susceptible they are to measurement and the form that measurement will take[2] (Figure 10.1).

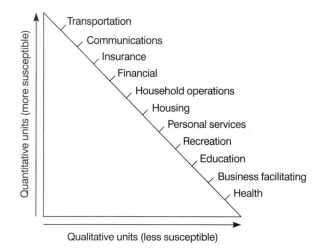

Figure 10.1 Productivity of services: susceptibility of output to measurement. *Source*: Rathmell (1974)[2]

Established productivity measures are less easily applied as one moves from the left to the right of Figure 10.1. Measuring productivity in a transportation service poses fewer problems than in a counselling service.

For a transportation service input (e.g. driver hours) and output (e.g. tonne-miles) and the relationship between the two offers a clear measure of productivity. For a counselling service, quantitative input and output measures and the relationship between the two are not so readily available. Counselling involves advice and human relationships, and because of that, understanding the process and impact of such a service is far from straightforward. It is a service where the proper application of knowledge and skills should take precedence over attempts to apply input/output ratios.

The productivity framework

To develop our understanding of productivity we need to add to the ideas of input and output already mentioned (Figure 10.2).

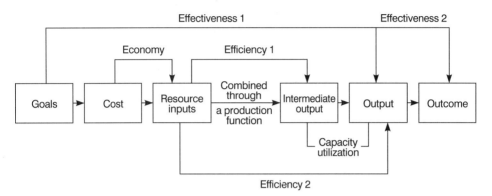

Figure 10.2 The productivity framework

Two words in Figure 10.2 are frequently mentioned in everyday discussion often without clear understanding of their meaning. They are used loosely and often interchangeably. The words are, of course, efficiency and effectiveness. The meanings will become clearer as we look at some examples. However, in general they can be defined as follows:

- *Efficiency* – rate at which inputs are converted into outputs, e.g. calls per sales representative; customers served per catering assistant. The emphasis is often on quantitative measurement and the objective is one of securing the maximum output from the minimum input.
- *Effectiveness* – extent to which purposes/goals are achieved, e.g. the number of productive and profitable calls per sales representative and the nature of customer relationships established and fostered; the number of satisfied customers served per catering assistant. The emphasis is on qualitative measurement and the objective one of meeting customer needs and delivering service quality.

The distinction between efficiency and effectiveness has been defined as 'doing things right' (efficiency) and 'doing right things' (effectiveness).[3] What this amounts to is that efficiency is 'the rate of which inputs are converted into outputs' and effectiveness 'the extent to which purposes are being achieved'.[4]

Figure 10.2 offers a guide to developing an understanding of the various elements and their relationships:

- *Economy*: the cost of selecting and hiring people, materials and equipment and conversion through training and installation into resource inputs capable of providing service. It is not a measure of performance, but can have an impact on the level of performance.
- *Efficiency 1*: the ratio of inputs to intermediate outputs, e.g. the cost per unit of capacity (cost per place in a private nursing home) or cost per anticipated level of demand (cost per meal prepared in a hotel).
- *Production function*: all the resources (staff, buildings, equipment, consumables) are combined to produce intermediate outputs, i.e. the capacity to produce the relevant service (school places, hospital beds, train seats, restaurant seats).
- *Efficiency 2*: the ratio of inputs to outputs, e.g. the cost per college graduate or cost per number of meals sold in an hotel.
- *Capacity utilization*: the ratio of intermediate output to final output, i.e. how good is management at converting the intermediate output into customer take-up. For example, what percentage of seats will be taken up by customers in a restaurant or what percentage of places will be taken up in a residential home. For services in general, and in particular where advance preparation is involved (meals in a restaurant), accurate demand forecasting will become part of effective marketing management.
- *Effectiveness 1 and 2*: there is no overall agreement as to how effectiveness should be defined. Is it to be in terms of 'output' or 'outcome'?

Output means the service actually delivered to customers. Outcome, on the other hand, is the impact which the service may have on the recipients. It is the quality of the service delivered and its effectiveness in meeting users' needs or achieving its underlying purpose (Audit Commission)[5]. For example, a college educates students (output) but has a certain responsibility for graduate employability and destination (outcome). A management consultancy produces a report and advises a client (output) but has a certain responsibility for the impact of the report on the performance of the client company (outcome). In both cases, however, the outcome measure is not completely under the control of the service provider.

For many services, output is defined in a straightforward manner, as in:

- Number of commuters transported
- Number of home help clients assisted
- Number of restaurant meals served
- Number of admissions to a leisure centre

What is missing is any reference to the quality of service delivered.

Some services simply have no output or outcome that can practically be measured in quantitative terms; for example, a counselling service.

If the output of a process appears to defy identification with precision, a surrogate measure of output may be used. For example, the true output of the police force could be its contribution to the maintenance of a peaceful, crime free, ordered society, or a public library's true output might be the contribution it makes to expanding the knowledge base of, and to entertaining, the constituent community. As both of these outputs are likely to prove difficult to quantify, proxy measures in the form of 'percentage of reported crime solved' and 'ratio of loans to book stock' are used.[6]

The difficulties surrounding the measurement of output and outcome has led to the development of a different approach which is known as process productivity. It has been argued as being a more realistic and expedient measure.[7] How well the service is delivered is, arguably, a better way for a service like health, where it is difficult to measure changes in health status and where factors other than medical care affect health outcome.

Improving productivity

Given the standard ratio there are, in theory, five ways to increase productivity:

1 Output increases faster than input
2 Output remains unchanged with fewer inputs
3 Output increases from the same inputs
4 Input decreases more than output
5 Maximum increase in the ratio through an ideal combination of outputs and inputs

Whatever method is selected the true test will be the effect on the quality of service delivered.

Improved productivity must, therefore, take into account effectiveness as well as efficiency. A number of practical steps can be taken to improve productivity in terms of efficiency and effectiveness:

1 Careful cost control, driven by a management desire to become 'leaner and fitter'.
2 Job design – management and employees in pursuit of productivity improvements, must attempt to answer questions such as.[8]

What work do we do?
How do we do it?
Why do we do it this way?
How can we do it better?

3 Replace human labour with automation.
4 Improve employee motivation:

How do employees perceive the organizational culture?
Do they feel part of the organization?
Are rewards commensurate with the tasks done?

5 Select people more predisposed for productivity, for example the predisposition of an air traffic controller is more important than that of a security guard in a low-crime area.
6 Isolate, and even extend, the back office so that the benefits of manufacturing technology can be achieved.
7 Schedule resource deployment to match fluctuations in the level of customer demand.
8 Involve customers more in the production and delivery of service.
9 Make sure that highly skilled employees are not doing jobs that could be undertaken by less fully trained staff.

Practical examples: some undesirable consequences

In the drive for greater efficiency, productivity increases may produce an adverse effect.

Example 1 – a 300-bedroomed hotel has reduced the number of chambermaids from thirty to twenty as a result of a productivity drive. There are to be no changes in time to do the job and materials/equipment available. The result is a reduction in the cleanliness of rooms, in particular those occupied by families who leave the room very untidy.

Example 2 – an insurance company decides to measure the productivity of its employees by client satisfaction. As a result, the claims department rapidly settled claims and nearly bankrupt the company.

Example 3 – a hospital increased patient throughput by decreasing the average duration of bed occupancy. Efficiency could be said to have increased. However, to achieve this efficiency, the hospital selected patients offering the likelihood of shorter lengths of stay. Fundamentally, a faster throughput may increase efficiency but at what cost to full and lasting patient recovery (effectiveness). An increase in the number of early deaths would certainly increase efficiency!

What these examples clearly demonstrate is an overriding concentration on increases in quantity and cost reduction. The consequence is an adverse effect on service quality. Greater efficiency is achieved by increasing the numerator (faster turnover of patients) while maintaining the denominator or maintaining the numerator and decreasing the denominator (fewer chambermaids).

There is often a tension between the drive for efficiency and the achievement of effectiveness[9] (Figure 10.3). A service can be efficient but ineffective; alternatively it can be effective but inefficient. This can be illustrated by a hypothetical emergency ambulance service:

> One can envisage an ambulance with a highly trained crew that is very efficient and dashes about from accident to accident promptly, treating injured persons with expert skill, placing them in the ambulance and rapidly driving them to the nearest hospital, then racing off to service yet another emergency. The unit would be extraordinarily efficient if it handled two such emergencies in an hour or about sixteen in an eight hour shift. However, it would be utterly ineffective if the actual number of emergencies in the area averaged twenty per shift. This would be an example of a highly efficient service that is utterly ineffective; more ambulances are needed. Alternatively, one can conceive of a very effective ambulance service where no-one has to wait more than five minutes to receive expert medical attention, ambulances are promptly dispatched, and many lives are saved. However such a service may be extremely inefficient, if in fact it is staffed with so many ambulances and crews that most of them sit around doing nothing for hours on end because there is little demand for their service.[10]

	Ineffective	Effective
Inefficient	Die quickly	Survive
Efficient	Die slowly	Thrive

Figure 10.3 The contrast between efficiency and effectiveness. *Source*: Brown (1987)[9]

Consumer participation and productivity

As the consumer is the central character in the provision of service the question arises, 'What contribution can the consumer make to the delivery of an efficient and effective service?'

To test the impact of the consumer's contribution to service productivity, consider the four following real-life service scenarios.[11]

Scene 1: a major hotel

Guest A called the desk right after check-in to report a burned-out light bulb and an absence of hot water; both were fixed in an hour.

Guest A also slept better, as the hotel assigned him a quiet room when he identified himself as a light sleeper.

Guest B did not communicate to management until check-out time, when he complained that there was no hot water and he had to read in the dark; he was overheard by new guests checking in, who asked if the hotel was undergoing a disaster.

Scene 2: an airline flight from New York to Los Angeles

Passenger A arrives for the flight with a portable tape player and tape, with a large supply of reading material, and wearing warm clothes.

Passenger A also booked a special meal ahead of time.

Passenger B, who arrives empty-handed, becomes annoyed when the crew runs out of blankets and magazines, complains about the lunch and starts fidgeting after the movie.

Scene 3: office of a professional tax preparer

Client A has organized the necessary information into categories that will help the accountant.

Client B has a shoe box filled with papers, including laundry receipts mixed in with cancelled cheques.

Scene 4: a health club

When a new aerobics instructor includes a routine that seems hard to follow, Member A modifies the steps and adjusts the pace to allow for her individual physical limitations.

Member B complains that the routine is too hard to follow and suggests that the instructor be fired immediately.

Reflecting on the four scenarios, two related questions are worth remembering:

1 How many of the Customer B type are there around?
2 What can a service provider do to encourage more of the Customer A type?

In trying to turn the service consumer into a valued participant in the service delivery process, the service provider must recognize the following factors and how they could be managed:

● Consumer predisposition, e.g. personality, attitudes, values – may be difficult to change.
● Consumer potential commitment/willingness to become involved – low to high.
● Consumer knowledge and skills – how easily can they be developed if need be?

In addition to the degree of consumer involvement, the service provider must consider the nature of consumer involvement, i.e. when, where and how in the service delivery process will customer involvement occur.

From self-service at a restaurant or petrol station through to interactions with a doctor, teacher or accountant, the potential for exploiting improvements in productivity can be substantial. Whatever changes in service delivery are proposed, the consumer must be the major beneficiary.

White-collar productivity

The working day for a blue-collar worker is often prescribed down to the finest detail (tasks to be done and time taken to do them). For the white-collar worker, what they do and how much time they spend doing it, is often left to their own judgement. The blue-collar worker can be defined as one category in which the tasks are largely standardized and repetitive, e.g. railway porter, catering assistant, bus driver, street sweeper. The white-collar category, on the other hand, includes a diversity of jobs, with differing sets of authority, responsibility and duties. Ruch sought to clear up the problem of the white-collar category by isolating two relevant dimensions.[12]

I The amount of discretion involved – not the amount of skill, but the degree to which there is a specified procedure to follow in the performance of the job. For example, the hotel receptionist's job is not highly skilled but judgement may be required in handling the different customer enquiries and complaints. On the other hand, the dentist's job is a highly skilled procedure in contrast to the procedure for handling complaints. It would be easier to measure, therefore, the productivity of the dentist (number of fillings, extractions per dentist) than the hotel receptionist's performance in handling customer enquiries and complaints. The general rule is that the less discretion there is in the job, the easier it is to measure. The dentist's job, in productivity terms, is, therefore, more akin to the blue collar worker.

2 The degree to which there is a physical product involved in the process. For the McDonald's cook or the dentist there is a tangible output that can be counted and checked for quality (the hamburger and the filling). The hotel receptionist's job has to be experienced, as once it is performed, the evidence disappears. There is no output left to count or check for quality. The general rule is that the more there is a tangible output, the easier it is to measure.

There are problems then in measuring white-collar productivity.[12]

- Difficulties in determining the output or contribution
- Tendency to measure activities rather than the results, e.g. number of reports created says nothing about the quality of these reports.
- The input may not show up in output until some time later. There is a lagged effect
- Quality of output is even more difficult to determine than quantity.
- Distinction is often not made between efficiency and effectiveness. The white collar worker may be efficient at developing reports but ineffective by not having enough to do, attending unproductive meetings, or assigned work outside the area of expertise.
- White-collar workers are not accustomed to being measured.

Although there are difficulties, effort should be made to measure white-collar productivity. The inputs may be relatively straightforward, e.g. number of hours worked, number of hours paid, resources used. It is the process and the output that pose the difficulties. The following issues are worth consideration:

- How creative are the white-collar employees in the sense of developing and implementing new ideas.
- How efficient and effective is the utilization of the working day – this is an over-riding factor upon which everything else depends.
- How satisfied are the customers – care needs to be exercised since no matter what the white-collar worker does, the customer may remain dissatisfied, e.g. lecturer and student, doctor and patient.
- Ability to handle non-standard situations, i.e. crisis management.
- Communication skills and success in keeping people properly informed.

The above list is by no means exhaustive but simply indicates the kind of analysis that needs to be undertaken.

The single greatest challenge facing managers, according to Drucker[13] is to raise the productivity of knowledge and service workers. He stresses that for all their diversity in knowledge, skill, responsibility, social status and pay, knowledge and service workers are remarkably alike in terms of:

What does and does not work in raising their productivity.

The first lesson that came as a rude shock, according to Drucker, is that the replacement of labour with technology does not, by itself, raise productivity. The key to raising productivity is working smarter rather than harder or longer. Drucker believes that fundamental questions need to be asked if the productivity of knowledge and service workers is to be raised. For example:

● What is the task?
● What are we trying to accomplish?
● Why do it at all?

Drucker bemoans the fact that in many professional service jobs, e.g. nursing, teaching, a great deal of effort and time is taken up with paperwork and meetings, much of which contributes little if any value and has little if anything to do with what these professionals are qualified and paid for. The result is job impoverishment rather than enrichment and a reduction in motivation and morale.

Drucker recognizes that for a good many service jobs, e.g. making hospital beds, handling insurance claims, performance is defined on a quantity basis, very much like production jobs. The application of industrial engineering techniques will determine how long it should take, for example, to make up a hospital bed properly. For other service jobs, e.g. knowledge based, raising productivity, in Drucker's view, requires asking 'What works?' plus analysing the process step by step and operation by operation.

Process is the subject of a new approach that could achieve for office productivity what just-in-time techniques did for manufacturing practice. Business process redesign (BPR) looks at procedures and the way things are organized. BPR is attracting the interest of large service organizations looking for new ways of raising productivity and cutting costs. By simplifying the workflow and reducing the number of stages involved in a procedure, BPR can speed up customer service and involve fewer staff.

The development of schemes relating pay to individual performance has grown dramatically in recent years. According to one survey,[14] 47 per cent of private sector companies have performance related pay (PRP) schemes for all non-manual grades and a further 21 per cent were using it for some non-manuals. There was no significant difference between manufacturing and service industries, but there was a difference between the public and private sectors. In the public sector 37 per cent of organizations in the survey were operating PRP schemes for some of their non-manual grades, but only 6 per cent covered all non-manuals. Non-management grades in the public sector were significantly less likely to be covered by PRP than in the private sector, and those employed in senior management. Management and professional occupations were nearly twice as likely to be eligible for PRP in the private sector as those in the public sector.

The supporters of PRP put forward a number of reasons for introducing it, e.g. it's a motivator, it improves quality and productivity and it's fair. The evidence in support of these claims is inconclusive. Instead it can be argued that the actual assessment of performance is open to charges of unfairness. Questions are raised about who does the assessment and how it is done. Furthermore is PRP appropriate to all organizational cultures? Even if it is appropriate, how far can PRP help to promote changes in organizational culture? Can it make organizations more customer performance oriented through improved productivity and service quality?

The challenge of implementing PRP is arguably greater for service organizations than their manufacturing counterparts. There is more uncertainty in terms of process and output and factors outside their employees' control may figure prominently in service situations, e.g. infinite variety of possible breakdowns in the service delivery system, difficulties in managing customers.

Some jobs or tasks may not easily lend themselves to concrete performance measures. It is easier to evaluate if hard quantifiable, technical measures can be set. However, softer measures, e.g. related to communication skills should also be encouraged.

It is argued that PRP is a distinct improvement on previous incentive schemes. According to Kessler and Purcell,[15] the link between pay and performance remains as obscure as ever and further research is necessary to throw some light on this vexed issue'.

Of course, the most radical question of all in any discussion of white collar productivity would be, 'Why not give the workers a say?'

Giving subordinates a 'voice' in formal performance evaluation of their bosses can prove invaluable as a source of feedback for everyone concerned.[16] Employees can be asked their view of how effective the bosses are in, for example:

- Providing feedback on performance
- Looking for ways to improve existing systems
- Taking action on urgent requests
- Keeping people well informed
- Handling a disruptive employee

Care must be exercised over what to appraise and how to do it. Some might question the accuracy of subordinate appraisals. To some extent this misses the point. Their true value is in offering a view of management performance from those directly affected by it. That view can then be compared with management's view of itself. One study[17] found that managers who perceived themselves to be effective at 'providing clear instruction and explanation to employees when giving assignments', were not perceived as such by those persons supposedly on the receiving end of the instructions!

Involving employees in management appraisal can influence their own productivity as well. What they believe and say about management's expectations of them may hold the key to explaining levels of productivity. The 'Pygmalion in Management' view suggests that most managers unintentionally treat their subordinates in a way that leads to lower performance than they are capable of achieving.[18]

The way subordinates are treated is very much influenced by management expectations of them. The result is that high expectations lead to high productivity and low expectations lead to low productivity. However, expectations must, in the view of the subordinate, be realistic and achievable.

A concluding comment about white-collar productivity – it is not so readily observable and measurable as blue-collar productivity, e.g. the bricklayer is both easily observed and measured – number of bricks laid per hour; whereas a nurse comforting a patient after a major operation may not be viewed as productive activity in the conventional wisdom.

Service productivity as a relationship between input and output

Efficiency and effectiveness in a service organization are measured in terms of inputs and outputs. But unlike manufacturing or extractive industries, service is a process with customer involvement. Understanding the process is fundamental to explaining the relationship of inputs to outputs. This process, and the inputs and outputs, can be portrayed as approximating to a triangle. The base could be a point (making it truly a triangle) or as wide as the top (making it a square) (Figure 10.4).

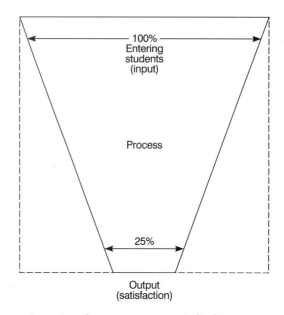

Figure 10.4 The service triangle: percentage satisfied

An example will serve to illustrate. Colleges take in students who have expectations. After a period of time one output will be student satisfaction. The width of the base will indicate that of those who have entered, what percentage at the finish were satisfied with what they received. In this case (Figure 10.4) the percentage satisfied would be of the order of twenty five per cent. The dotted line would represent a situation where all the customers who used the service were satisfied. Of course, in addition to determining how many customers were satisfied, consideration would have to be given to how satisfied they were. Notwithstanding dropouts and failures, the percentage satisfied will serve as a measure of how effective the process they have gone through has been. This kind of analysis could apply to many services, e.g. hotels, package holidays, rail commuters.

Equally, the triangle could be portrayed another way (Figure 10.5). This time the emphasis is on the value added by the process. Students enter with qualifications, e.g. A-levels and finish with a qualification. But how effective has the process been in developing skills and abilities valuable for entering the world of work? The wider the base (dotted line) the more effective the process has been. Unlike the percentage satisfied measure, the value added approach is more difficult to determine.

Heaton[19] suggested that the productivity of service organizations could be calculated as the product of four operating functions: input, processing,

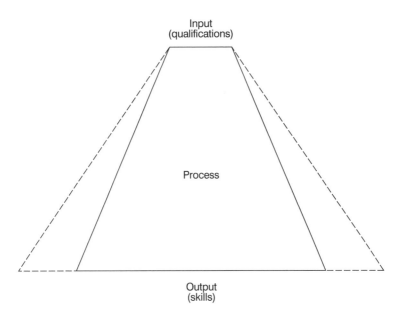

Figure 10.5 The service triangle: value added

output or follow-up and timing and coordination. He applied this to the unusual example of a mental hospital:

Input: 30 per cent of those admitted do not require hospitalization – gross rating then of 70 per cent.

Processing: only 50 per cent of those needing help receive it due to overcrowding, under staffing and a general lack of skills, understanding and care – gross productivity measurement is then 35 per cent (50% × 70%).

Output or follow-up: on release, only 20 per cent is offered appropriate follow-up and assistance due to limited outpatient services – gross productivity measurement is now 7 per cent (50% × 70% × 20%).

Timing and coordination: there is a time and place for everything. Too little too late is as wasteful as too much too soon. Of the 7 per cent only 50 per cent were admitted; treated and released at the proper time and helped by the proper agencies – gross productivity measurement is now 3.5 per cent (70% × 50% × 20% × 50%).

Therefore out of an initial one hundred patients only three to four were effectively helped. It is hardly the mark of an effective service organization.

Analysis similar to Heaton's is a must for service organizations as it focuses on the process and facilitates understanding of the progress from the input to the output stage. As with the college example mentioned earlier, there will be a number of variables that require investigation. Some of these will be under the control of the service organization and others may be more difficult to control. The nature and deployment of employee skills, materials and equipment are far more controllable than the customers' behaviour and demand levels.

Technology and productivity

Given the characteristics of services it is difficult to measure productivity with the same precision as exists in the manufacturing sector. To what extent can the adoption of technology improve productivity? A distinction must be drawn between hard technology and soft technology. Hard technology means the computers and other equipment e.g. ATMs, automatic car washes, airport X-ray surveillance equipment. The soft technology involves the systems and processes in operation, e.g. fast-food outlets, pre-packaged tours.

Quinn and Paquette[20] suggest that service technologies can deliver lowest cost outputs and maximum personalization and customization for customers.

Production, efficiency and customer customization are achieved, according to them, by 'seeking the smallest possible core unit at which production can be replicated and repeated; then developing micro-measures to manage processes and functions at this level, and finally mixing these micro units in a variety of combinations to match localized individual customers' needs'. This smallest replicable unit will vary by industry but they quote the example of American Express's credit card and travel service operation. 'It can capture in the most disaggregated form details that its various traveller, shopper, retailer and transportation company customers put through its credit card system. American Express can then mix and match the patterns and capabilities of each group to add value for them. It can identify life style change or match forthcoming travel plans with customers' specific buying habits to notify them of special promotions, product offerings or services'. This example illustrates the impact of service technologies on both efficiency and effectiveness. Technology enables such a process to be possible. Precision, speed and accuracy are the hallmarks of the process.

It has been suggested that 'technology gives the quality to service organisations to handle larger volumes of service, to offer a wider range of services, to provide quicker and more accurate services and to permit more efficient management'.[22]

In addition to achieving cost effectiveness and customer satisfaction, the frontline employee becomes more efficient by working faster and smarter. The employee is also empowered to be much more capable of meeting customer needs, and according to Quinn and Paquette, 'it allows relatively inexperienced people to perform very sophisticated tasks quickly, increasing the value-added per employee'.[20] The frontline employee, in effect, has access to information which can be accessed and customized to meet the needs of particular customers. Information is, of course, the key for effective management and marketing of many service organizations.

Customer retention and lifetime value

The retention perspective

The traditional role of marketing has been to win customers. Little attention or effort was devoted to keeping them. This preoccupation with customer acquisition rather than customer retention has been criticized as a 'leaky bucket' approach to business. So long as new customers are acquired to replace those existing customers lost through the hole in the bucket, success in the form of sales is achieved.

It has been estimated that most organizations lose significantly more than 30 per cent of their customers before or at the time of a repurchase decision, mainly through poor service; and the only reason market shares do not drop is because competitors are usually in the same position and are losing customers to their rivals.[21] What all this means is that there is a high turnover of dissatisfied customers searching for a company that they can trust and have faith in. As one observer points out:

> It has always been incredible to me how insensitive companies can be to their customers. Most of them don't seem to understand that their future business depends on having the same customer come back again and again.[22]

Support for retention over acquisition came in a report[23] claiming that a reduction in customer defections by just 5 per cent across a range of service industries generates an increase in profits anywhere from 25 to 85 per cent (for an illustration of the profit impact of customer retention see Appendix 10.3). More recent work has confirmed the earlier finding.[24] Two previously unidentified factors evidently explain such an impact on profits.[25] The first factor is the customer volume effect – the bigger the leak of customers from the bucket, the harder a company must work to fill it up and keep it full. Consider two companies, one with a customer retention rate of 95 per cent, the other with a rate of 90 per cent. The leak in the first company's bucket is 5 per cent per year and the second company's leak is twice as large, 10 per cent per year. If both companies acquire new customers at the rate of 10 per cent per year, the first will have a 5 per cent net growth in customers per year, while the other will have none. What this means is that the first company will double in size over fourteen years. while the other will have no growth at all (see Appendix 10.4 for calculations). The second factor is the profit per customer effect – this is more difficult to see than the customer volume effect but evidently the effect on profits is even bigger.

Retention rate and average customer lifetime

The measurement of customer loyalty is known as the 'customer retention rate'. As a company's retention rate improves, the average 'life' of a customer increases. For example, if a company can find a way of increasing its average retention from an annual 80 per cent to 90 per cent it will actually double the average customer lifetime from five to ten years (Figure 10.6)

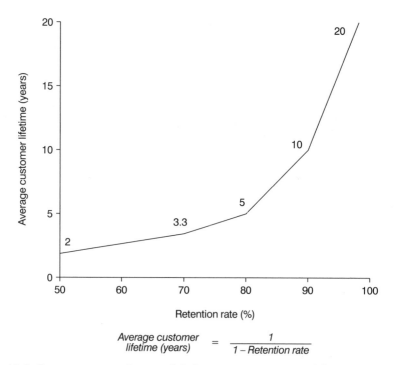

Figure 10.6 Customer-retention model: impact on customer lifetime. *Source*: Bain & Co.

If it retains 80 per cent of its customers it will have had to replace all of them over a five year period (5 × 20 per cent). If it retains 90 per cent it will lose just half of them over the same period (5 × 10 per cent = 50 per cent). Increase in retention is one means of increasing profitability.

Why loyal customers are more profitable

According to Bain & Co. a number of factors are deemed important for understanding profit enhancement from customer loyalty. The factors cited are:[25]

- **Acquisition cost** – money has to be invested to bring in new customers, e.g. cost of selling, advertising etc.
- **Base profit** – all customers buy some product or service and the prices they pay are usually higher than the company's costs. The longer you keep a customer, the longer you will earn this base profit.
- **Per customer revenue growth** – customer spending tends to accelerate over time.
- **Operating costs** – as customers get to know a business and company employees get to know their customers, efficiencies in doing business arise and thereby reduce costs.
- **Referrals** – satisfied customers are more likely to introduce new customers to the company through word of mouth recommendation.
- **Price premium** – satisfied customers are often willing to pay premium prices to a supplier they know and trust.

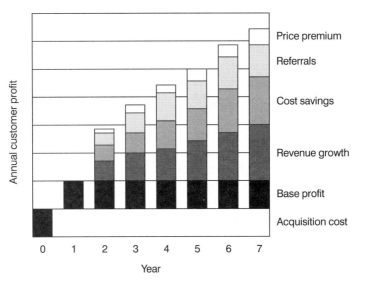

Figure 10.7 Why loyal customers are more profitable. Source: Bain & Co.

Figure 10.7 illustrates the root causes of, and their respective contribution to, increased profitability over time.

A key criticism made of the customer retention concept is that customer longevity does not always result in significant profitability improvement.[26] Bain & Co's response has been that 'Our position has never been that simply increasing retention rates will magically produce profits. For example, foolish investments to retain hopelessly unprofitable customers would destroy profits. Our point is that substantially higher profits require high retention. Therefore, understanding the link between retention and profits is essential.[27] The argument revolves around the types of customer retained'. One critic (of Bain & Co.'s argument) gave the following example to illustrate the point:[26]

Three types of retail banking customer:

A customers: acceptable annual contribution
B customers: unacceptable but positive annual contribution
C customers: negative annual contribution

In the first quarter of year 1:   1000 new customers

In the second quarter of year 1:   500 lost money (Type C)
                                   200 made a little but not much (Type B)
                                   300 were strong contributors (Type A)

By the end of year 3, there are 500 customers left:

Of the 500 initially unprofitable, 150 remain
Of the 200 who made a little, 100 remain
Of the 300 who made strong contributions, 250 remain

Type A customers now made up to 50 per cent of that total, as against 30 per cent at the beginning.

The resulting improvement in profitability has been caused by the departure of Cs, not by the change of status of Cs to Bs and Bs to As.

If an A customer is worth £250 a year, a B customer is worth £50 per year and a C customer is worth £150 a year, what change has there been in the average annual contribution between early in year 1 and the end of year 3? Table 10.2 tells us that the average annual contribution has gone from £10 to £90 owing to the rise in the proportion of A customers, the most profitable type.

Table 10.2 Customer retention and profitability: comparison of average annual contributions

	Customer	Number of customers	Profit per Customer (£)	Total Profit (£)
Year I, quarter 2	A	300	250	75 000
	B	200	50	10 000
	C	500	(150)	(75 000)
		1000		10 000
	£10 000 ÷ 1000 = £10 per customer			
End of year 3	A	250	250	62 500
	B	100	50	5 000
	C	150	150	(22 500)
		500		45 000
	£45 000 ÷ 500 = £90 per customer			

Lifetime value of a customer

To understand the full impact of defections, companies must calculate the lifetime value of a customer. It is defined as the total revenue received from a customer during his or her 'lifetime' with a company, less the costs of servicing and marketing. In effect the total profit received from having that customer over time. Where there is a difficulty in calculating profit, contribution margin (revenue minus variable cost) or sales revenue can be used.

In general terms, lifetime value of a customer can be calculated as follows:

Lifetime value = Average transaction value
× frequency of purchase
× customer life expectancy

To take a simple example, just one loyal customer paying an average £100 per week over ten years for office-cleaning services would be worth £520 000 to the provider.

A relatively simple scenario using contribution margin (CM) as the financial measure of success will demonstrate lifetime value in practice[28] (Table 10.3). From an initial acquisition of 1000 new buyers, the lifetime value over a twelve-year period is determined.

In year 1 the company acquires 1000 new buyers. The average contribution margin per buyer (CM/buyer) is £1 owing to a large proportion of the contribution margin having been used to cover the cost

Table 10.3 Lifetime value

	Acquisition year											
	1	2	3	4	5	6	7	8	9	10	11	12
Buyers	1000	250	150	105	84	67.20	53.76	43.01	34.41	27.53	22.02	17.62
Retention (%)		25	60	70	80	80	80	80	80	80	80	80
Contribution margin (CM) per buyer	£1	£20	£20.40	£21.01	£21.85	£22.95	£24.09	£25.30	£26.56	£27.89	£29.28	£30.75
CM % increase		2%	2%	3%	4%	5%	5%	5%	5%	5%	5%	5%
Total CM	£1000	£5000	£3060	£2206	£1836	£1542	£1295	£1088	£914	£768	£645	£542

Source: Wang and Splegel (1994)[28]

of new customer acquisition. Therefore, the total annual contribution for these buyers is £1000. The following year, 250 of the original buyers made repeat purchases from this company. The average contribution per customer increases to £20. The increase in the contribution margin is due to the significant decrease of variable marketing costs by the second year. Over subsequent years we witness an increase in the average contribution per buyer due to the improving quality of repeat customers. From year 6, a contribution margin of 5 per cent is sustained till year 12. The lifetime value of this customer group over the 12 years is £19 896, being the sum of the 12 yearly contribution.

Present value

The problem with Table 10.3 is that we are unable to make direct comparisons between the cash received in year 12 and that received in year 1 in terms of how much each is worth. Clearly £542 received today is worth much more than £542 received in 12 years' time. In fact £542 invested today for 12 years at an annual interest rate of 10 per cent would give a cash amount of £1701 (i.e. £542 $\times$ 1.10^{12}). We have in effect converted today's money (£542) into an equivalent amount (£1701) 12 years in the future by using a rate of interest.

A better way of making all the cash flows comparable is to bring all of them back to today's values rather than to project forward. The technique uses the same logic but in reverse: the objective is to find an equivalent present value for any future cash flow. Instead of applying compound interest we apply a negative interest rate to reduce the future value to the present value. This negative interest rate (or discount rate, as it is called) is the annual cost associated with having to wait to receive the cash. The present value (PV) of a future sum as given by the formula:

$$PV = \frac{1}{(1 + R)^n}$$

where R equals the rate of interest per period and n the number of the periods to be discounted. Returning to Table 10.3 and using a standard discount rate of 10 per cent the £19 896 in cumulative contribution translates to a present value of £13 111 (Table 10.4).

What does this £13 111 mean? It gives some sense of how much this customer group is worth in today's money. Furthermore, it guides the amount that can be spent today on acquiring customers. Spending sums today in excess of £13 111 on acquiring customers would do little for the company's profitability.

The above calculations and frameworks form the basis for what can become a complex, intricate process. What is at issue here is growth and

Table 10.4 Present value

Year	Total CM £	Discount factor	Present value £
1	1000	$1/1.10^1$	909.1
2	5000	$1/1.10^2$	4 132
3	3060	$1/1.10^3$	2 298.9
4	2206	$1/1.10^4$	1 506.6
5	1836	$1/1.10^5$	1 139.9
6	1542	$1/1.10^6$	870.4
7	1295	$1/1.10^7$	664.5
8	1088	$1/1.10^8$	507.5
9	914	$1/1.10^9$	387.6
10	768	$1/1.10^{10}$	296
11	645	$1/1.10^{11}$	226
12	542	$1/1.10^{12}$	172.6
			13 111.1

profitability. The task of balancing what is spent on customer acquisition with what is spent on retention will require knowledge of returns from spending in terms of acquisition and retention rates and subsequent present values. In essence all companies face the following questions:

How does the current rate of acquisition/retention compare with the highest possible number of customers that could be acquired/retained?

How would the acquisition/retention rate respond to variations in expenditure allocated for acquisition/retention?

Who are our most profitable customers and why? Is it one or a mixture of factors such as customer characteristics, loyalty behaviour, response to marketing stimuli etc.

Summary

Productivity is an issue that has been around for some time. It is concerned with the efficiency of converting inputs into outputs. For service organizations, unlike manufacturing, productivity management is more difficult. This is because the input, process and output are not always susceptible to objective definition and measurement.

A number of steps can be taken to improve productivity but care must be exercised when devising an efficiency programme because effectiveness may diminish as a result.

Consumers play a pivotal role in services. Strategies must therefore be devised for developing consumer participation in the drive for increased productivity. In doing so, recognition must be given to the difficulties involved in obtaining this participation.

Productivity measures have usually been applied to the blue-collar employee but the white-collar employee performance and the impact of technology are becoming more important in the pursuit of efficiency and effectiveness.

In addition to the quest for increased productivity organizations are seeking to retain customers in preference to the traditional way of acquiring them. The attractiveness of this approach has accelerated since evidence showed increasing returns from customer retention. However, it has also been recognized that not all long-term customers are profitable. Nevertheless, with the increasing emphasis on database technology and loyalty cards, the opportunity for establishing the economics of loyalty is self-evident.

Appendix 10.1 A sample of indicators from selected service organizations

1 British Rail

Passenger business

(a) *InterCity*

- PROFIT/(LOSS) as a percentage of receipts %
- Receipts per train mile £
- Receipts per passenger mile pence
- Passenger miles per loaded train mile (average train load) passengers
- Total operating expenses per train mile £
- Percentage of trains arriving within ten minutes of booked time %
- Percentage of trains cancelled %

Similar indicators for other aspects of the business

Source British Railways Board Annual Report and Accounts 1990/1991

Note: Performance on the railways is judged mainly in terms of:
Punctuality – percentage of trains arriving within a defined number of minutes of the scheduled time. Surprisingly, this can stretch to 20 and 30 minutes in the case of two rail operators!
Reliability – percentage of trains that actually run.

2 Museums

(a) Education

- Number of courses/workshops arranged and their take-up
- Number of school visits
- Percentage of schools in the target areas reached

(b) Enquiries

- Number of enquiries dealt with each year
- Percentage of total enquiries successfully dealt with
- Average time/cost per specific enquiry

(c) Access

- Length of stay
- Number and type of visitors
- Return visitors
- Percentage from a given catchment area
- Relative performance with competition
- Measurement of visitor satisfaction

Other indicators for other aspects of the service.

Source: *Museums Year Book 1991–1992*, Museums Association, published by Rhinegold Publishing Ltd, London.

3 Further education

(a) Student success ratio

$$\frac{\text{Number of students obtaining a qualification}}{\text{Number of enrolled students}}$$

(b) Post-course success ratio

$$\frac{\text{Number of successful students who gain employment or progress to more advanced education or training}}{\text{Number of successful students}}$$

(c) Client satisfaction

$$\frac{\text{Number of clients expressing satisfaction}}{\text{Number of clients responding to requests for opinions}}$$

(d) Utilization of teaching accommodation

$$\text{Room utilization factor} = \frac{\text{Room-hours used} \times 100}{\text{Room-hours available}}$$

That is, the percentage use of available rooms

$$\text{Seat utilization factor} = \frac{\text{Seat-hours used} \times 100}{\text{Seat-hours available}}$$

That is, the percentage use of available seats.

Source: Measuring Up: Performance Indicators in Further Education, A report by HM Inspectors of Schools, Scottish Education Department, HMSO, London, 1990.

4 Hospitals

Acute Health Services

(a) *Activity indicators*

- Average length of stay
- Average number of patients per bed per year
- Admission waiting lists in relation to the population served
- Turnover interval: average length of time a bed lies empty between admissions
- Urgent, immediate or emergency in-patient admissions in relation to the population served

(b) *Financial indicators*

- Cost per day and cost per case by hospital and district
- Actual and percentage component cost by hospital
- In-patient catering costs per in-patient day by hospital
- Domestic and cleaning cost per cubic metre by district

(c) *Manpower indicators*

- Percentage breakdown of registered, enrolled, learners, auxiliary nursing and midwifery staff for all acute and mainly or partly acute hospitals
- Ratio of acute sector nursing staff to:
  - (i) Number of day cases and in-patient cases
  - (ii) Number of day cases and in-patients days
- Ratio of nursing auxiliaries/assistants to domestic staff in acute and mainly or partly acute hospitals

Similar indicators for other aspects of the service.

Source: Clinical Performance Indicators: A Background to Their Use, Northwest Thames Regional Health Authority, December, 1984.

Appendix 10.2 Local authority performance indicators

As part of the Citizen's Charter, councils and police forces have to publish details of their performance in local newspapers, using a standard set of 'performance indicators'. The Audit Commission in 1996 pulled all this information together in three volumes. The performance indicators mentioned below are a sample and they refer to councils in England and Wales. Two basic questions require to be answered:

How well is your council doing its job?
Is the money you pay for council services being well spent?

In attempting to answer these questions, account needs to be taken of local circumstances. There are often good reasons why it is harder or dearer to provide certain services in some areas of the country than in others.
   Some of the circumstances that influence council services are:

- Population density
- Social deprivation
- Daily or seasonal changes in population
- Age of population
- Language and cultural differences
- Geographical differences
- Housing and historical differences
- Regional pay and cost differences

Sample of indicators:

Libraries
- The number of books and other items issued by libraries per head of population

Crime and detection
- The percentage of all crimes cleared up by primary means (where the police need to carry out an investigation to solve the crime)

Police resources
- The proportion of police officers' time spent in public

999 calls and emergencies
- Percentage of calls answered within target time

Council tax collection
- The cost of collecting council tax per chargeable dwelling
- The amount of council tax collected by the council as a percentage of the amount which they anticipated collecting

Recycling
- Percentage of household waste recycled

Source: Audit Commission, *Local Authority Performance Indicators, Volumes 1–3, 1994/1995*

Appendix 10.3 Customer retention

A service organization has made available the following information:

Starting point – at current levels of retention, cross-sales and referrals

Key data

Marketing budget, acquisition	£2 325 000
Marketing budget, retention	£0
Total number of customers	50 000
Average acquisition rate	33.75 (weighted average = 31.5)
Total, new customers p.a.	15 750
Average retention rate	71% (weighted average = 70.5)
Total, customer lost p.a.	(14 750)
Growth/decline in customer file	1000
Growth/decline in customer file, %	2.0%
Average customer lifetime	3.29 years (weighted average = 3.4)
Average profit contribution per cust. p.a.	£300

Segmentation	*Segment 1* *18 to 29*	*Segment 2* *30 to 39*	*Segment 3* *40 to 49*	*Segment 4* *50 plus*
Revenue per customer, p.a.	£400	£500	£650	£750
Servicing costs per customer, p.a.	£250	£320	£400	£480
Acquisition costs per customer	£70	£100	£220	£250
Cross-sales ratio, (1 to . . .)	1.07	1.22	1.31	1.12
Referral ratio (1 to . . .)	1.05	1.13	1.18	1.31
Total customers per segment	5000	20 000	15 000	10 000
Retention rate per segment	60%	70%	75%	70%
Acquisition rate per segment	50%	35%	25%	25%
Lifetime per customer, years	2.50	3.33	4.00	3.33
Customers acquired p.a.	2500	7000	3750	2500
Customers lost p.a.	(2000)	(6000)	(3750)	(3000)
Growth in customer file p.a.	500	1,000	0	(500)
% Growth in customer file	10%	5%	0%	–5%

At stage 2: Marketing expenditure switches from
100% acquisition to
75% acquisition and
25% retention. We assume that this will increase retention by
5% in all segments, (i.e. one in 20 more customers will be retained).

We also assume that this will encourage

10% more cross-sales to occur and
7.5% more referrals to occur

Key data:

Marketing budget, acquisition	£2 325 000	changing to £1 743 750
Marketing budget, retention	£0	changing to £581 250
Total number of customers	50 000	
Average Acquisition Rate	25.5	(weighted average = 23.7)
Total, new customers p.a.	11 850	
Average Retention Rate	73.75%	(weighted average = 75.5)
Total, customers lost p.a.	(12 250)	
Growth/decline in customer file	(400)	
Growth/decline in customer file, %	(0.8%)	
Average customer lifetime	3.965 years	(weighted average = 4.186)
Profitability per annum	£300	

Segmentation	*Segment 1* *18 to 29*	*Segment 2* *30 to 39*	*Segment 3* *40 to 49*	*Segment 4* *50 plus*
Revenue per customer, p.a.	£400	£500	£650	£750
Servicing costs per customer, p.a.	£250	£320	£400	£480
Acquisition costs per customer	£70	£100	£220	£250
Cross-sales ratio, (1 to . . .)	1.07	1.22	1.31	1.12
Referral ratio (1 to . . .)	1.05	1.13	1.18	1.31
Total customers per segment	5000	20 000	15 000	10 000
Retention rate per segment	65%	75%	80%	75%
Acquisition rate per segment	38%	26%	19%	19%
Lifetime per customer, years	2.86	4.00	5.00	4.00
Customers acquired p.a.	1900	5200	2850	1900
Customers lost p.a.	(1750)	(5000)	(3000)	(2500)
Growth in customer file p.a.	150	200	(150)	(600)
% Growth in customer file	3%	1%	−1%	−6%

Question
Determine the impact on profit from stage 1 to stage 2.

Stage I

Customer value	Segment 1 18 to 29	Segment 2 30 to 39	Segment 3 40 to 49	Segment 4 50 plus
Profits in year 1 from core product sales	£80	£80	£30	£20
Profits in subsequent years from product sales	£150	£180	£250	£270
Total net profit per customer from product sales	£305	£500	£780	£650
Profit from cross-sales over lifetime	£21	£110	£242	£78
Profit from referrals	£15	£65	£140	£202
Total customer value	£341	£675	£1162	£930

Summary

Customer value	Segment 1	Segment 2	Segment 3	Segment 4
Total customer value in segment	£1 705 000	£13 500 000	£17 430 000	£9 300 000
Customer value contributed p.a.	£682 000	£4 050 054	£4 357 500	£2 792 792

Total customer value across all segments   £41 935 000

Total annual customer value across all segments   £11 882 346

Stage II

Customer value	Segment 1 18 to 29	Segment 2 30 to 39	Segment 3 40 to 49	Segment 4 50 plus
Profits in year 1 from core product sales	£80	£80	£30	£20
Profits in subsequent years from product sales	£150	£180	£250	£270
Total net profit per customer from product sales	£359	£620	£1030	£830
Profit from cross-sales over lifetime	£28	£150	£351	£110
Profit from referrals	£19	£87	£199	£277
Total customer value	£406	£857	£1580	£1217

Summary

Customer value	Segment 1	Segment 2	Segment 3	Segment 4
Total customer value in segment	£2 030 000	£17 140 000	£23 700 000	£12 170 000
Customer value contributed p.a.	£707 790	£4 285 000	£4 740 000	£3 042 500

Total customer value across all segments	£55 040 000
Total annual customer value across all segments	£12 775 290
At 100% of marketing budget spent on acquisition	£41 935 000
At 75% spent on acquisition, 25% spent on retention	£55 040 000

The impact on profit is an increase of 31% from stage 1 to stage 2.

Appendix 10.4 The customer volume effect

Growth rate r% per annum (r expressed in decimal form)

Initial number of customers $= A$

At the end of year 1 the number of customers $= A + Ar$
$= A(1 + r)$

At the end of year 2 the number of customers $=$ the number of customers at the beginning of year 2 + number acquired during year 2 $= A(1 + r) + A(1 + r)r = A(1 + r)(1 + r) = A(1 + r)^2$

At the end of year 3 the number of customers $=$ the number of customers at the beginning of year 3 + number acquired during year 3 $= A(1 + r)^2 + A(1 + r)^2 r = A(1 + r)^2(1 + r) = A(1 + r)^3$

At the end of year n the number of customers $= A(1 + r)^n$
Over what period of time will the firm double in size?
If the initial number of customers is A, we wish to solve

$$A(1 + r)^n = 2A \qquad (1 + r)^n = \frac{2A}{A} \qquad (1 + r)^n = 2$$

Taking logs of both sides

$$\log(1 + r)^n = \log 2$$
$$n\log(1 + r) = \log 2$$
$$n = \frac{\log 2}{\log(1 + r)}$$

A range of net growth customers per year and how long it will take to double in size is considered below:

Net growth (%)	Calculation	Years
2.5	$\dfrac{\log 2}{\log 1.025}$	28.07
5.0	$\dfrac{\log 2}{\log 1.05}$	14.20*
10.0	$\dfrac{\log 2}{\log 1.10}$	7.27
20.0	$\dfrac{\log 2}{\log 1.20}$	3.80

*Example in text

References

1. Ball, S. D., Johnson, K. and Slattery, P. (1986) 'Labour productivity in hotels: an empirical analysis', *International Journal of Hospitality Management* **5**(3), 141–147.
2. Rathmell, J. M. (1974) *Marketing in the Service Sector* Winthrop, Cambridge, MA.
3. Drucker, P. (1973) *Management: Tasks, Responsibilities, Practices*, Harper & Row, New York.
4. Butt, H. and Palmer, B. (1985) *Value for Money in the Public Sector*, Blackwell, Oxford.
5. Audit Commission (1989) 'Managing services effectively', *Performance Review*, **5**, December.
6. Whynes, D. K. (1987) 'On assessing efficiency in the provision of local authority services', *Local Government Studies*, January–February, 53–68.
7. Mersha, T. (1989) 'Output and performance measurement in outpatient care', *Omega*, **17**(2), 159–161.
8. Heskett, J. L., Sasser, W. E. and Hart, C. W. L. (1990) *Service Breakthroughs*, Free Press, New York.
9. Brown, R. (1987) 'Marketing – a function and a philosophy', *Quarterly Review of Marketing*, **12**(3 and 4), 25–30.
10. Savas, E. S. (1978) 'On equity in providing public services', *Management Science*, **24**(8), April, 800–808.
11. Goodwin, C. (1988) ' "I can do it myself": training the service consumer to contribute to service productivity', *Journal of Service Marketing*, **2**(4), 71–78.
12. Ruch, W. A. (1982) 'The measurement of white-collar productivity', *National Productivity Review*, Autumn, 416–426.
13. Drucker, P. F. (1991) 'The new productivity challenge', *Harvard Business Review*, November–December, 69–79.
14. Cannell, M. and Wood, S. (1992) *Incentive Pay: Impact and Evolution*, National Economic Development Office and Institute of Personnel Management.
15. Kessler, I. and Purcell, J. (1992) 'Performance related pay: objectives and application', *Human Resource Management Journal*, **2**(3), 16–33.
16. Bernadin, H. J. and Beatty, R. W. (1987) 'Can subordinate appraisals enhance managerial productivity?' *Sloan Management Review*, Summer, 63–73.
17. Mount, M. K. (1984) 'Supervisors, self and subordinate ratings of performance and satisfaction with supervision', *Journal of Management*, **10**, 121–130.
18. Livingston, J. S. (1988) 'Pygmalion in management', *Harvard Business Review*, September–October 121–130.
19. Heaton, H. (1977) *Productivity in Service Organisations*, McGraw-Hill, New York.
20. Quinn, J. B. and Paquette, P. C. (1990) 'Technology in services: creating organisational revolutions', *Sloan Management Review*, Winter, 67–87.
21. Smith, S. (1994) 'Building loyalty through communications', *Marketing Business*, November.
22. Davidow, W. H. (1986) *Marketing High Technology*, Free Press, New York.

23. Reichheld, F. F. and Sasser, W. E. (1990) 'Zero defections: quality comes to services', *Harvard Business Review*, September–October.
24. Reichheld, F. F. (1994) 'Loyalty and the renaissance of marketing', *Marketing Management*, **15**.
25. Reichheld, F. F. (1996) *The Loyalty Effect*, Harvard Business School Press, Cambridge, MA.
26. Carroll, P. (1991/92) 'The fallacy of customer retention', *Journal of Retail Banking*, **XIII**, 4.
27. Reichheld, F. F. (1991/92) 'The truth of customer retention', *Journal of Retail Banking*, **XIII**, 4.
28. Wang, P. and Splegget, T. (1994) 'Database marketing and its measurements of success', *Journal of Direct Marketing*, **8**, 2.

Chapter 11

Delivering satisfaction

Introduction

Complete or total customer satisfaction is a goal that more and more service companies are striving to achieve. Many organizations in the public sector now refer to their users as customers, and customer views are taken into account in the design and monitoring of the service. This is done in the belief that higher levels of satisfaction will be built in this way. The Audit Commission, whose job it is to control local authorities, stated that 'services need to be provided *for* the public, rather than simply *to* it'[1]

However, the totally satisfied customer is becoming an increasingly elusive creature. As Sir James McKinnon, the first director-general of OFGAS (the gas industry regulator) says, 'customers are increasingly aware of their rights and are more confident about seeking redress'.[2]

Increasing confidence levels is only partly responsible for declining levels of satisfaction. Many would argue that the increasing expectations that consumers hold is at the root of this problem. Therefore, it is simply unrealistic to expect that there will be no dissatisfied customers. Of course, companies should attempt to minimize levels of dissatisfaction by providing a better service. However, at the same time they should also consider what to do for those who are dissatisfied. Analysing dissatisfied customers, designing efficient systems for handling complaints, and the provision of guarantees are ways in which management can build levels of satisfaction.

Why try to make customers satisfied?

In general, the response to a satisfactory experience will contain both emotional and behavioural elements (Figure 11.1). So customer satisfaction will result in positive emotional states. These, in turn, mediate the

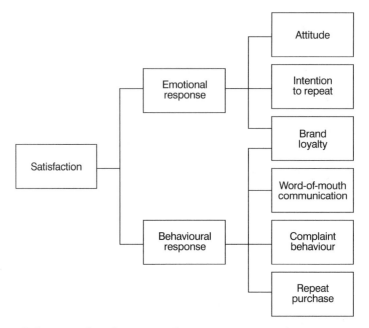

Figure 11.1 Behavioural and emotional responses to satisfaction

response between customer satisfaction and behavioural responses – positive word-of-mouth, no complaint behaviour, and repeat purchase.

What does 'satisfaction' mean? The concept itself is an abstract one. The achievement of satisfaction can be a complex and precarious process. The roles played in the service encounter by individual personalities contribute to this.

In the same way that totally satisfied customers are hard to find, the totally dissatisfied customer is also an elusive creature. Most consumers are satisfied to some extent and there are various research techniques that attempt to measure this (see Chapter 12). While one should understand the extent of customer satisfaction, it is perhaps more important to understand the underlying cause of this satisfaction.

What is satisfaction?

The model used to explain the occurrence of satisfaction is known as the expectancy-disconfirmation model (Figure 11.2). It was first proposed by Oliver in 1977[3] And has subsequently been tested in a variety of different industries.

The model suggests that satisfaction is dependent on the customer's expectations, and their perceptions of performance exceeding those expectations. One implication of this model is that to secure satisfaction,

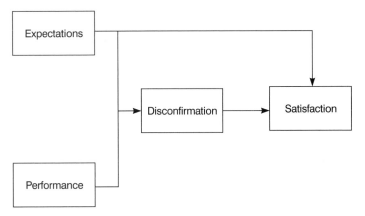

Figure 11.2 Expectancy-disconfirmation model of consumer satisfaction

management need not (and indeed should not) focus exclusively on improving its performance. Resources should also be devoted to managing customer expectations. As Peters and Austin state:[4] 'Managing expectations is all about under-promising and over-delivering.'

There are five key factors that influence a customer's expectations: previous experience; personal recommendation; personal needs; marketing communications; and the level of involvement in the purchase (Figure 11.3). Research suggests that the most important of these factors in shaping expectations is the consumer's past experience of the service and what other people say about it.

Customers complain less about services than products even although they are more likely to be dissatisfied with services.[5] One reason why they

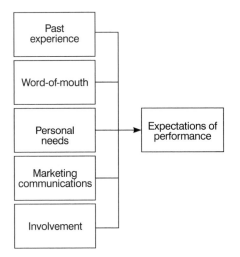

Figure 11.3 Antecedents of expectations

do not complain as much comes from the active part that they play in specifying the service. If a trip to the hairdresser results in a bad haircut, who is to say that it is because the hairdresser is lousy? It may be that the client did not communicate clearly enough what he or she wanted.

Prior to using a service, consumers may have in mind four different scenarios of the service that they might experience:

- The ideal
- The anticipated
- The deserved
- The minimum tolerable

The consumer can expect any of these (Figure 11.4). As we have seen, expectations shape satisfaction. If the 'minimum tolerable' is expected then this or anything better may lead to satisfaction. Equally, anyone expecting the 'ideal' will be dissatisfied with anything less.

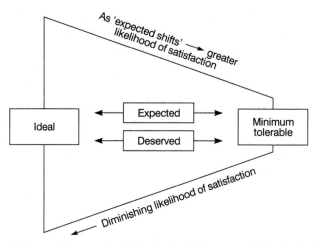

1. The closer 'expected' expectations are to the 'minimum tolerable' the greater the likelihood of satisfaction.
2. Satisfied customers can appear anywhere on the spectrum. What determines their position is the position of 'expected' outcome.

Figure 11.4 Impact of expectations on satisfaction

Sometimes customers have a view about what they 'deserve', even if these are set at a low level. For instance, patients may believe that at the very least they 'deserve' to return from surgery alive. (This may also be the minimum tolerable!)

If a customer has a strong idea of what he or she deserves, perhaps formed from a guarantee, or previous usage, then expectations will be set at that level. Expectations will be more firmly held and will probably result in greater levels of dissatisfaction if the service fails to deliver.

Figure 11.5 Levels of expectations. Based on Parasuraman, Zeithaml and Berry (1990)[5]

The 'deserved' outcome can also modify expectations downwards, e.g. if a builder is instructed to build a house that must be finished in two months, then the level of workmanship that the customer receives is likely to suffer from corner-cutting as the builder struggles to meet the deadline. If the customer realizes the constraints that they have forced the builder to work to, then their 'deserved' outcome should be set at a low level.

What the customer believes he or she deserves, may however, still be lower than his or her 'anticipated' or expected outcome. If this arises then the customer will be dissatisfied. He or she may have chosen not to believe what the builder told him or her at the outset about the most likely consequences of the tight schedule, choosing instead to expect the outcome to be better than the picture painted.

Parasuraman, Zeithaml and Berry[5] define a narrower band for expectations. They describe a 'zone of tolerance' between adequate service provision and the desired service provision (Figure 11.5). This zone expands and contracts. It can also remain unchanged in magnitude, while moving up or down the spectrum. It varies according to the service and to the individual customer. More recently, it has been shown that expectations and the zone of tolerance can fluctuate *during* service consumption.[6,7]

Relationship marketing

The pivotal role of customer satisfaction to marketing arises because, satisfying customers with the current service offering is generally a prerequisite to retention or repeat purchase.[8] It is important for companies to retain existing customers for the financial business benefits that accrue. Organizations can grow business by attracting new customers, losing fewer customers, and doing more business with existing customers. A combination of the latter two is generally a more efficient way of utilizing resources.[9] Recruiting new customers costs considerably more than retaining existing ones. Furthermore, since the majority of consumer markets are operating in the mature stage of their service life cycle, attracting new customers becomes increasingly difficult. This focus on the retention of existing customers underspins the recent shift in marketing from transactional (or acquisition) marketing to relationship (or retention) marketing. See Chapter 10 for a more extended discussion of customer retention.

Relationship marketing has been defined as a data-driven, quantifiable marketing tool, and is driven by a desire to keep customers loyal. The practice of relationship marketing relies on an organization's ability to identify, target, communicate and reward valuable customers. Therefore establishing a one-to-one dialogue (not monologue) with customers is important. This is the reason why the building of customer databases is important for the practice of relationship marketing. Relationships that endure are built on trust and open dialogue. Transactional marketing does not nurture customers. Consequently, there is a greater likelihood of customer defections and dissatisfaction.

Dissatisfied customers

What do they do?

Customers who are unhappy with a service are less likely to complain about the situation than they are when they are unhappy with a product.[10] But even within the services sector, dissatisfied consumers complain in varying proportions. Over 80 per cent of dissatisfied consumers complain to supermarkets, credit card and cable companies, whereas, just over 30 per cent complain to their GP or dentist (Figure 11.6).

However, dissatisfied customers are not likely to keep the bad news to themselves. At the same time as deciding not to buy the service again they are probably spreading the bad news.

Customer complaint are actually helpful to the organization for several reasons. First, they give the organization a chance to recover its original customer. Indeed, there is some evidence to suggest that customers whose complaints lead to a successful recovery of the service experience end up more satisfied than those customers who found the initial service encounter satisfactory. It also diminishes the risk of bad publicity, either from personal word-of-mouth communication or in more damaging leaks through the press to the general public, and it provides information that should be useful for development of the service.

Historically companies have shied away from the whole issue of customer complaints preferring instead to devote resources to generating business. Retaining business through service recovery is still not wide-spread. However, while we would suggest that the handling of complaints

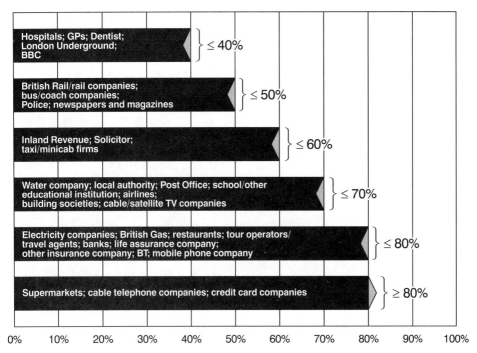

Figure 11.6 Percentage of dissatisfied customers who complained. *Source*: Consumers' Association (1998)[11]

should be resourced, it has been shown that even those customers who had their complaints satisfactorily resolved were more likely to switch service provider than those who had not been dissatisfied in the first place.[12]

Who complains?

Research has shown that those consumers who do complain about the service they receive, tend to be the loyal users of the service. In terms of numbers, they represent only a tiny fraction of the total number of dissatisfied customers. Bell and Zemke[13] estimate that only 4 per cent complain.

A great deal of research has been carried out to establish the characteristics of those who complain. Zemke and Bell[14] and Warland, Hermann and Willits[15] found them to be predominantly young women, who were intellectually, socially, and economically upmarket. Perhaps they complain more because they are less daunted by confrontation. Perhaps it is because their expectations are higher than for many other groups of consumers. There is certainly evidence to support this latter view. Studies have found that these consumers are the ones most likely to be unhappy about the performance of the services that they purchase.[16,17]

Of the three possible outcomes of poor service delivery (illustrated in Figure 11.7) not upset, upset/complain, and upset/no complaint, it has been found that the two groups that were furthest apart demographically were the upset/complain, and the upset/no complaint. Those that were not upset tended to be the older, more conservative members of society.[15]

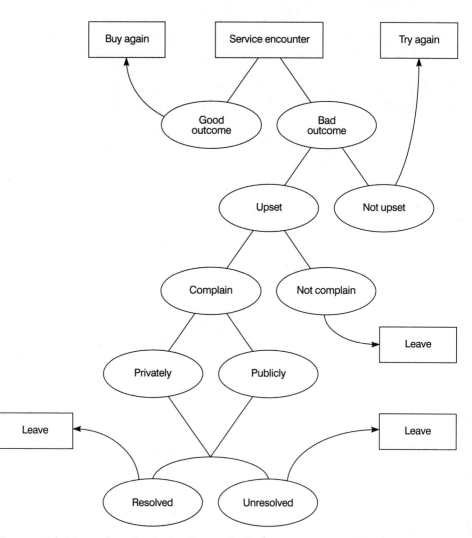

Figure 11.7 Means by which the dissatisfied consumer can tackle the issue

To whom do they complain?

Channels for making a complaint

Complain to the service provider
There are a number of options open to the customer who decides to complain (Table 11.1). He can go back to the company and complain to them. This is in fact, the most likely first course of action. Best and Andreasen,[17] found that, on the whole, sellers have a virtual monopoly on complaints handling. The company imposes their own standards, sets the resolutions and decides on any level of compensation.

Table 11.1 What the dissatisfied customer can do

Complain to seller
Write or phone manufacturer
Write or phone the head office
Write or phone trade association
Contact TSO
Consult CAB
Consult a solicitor
Write or phone OFT

The unhappy customer can complain in private, e.g. by writing a letter of complaint, or in public, e.g. by creating a scene on the premises.[18] The public complaint is most feared by those companies that do not provide a good service in the first place, or do not have a good complaints handling procedure. Customers sometimes choose to air their grievances publicly in the belief that they are more likely to have them satisfactorily resolved by behaving in this manner in front of other customers.

Successful resolution of complaints by the company also reduces the risk of attracting the attention of the legislature or even the voluntary consumer watchdog. The vociferously negative comments of the *London Evening Standard*'s commuter watchdog no doubt played a part in the establishment of the Passenger's Charter. Had there been no cause for complaint there would have been no watchdog. Had there been no watchdog there would have been less incentive to change.

Complain to a consumer watchdog
So instead of approaching the offending company, the consumer can take a complaint to an organization that has been set up to protect or promote consumers' interests. Some of these organizations deal with all kinds of

problems and enquiries, e.g. the Citizen's Advice Bureau, which receives public funding, and the Consumers' Association which has no grants or subsidies from government or industry.

There are also industry-specific bodies, e.g. OFGAS for the gas industry, OFFER for the electricity industry, or Greenpeace for the environment. The first two were set up when these industries were privatized. They were given statutory powers to protect consumers' interests. The smaller ones rely on voluntary help and fund-raising for their existence. If these organizations cannot resolve the complaint by conciliation then, in some cases, the aggrieved customer can seek redress through arbitration.

Take legal action

If dissatisfied consumers find no joy through any of the above channels they must then resort to the final method of redress and take the matter to court. They can raise an action of damages for breach of contract. In so doing, they can seek compensation for any loss which occurs as a result of the failure, or reimbursement for the cost of having the fault put right. This course of action is open to consumers regardless of whether the original contract was written or merely spoken.

The scope of the law of contract has been modified by various statutes specifically related to the purchase of services by consumers. Statutory changes in recent times have reflected the growth in consumer movement. The Consumers' Association believes that it was as a result of their campaigning that the Unfair Contract Terms Act was passed by Parliament in 1977.[19] Some of the more significant pieces of legislation in this area are the Consumer Credit Act 1974, the Unfair Contract Terms Act 1977, the Sale of Goods Act 1979, and the Supply of Goods and Services Act 1982.

At common law people are free to agree between themselves whatever they choose. This is fair practice where both parties have equal power. However, in many exchanges this power is not equally distributed, and it tends to be the relatively uninformed consumer that is in the weaker position. Thus the Consumer Credit Act 1974, among other things, introduced a system of licensing of consumer credit business; the Unfair Contract Terms Act 1977 curtails the extent to which a supplier can introduce exclusion or restriction from liability clauses into their contracts with individual consumers; the Sale of Goods and Services Act 1982 entitles consumers to a 'reasonable standard of service'. In very extreme cases, for example where the supplier has made absolutely no attempt to carry out the service, it may be open to the customer to report the matter to the police as a case of fraud. While this course of action is unlikely to provide the customer with any recompense, the threat of it may act as a powerful bargaining tool.

Why do they complain?

Consumers complain because they are dissatisfied. They are dissatisfied because their expectations are not met, and obviously the higher their prepurchase expectations, the more likely they are to be dissatisfied. This is why a key role for communications in service marketing is the management of expectations. To understand more fully why they complain, we have to examine the reasons why their expectations may be unfulfilled.

Miscommunication on a customer's part is only one reason why expectations may not be fulfilled (Figure 11.8). Some of these factors are within the control of the service provider, some are not. It is certainly up to the provider to reduce the likelihood of miscommunication or misinterpretation by making the service clearly understood. It is also the responsibility of the company to ensure both that it clearly understands a client's instructions, and that the client clearly understands what will be delivered. Service providers should take the lead in designing initiatives to reduce these problems.

Figure 11.8 Major causes of unfulfilled expectations

However, it is not only prepurchase expectations that condition whether or not a complaint is made. It is also the expectation of the likely outcome from complaining. If consumers expect to achieve something by complaining then they are much more likely to complain. Some psychologists would go even further, by suggesting that even if there is no possibility of rectifying the situation, it is still best to express anger, in order to accept the dissatisfaction.[20]

The average consumer would probably not take this advice too seriously no matter how beneficial it may be to them psychologically. They

Table 11.2 The costs and benefits of complaining

Costs	Inconvenience	Special trip to complain Form-filling, letter writing Forgo service during complaint process
	Uncertainty	Difficulty finding correct complaint procedure No indication of the action that will be taken
	Unpleasant	Treated rudely, have to hassle Feel guilty, embarrassed
Benefits	Emotional	Chance to assert rights, chance to vent anger, receive an apology
	Functional	Refund, replacement, repair
	Altruistic	Other customers prevented from experiencing dissatisfaction Would feel guilty about not complaining
	Product improvement	Organization would improve its offering

Based on Richins (1990)[21]

are much more likely to weigh up all the costs and benefits associated with complaining. Their emotional well-being will be only one factor. If they perceive the benefits to outweigh the costs then they will complain. Table 11.2 lists the factors that help fashion the costs and benefits of complaining.

What do they complain about?

As we have stated, there is a lower incidence of complaining in the service sector than there is for manufacturing. Of the complaints that are made a lower proportion of these are resolved, and the ones that are, take longer to clear up.[22]

Once again some service sectors appear to be better than others at handling customer complaints. So although supermarkets received the highest proportion of complaints, they were also the best at satisfactorily resolving them. However, the picture for life and other insurance companies is not as positive with less than 30 per cent of complainants being satisfied with how their complaint was handled (Figure 11.9).

One of the main reasons for this is that nearly all problems that occur with products can be openly demonstrated and discussed. If a car does not start, it does not start. If a vacuum cleaner fails to clean carpets then this too can be demonstrated. Whereas, who is actually to blame for problems

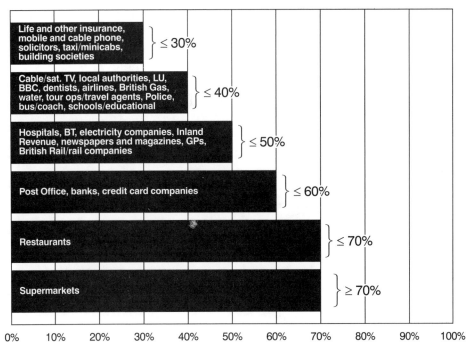

Figure 11.9 Percentage of complaints satisfactorily resolved. *Source*: Consumers' Association (1998)[11]

that arise in the consumption of services is often open to judgement and debate. Even where the complaint is justified, service providers may still feel that their own position is also quite defensible. This is often to do with verbal and non-verbal signals from the consumer that the service provider attempts to interpret. Communication is a transactional process.

Imagine a company rings a courier in a panic. It desperately needs to get a document to Paris the following day. The courier goes to extraordinary lengths to see that it gets there, and this results in some extra costs. When the company receives the invoice it is outraged by the price. The service provider misinterpreted the signals about urgency from the company.

A large party in a restaurant spends a long time deciding what they want to eat, apparently preferring to chat with fellow diners. They do not appear to be in any hurry, or to want an attentive waiting staff. When the bill arrives they leave no tip, saying that they were disappointed with the time that they spent waiting for their food.

These are two examples of service scenarios where the service provider would feel that the complaint was unjustified. However, the customer would feel that the service provider was to blame. After all, he misjudged the customer's requirement.

Customers complain about different problems in different industries (Table 11.3). In banking, account errors are the biggest source of complaints, whereas in air travel, cancellations and flight delays generate the most complaints. Even within an industry, there will be varying weaknesses from different service companies. Each operator should have an understanding of his or her own weaknesses, and those of the main competitors.

Table 11.3 Major sources of complaint

Reason	Total	Auto repair	Bank	Insurance	Government	Hospitals	Airline
Not done right	**	***	*	*	*		
Too slow	**	*	**	**	**	**	
Too expensive	**	**		*		**	
Indifferent personnel	**		*	*	**	**	*
Unqualified personnel	*		*	*		*	*
Lack of courtesy	*		*			*	
Lack of personnel						*	
Poor scheduling							**
Reservations							*
Poor food							
Music	*				*		
Unspecified	*	*					

Source: American Society for Quality Control. Gallup Survey (Autumn 1985)

<10%	–
10–20%	*
20–60%	**
60%+	***

The value of the purchase that consumers complain about in services is also different. The cheaper the service, the more likely there are to be complaints. Quite the reverse is true *for* products. This has much to do with the intangible nature of services. Higher-cost services tend to be more complex, which tends to lead to greater intangibility, and therefore more ambiguity about the exact nature of the service provision.

Expensive services probably also attract fewer complaints because they are offered by experts or professional people.[16] This leaves the service provider in a position of authority and power. The consumer feels more intimidated by this apparent superiority and is less likely to make a complaint. Most people no longer feel intimidated about complaining in a restaurant. Many more would think twice about complaining to their lawyer.

The organization's role in minimizing dissatisfaction

Total customer satisfaction is unlikely to be achieved even on a temporary basis. However, improvements in the level of satisfaction can often be achieved through the development of an augmented service. The core service can be augmented by providing a guarantee, or by providing good after-sales service. Today's increasingly competitive environment means that it is foolish to hold on to the old adage 'customers come and customers go'. As *Serving Them Right*[23] notes, this is foolish not only because it is expensive to recruit new customers, but also because they are harder to find. Part of a good after-sales service policy should be the provision of an efficient and effective means for handling complaints.

Even just allowing the customer to let off steam can help. Perceptions of satisfaction and fairness will be enhanced if this is then acknowledged with an apology which provides even a small 'tangible token of restitution'.[24]

Effective complaint-handling procedures

Companies that take a pragmatic view will accept that they can make mistakes. They will recognize that customers will occasionally have a better idea of the way that the service should be delivered. Indeed a dearth of complaints is more often a danger signal than a cause for celebration. It is to the organization's advantage to encourage customers to air their views, and it must set up a complaint-handling procedure that does just that. As the President of world-wide quality at American Express says, 'the formula that I use is: better complaint handling equals higher customer satisfaction, equals higher brand loyalty, equals higher profitability'.[25]

When designing a complaint handling system, it can often be difficult to strike the right balance between making the system easily accessible, and making it too accessible. The organization wants to encourage users to make justifiable complaints, but it is counterproductive to set up a complaints procedure that creates the impression that the organization is expecting lots of complaints. This usually means that the service provider does not believe that he is offering a good service. Customers will very quickly pick this up, and begin to start looking for problems. It would be much more productive to provide a better service in the first place.

Historically, dealing with customer complaints was considered a second-rate occupation for marketing professionals. It was much more stimulating and glamorous to be developing new products and advertising campaigns. Customer complaint-handling was regarded as a maintenance function and a cost centre to the business.

Fortunately nowadays, many companies take a more enlightened view. They incorporate complaints handling into their strategic mix, and call it Customer Service or Customer Care. Until the late 1990s it was common practice in those companies to staff these operations with marketing personnel, thereby allowing them to experience first-hand the voices of consumers. There is an old management saying, 'If you're going to be a general, you have to remember what its like to be a private'. The organization benefits in several ways by staffing customer service with these employees. It raises the profile of the department in the company. It makes a statement to all employees about the importance that the company attaches to the resolution of complaints. In doing so, it communicates the significance of providing a quality service, and finally, it generally also leads to improvements in the way that complaints are handled. Employees charged with complaint-handling will often make suggestions about the powers they need to do the job well, and ways in which the department could be run more effectively. However, more recently there has been a trend towards outsourcing this function to call centres.

The benefits of effective complaint handling

Companies that devote resources to an effective complaints procedure benefit in many ways:

- They are given a second chance to make good their relationship with a dissatisfied customer.
- Adverse word-of-mouth publicity is avoided.
- They will understand what would improve their current service.
- They will know where their operations problems lie.
- Employees may be motivated to provide a better-quality service.

To make the best use of a customer service department it is not enough to deal expediently with each complaint as it is received. Naturally, this is all that the aggrieved customer is interested in. Initially, it should also be what interests the company most.

There are many examples of companies who have gone to extraordinary lengths to try to please a dissatisfied customer. Most of them are American. As a nation they seem to be more clued up to the benefits of dealing with complaints effectively. They are less reticent about going 'over the top' in an overt attempt to keep a customer.

However, in addition to dealing with complaints, the company should also attempt to learn from its mistakes. It does this by putting in place

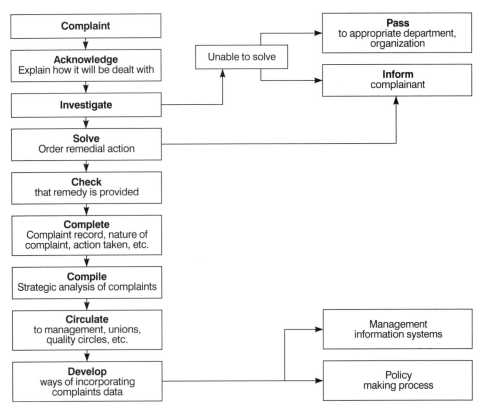

Figure 11.10 Effective complaints handling process

management information systems that enable customer service staff to record every complaint that is made and then to report these complaints (Figure 11.10). Management must be able to identify the cause of complaints if they are to aid the development of the service.

For example, it has been estimated that British banks spend more than twice what they ought to in order to operate their service. This is because their procedures are so error-prone that they keep losing documents and waste precious time and money tracking them down, or regenerating them. This problem has come to light because customer complaints were monitored. They now know the source of the problem so all they need to do is deal with it. As Einstein said, 'The formulation of a problem is far more essential than a solution'.[26]

The success of a complaint management process can also be examined by checking complaining data against satisfaction and retention. This is illustrated in Figure 11.11 using data adapted from a survey of hotel guests.[27] The first diagram shows an organization's complaint resolution performance. In this case, 25 per cent of customers have a problem with

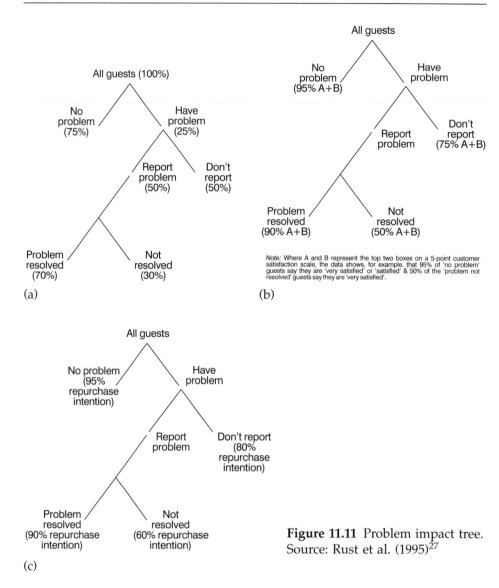

Figure 11.11 Problem impact tree.
Source: Rust et al. (1995)[27]

the service. Only half of those report the problem, and of those that do, 30 per cent remain unresolved.

The Problem Impact Tree shown in Figure 11.11(b) displays satisfaction data from the same customers. The letters A and B represent the top two points on a five-point satisfaction rating scale. Among customers with a problem, satisfaction falls from 90 per cent for those whose problem is resolved to 50 per cent for those whose problem remains unresolved. In this case, satisfaction in the 'problem resolved' category is almost as high as for those in the 'no problem' category.

Customers who do not report a problem also end up with relatively low levels of satisfaction (75 per cent). But they are not as low as those whose complaints remain unresolved (50 per cent).

Complaint management also affects customer retention. Once again, Figure 11.11 illustrates the serious implications of not resolving complaints satisfactorily. If retention data is not available, then 'intention to repeat' survey data can be used. Combining satisfaction and retention data with complaint management information enables management to calculate the value of guiding the customer down different branches of the Problem Impact Tree. This will help the organization maximize its resources to greatest effect.

Service recovery

Successful complaints handling is known today as service recovery.[28] This is where the organization treats dissatisfied customers in such a way that it manages to hang on to their loyalty. Service recovery can take place where the service provider operates a comprehensive guarantee. It also occurs where the organization that is not working to any specified guarantee, meets or exceeds the expectations of the complaining customer in the way in which they handle complaints. However, efforts to recover potential defectors should not be treated uniformly. Organizations should base their offers on the potential profitability of individual customers.[29]

Dissatisfaction with the service can become more intense if the complainant does not feel that the complaint is being handled appropriately. This individual is already in an irritable frame of mind and therefore staff need to be trained to handle the situation sensitively. Ideally these employees should be empowered to take decisions about the best course of action. However, many companies find this an uncomfortable suggestion believing that the employee will always err on the side of the customer, and perhaps be over-generous with any compensation. Other companies take a more progressive view, as Jan Carlzon CEO of SAS said, 'What's the danger of giving away too much? Are you worried about an oversatisfied customer? That's not much of a worry. You can forget about an oversatisfied customer, but an unsatisfied customer is one of the most expensive problems you can have . . . the danger is not that employees will give away too much. It's that they won't give away anything because they don't dare'.[30]

If the empowerment of these frontline employees is not possible, then senior management themselves must be prepared to play an active part in the resolution of complaints. Top management involvement usually goes down well with customers, because customers like to deal with those who have the power and confidence to act on their behalf. They should be called in at the slightest hint that the customer might be dissatisfied with the way a complaint is being handled.

A recent empirical study suggests that from the complainant's viewpoint the most important aspect of service recovery is for the organization to accept responsibility for the problem (even if in approximately one-third of complaints, the customer is in fact responsible). The empowerment of frontline staff to resolve complaints was the next most important factor. Receiving an apology was the least impressive recovery strategy. A personal apology either face to face or by telephone was preferred to that of a written one.[31]

This study also found evidence to suggest that the way that an organization recovers is situation-specific. So however well it has performed in the past, and consequently has satisfied the customer, none of this will have any bearing on a customer's satisfaction with service recovery procedures.[31]

Customer defections

We have previously suggested that organizations should attempt to minimize customer defections. However, it has been suggested that the best defections management processes do not attempt to eliminate all defections.[32] Some will defect regardless of what a company does to tempt them to stay. Furthermore, attempting a zero defections strategy is likely to represent an inefficient use of resources.

A good defections management programme will attempt to identify those who have or are about to leave. However, it is not always easy to identify those customers who are about to defect. It is easier in those services where a contractual agreement is in place. In such industries, customers may begin to complain, or suggest that a competitor is offering a lower price, as the original contract comes up for renewal.

In consumer services, building a database that records purchase frequencies and values will help pinpoint potential defectors. Such a database is relatively easy to establish in services where reservations or appointments are necessary. Another means of capturing the information is to design a loyalty card or frequent purchase programme where customers are rewarded for their loyalty. The service operator can then spot customers whose purchase frequency has declined. Or those who buy with the same frequency but purchase less at each occasion. Both are indicators that the customer may be about to detract.

Although we have suggested that it is pointless for a service company to expect zero defections, the possibility of this is increased by the provision of an unconditional guarantee.

The provision of guarantees

The function of the guarantee is that it reduces risk to consumers both before and after purchase. It also conveys a powerful marketing message and helps to shape customers' expectations of a quality service. Pizzaland guarantees its customers their pizzas in five minutes or they get their money back (and the late pizza besides!). In this situation, customers know that once they have placed their order the delivery of their food is imminent. They also know what to expect if it does not appear.

In reducing risk, the guarantee often diminishes much of the ambiguity often associated with service provision. However, ambiguity often arises from the intangible nature of the service, and the more intangible the service, the more difficult it is to provide guarantees (Figure 11.12).

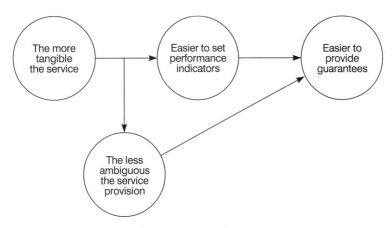

Figure 11.12 Tangibility and the provision of guarantees

For example, it is easy for a cobbler to guarantee to repair shoes in 24 hours or to provide his service free of charge. The smart cobbler should rarely find himself working for nothing. If he expects to turn round all shoes in a 24-hour period, then once he has taken on all that he can manage in this time, he can just refuse to accept any more under the conditions of the guarantee.

It is more difficult for a tutor to guarantee the results of his students. There are many intangible aspects of such a service, and not all of these are under the control of the tutor. This is not to say that those responsible for providing services with some intangibility should not provide guarantees. Indeed, guarantees have been developed for services as intangible as education, and driving instruction.[33] In both cases, free additional instruction was offered to those who did not successfully complete their course. However, too often those who provide the more intangible services shelter behind the shield of difficulty when it comes to the provision of guarantees. These companies will often regard a sincere apology as sufficient acknowledgement of a complaint.

Is an apology enough for the consumer who goes to all the trouble of complaining? Even those offering intangible services can offer something a bit more tangible than an apology when it comes to compensating the aggrieved customer. This also applies when the situation giving cause for complaint cannot be retracted or rectified at a later date, e.g. if a retailer refuses to accept payment by credit card because the credit card company has mistakenly refused to authorize the customer's use of the card, the customer will be embarrassed. No matter what the credit card company now does it cannot retract that situation. Sending the customer a bunch of flowers will probably be greeted with more enthusiasm than a wordy apology, and may stand a greater chance of effecting service recovery.

Many companies operating in such industries, particularly where the market is competitive, use guarantees as a positioning tool. They use it as a means of differentiating themselves from the competition, e.g. when Thomson Holidays first offered 'No surcharges guaranteed' it was the first tour operator to do this. However, the uniqueness of this benefit was short-lived. Like so many service developments, it was easily copied. Note also that this particular guarantee only applied to one aspect of the service.

Sometimes companies adopt a more all-embracing approach. Instead of providing a specific guarantee, they guarantee total customer satisfaction. We can probably all think of services that provide 'satisfaction guaranteed'. Whether or not we believe them is another matter. Many such companies attach no meaning to these statements. Using them merely as a form of words intended to convey a quality service.

Other more reputable companies that provide this sort of guarantee, probably suffer as a result. They genuinely mean that they will do everything in their power to make customers satisfied. The principle is part of the company's philosophy, and employees are aware of the importance that is attached to satisfying the customer. The customer however, may well remain sceptical.

Designing a guarantee

The all-embracing guarantee of the sort just described, is in fact, not the best type of guarantee that a company can offer. The best guarantees meet the criteria set out in Table 11.4

Table 11.4 Qualities of the ideal guarantee

Guarantees should be:
Easy to understand
Easy to invoke
Unconditional
Credible
Focused on customer needs
Meaningful (significant penalty or payout)
Provide clear performance standards

Easy to understand

The guarantee should be as short and simple as possible. It should be written in clear, plain English to help prevent any ambiguity from creeping in. The ideal is to think of an advertising endline; normally only one sentence in length, and with the intention of being highly memorable.

Easy to invoke

Companies are often fearful of making guarantees easy to invoke because they are frightened of the potential cost. They can see the benefits of offering guarantees to consumers, but cannot see what benefits are to be gained by making them easy to invoke.

Unconditional

For the same reasons that it is important to make it easy for dissatisfied customers to complain, it is best to make the guarantee as unconditional as possible. This type of guarantee communicates to staff and customers that the service provider believes in the quality of their offering. Naturally, it is only sensible to offer such a guarantee if the service is a quality one.

Credible

To provide a guarantee that customers regard as incredible casts doubt on everything that the company does. Driving schools that guarantee learner drivers will pass first time are making unbelievable promises. The learner will know that there are many factors affecting whether or not they pass the driving test that are outside the control of the instructor, e.g. the nerves of the learner, or the mood of the test instructor. A table of pass rates relative to other driving schools would probably prove more credible, and would serve the main purpose of providing a guaranteed risk reduction.

Focused on customer needs

A guarantee should be guaranteeing aspects of service that are important to customers. It should not be focusing on what the company regards as important, or on what the company thinks customers regard as important.

Enlightened service providers should have identified those aspects of their service that are critically important to customers, not only to aid the design of a guarantee, but also to enable them to design a quality service.

Meaningful (with significant penalties or payouts)

The guarantee is not meaningful if the penalties that accrue to the provider, or the levels of compensation paid to the customer are insignificant. In both these cases there is little incentive for the company to improve its service offering. Most dissatisfied customers will not take the trouble to complain. Even if they did, the company would not suffer high payout costs and so is less likely to work on service improvements.

Rail operators have come in for a lot of criticism in this respect, over the low targets that they have set themselves in the Passenger's Charter. The Consumers' Association called it 'little more than a glossy public relations con'.[34] Many factors affect what customers regard as significant levels of compensation. These include the cost of the service, the seriousness of the failure, and customers' perception of what is fair (deserved) for that service.

Provide clear performance standards

Employees should know the targets they are trying to meet. The achievement of these standards generally denotes the provision of a good service. The Pizzaland guarantee already mentioned states what the company regards as the maximum time that a customer should have to wait for a pizza. This guarantee has given kitchen and waiting staff clear performance standards.

Recent market developments

Privatized industries

Over the past twenty years a number of nationalized industries have been privatized. In dismantling these monopolies the government needed to ensure that they operated in the best interests of the customer. They tackled this in two ways. First, as they legislated for the powers needed to divest of these assets, they made provision for other companies to enter the market. Thereby eroding the monopoly power which has been suggested was the main reason for lower levels of customer satisfaction in the nationalized industries. It also made provision for the voice of the consumer in the privatization legislation; watchdog bodies were set up to monitor their activities, e.g. the Gas Consumers Council (GCC) was set up under the Gas Act 1986, with statutory powers to protect customers' interests. In 1992 the GCC actually forced British Gas to lower their proposed price increase. This is the sort of protection that the consumer enjoys.

Public services

Many of the services that remain under the government's control have also been restructured for the benefit of customers. So the roles of purchaser and provider have been separated as is the case with hospitals with trust status, and the Training and Enterprise Councils.

In addition, the government launched the Citizen's Charter. At the time of its launch, it was believed that it would provide a strong catalyst for change that would reform these services to the benefit of consumers. As the prime minister of the day stated, 'the main thrust of the Charter is to empower the individual'.

The government, whether central or local, then becomes primarily a setter of standards. It raises taxes to pay for services which are provided by either private or public bodies. The Audit Commission, the local authority watchdog, has devised ways of measuring the effectiveness of these locally provided services, regardless of who actually provides them. Within its new powers and duties it is required to specify performance indicators, and produce league tables of good and bad performers. There will certainly be difficulties in comparing different levels of effectiveness. How does one compare an area that provides a few high quality places in nurseries, with an area that provides for every child but does so with reduced quality?

The Charter Mark

In order to provide impetus for the Citizen's Charter, the government launched the Charter Mark in 1992. Initially, the award was given to a maximum of 50 organizations a year. However, this limit has been abolished, and the award is now available to every organization that reaches the Charter Mark standard of excellence. In 1997, 365 awards were made.

During the early years, the award was restricted to public sector organizations that served the public direct, and to the privatized utilities. This has recently been extended to include housing associations, and voluntary sector schools and hospitals that receive at least 75 per cent of their income from public funds.

The criteria that the Charter Mark judges use to evaluate excellent performance are:

- **Performance standards** – 'Setting, monitoring, and publication of explicit standards for the services that individual users can reasonably expect. Publication of actual performance against those standards.'
- **Information and openness** – 'Full accurate information readily available in plain language about how public services are run, what they cost, how well they perform and who is in charge.'
- **Consultation and choice** – 'The public sector should provide choice wherever practicable. There should be regular and systematic consultation with those who use services. Users' views about services, and their priorities for improving them, should be taken into account in final decisions about standards.'
- **Courtesy and helpfulness** – 'Courteous and helpful service, from public servants who will normally wear name badges. Services available equally to all who are entitled to them and run to suit their convenience.'
- **Putting things right** – 'If things go wrong, an apology, a full explanation and a swift and effective remedy. Well publicized and easy-to-use complaints procedures with independent reviews wherever possible.'
- **Value for money** – 'Efficient and economical delivery of public services within the resources the nation can afford.'
- **User satisfaction** – 'Evidence must be presented that shows that users are satisfied with the quality of service they are receiving.'

Figure 11.13 The Charter Mark logo

- **Improvements in service quality** – 'Measurable or demonstrable improvements in quality of service over the last two or three years.'
- **Planned improvements and innovations** – This final section deals with the future. Charter Mark is about continuous improvement and a forward-looking approach to delivering services.

Charter Marks are awarded for a period of three years. In addition to a trophy and certificate, winners can use the Charter Mark logo on their stationery and vehicles and other items of corporate identity (Figure 11.13).

Summary

As consumers' expectations continue to rise, levels of dissatisfaction rise too. Companies with a long-term future are those that attempt to minimize dissatisfaction. Given that it may not always be possible to get it right first time, this means dealing with complaints effectively.

Dealing with complaints effectively has several benefits. It reduces the possibility of adverse word-of-mouth publicity. It also gives the organization a better chance of recovering the future loyalty of the aggrieved customer. Remember that loyal customers are more likely to complain. Finally, it provides management with information that will help them design an improved service offering.

The process of service recovery may be aided by the provision of a guarantee. The main purpose of which is to reduce risk both before and after consumption. Guarantees should aim to be: easy to understand; easy to invoke; unconditional; credible; focused on consumers' needs; meaningful (in terms of payout or penalty); and provide clear performance standards.

References

1. The Audit Commission for Local Authorities in England and Wales (1988) *The Competitive Council*, HMSO, London.
2. McKinnon, Sir J. (1992) Article in *Financial Times*, 12 February.
3. Oliver, R. (1977) 'Effect of expectation and disconfirmation on postexposure product evaluation: an alternative interpretation', *Journal of Applied Psychology*, **62**, August, 480–486.
4. Peters, T. and Austin, N. (1985) *A Passion for Excellence*, Random House, New York.

5. Parasuraman, A., Zeithaml, V. A. and Berry, L. L. (1990) *Delivering Quality Service*, Free Press, New York.
6. Johnson, R. (1994) 'The zone of tolerance exploring the relationship between service transactions and satisfaction with the overall service', *International Journal of Service Management* **6**, No. 2, 46–61.
7. Cottam, A. (1998) *The Experiential Nature of Service Consumption: An Investigation of the Formation of Customer Satisfaction*, Unpublished PhD thesis, University of Manchester Institute of Science and Technology.
8. Jones, T. O. and Sasser, W. E. (1995) 'Why satisfied customers defect', *Harvard Business Review*, November/December, 88–99.
9. Page, M. J. *et al.* (1997) 'Before they leave, switch on the light: knowing the value of keeping customers', *Journal of Targeting, Measurement, and Analysis for Marketing*, **5**, No. 3, 232–246.
10. Consumers' Association (1989) Annual Consumer Complaints Survey.
11. Consumers' Association (1998) Policy Report, *Handled with Care? Consumer Complaints* 1991–1997.
12. Bolton, R. N. and Bronkhurst, T. M. (1995) 'The relationship between customer complaints and subsequent exit behaviour'. In *Advances in Consumer Behaviour*, Vol. 22, (F. Kardes and M. Sujan eds) Association for Consumer Research, Boston, MA.
13. Bell, C. R. and Zemke, R. (1988) 'Do service procedures tie employees' hands?' *Personnel Journal*, September, 76–83.
14. Zemke, R. and Bell, C. (1990) 'Service recovery: doing it right second time', *Training*, June 42–48.
15. Warland, R. H., Hermann, R. O. and Willits, J. (1975) 'Dissatisfied customers: who gets upset and who takes action', *Journal of Consumer Affairs*, **9**.
16. Miller, J. (1977) 'Studying satisfaction: modifying models, eliciting expectations, posing problems and making meaningful measurement'. In *Conceptualisation and Measurement of Customer Satisfaction and Dissatisfaction* (Hunt, K. ed.), MSI.
17. Best, A. and Andreasen, A. R. (1977) 'Consumer response to unsatisfactory purchases: a survey of perceiving defects, voicing complaints and obtaining redress,' *Law and Society Review*, November, 701–742.
18. Dayand, R. L. and Landon, E. L. (1977) 'Towards a theory of complaining behaviour,' *Consumer and Industrial Buying Behaviour*.
19. Holmes, A. (1992) Quote in a letter from Ashley Holmes of the Consumers' Association.
20. Kubler-Ross, E. (1969) *On Death and Dying*, Macmillan, London.
21. Richins, M. (1990) 'Consumer perceptions of costs and benefits associated with complaining'. In *Refining Concepts and Measures of Consumer Satisfaction and Complaining Behaviour* (Hunt and Day eds).
22. Consumers' Association (1985) Dissatisfaction Survey.
23. Liswood, L. A. (1989) *Serving Them Right*, Harper & Row, New York.
24. Goodwin, C. and Ross, I. (1992) 'Consumer responses to service failures: influence of procedural and interactional fairness perceptions', *Journal of Business Research*, **25**, 149–163.

25. Sellers, P. (1988) How to handle customers' gripes, *Fortune*, 24 October.
26. Einstein, A. (1954) *Ideas and Options*, Crown, New York.
27. Rust, R. T. *et al.* (1995) 'Making complaints a management tool', *Marketing Management*, **1**, No. 3, 40–45.
28. Hart, G., Heskett, J. and Sasser, W. E. (1990) 'The profitable art of service recovery', *Harvard Business Review*, July–August, 148–156.
29. Brown, S. *et al.* (1996) 'Service recovery: its value and limitations as a retail strategy', *International Journal of Service Industry Management*, **7**, No. 5, 32–46.
30. Carlzon, J. (1989) *Moments of Truth*, Harper & Row, New York.
31. Bosoff, C. and Leong, J. (1997) 'Empowerment, attribution and apologising as dimensions of service recovery', *International Journal of Service Industry Management*, **9**, No. 1, 21–47.
32. Kurtz, D. L. and Clow, K. E. (1998) *Services Marketing*, Wiley, Chichester.
33. Heskett, J. L. *et al.* (1990) *Service Breakthroughs Changing the Rules of the Game*, Free Press, New York.
34. Consumers' Association (1992) Quoted in *The Times*, 5 March, Times Newspapers, London.

Chapter 12

Monitoring and evaluating the service

Introduction

Most markets are too competitive nowadays to leave anything to chance. They are usually populated by a growing number of service companies all attempting to build their own market niche. Thus it becomes more important to try to get it right first time. Putting aside luck and good fortune, the best chance a company has of achieving this is by incorporating market research into the development and evaluation processes. This means listening to the customers. The company should give them a voice even before it has anything to sell to them. By listening to what they want in the first place, the company is more likely to launch something that meets their expectations.

Giving the customer a voice and then listening to what they say is an integral part of a service marketing system. It is also an ongoing process. When the service becomes available, the company should begin to monitor and evaluate its performance with the help of its customers. An holistic approach to this evaluation means treating as customers, not only those who purchase the service, but also those who deliver it. This evaluation will often lead to improvements in the service being made. And so the whole process begins again.

In all of this it should be remembered that while market research can help to reduce risk, it does not eliminate it. Market research findings should be used as an aid to decision making. They should not be used to make the decision.

Information + Judgement = Decision

Better information + Judgement = Better decision

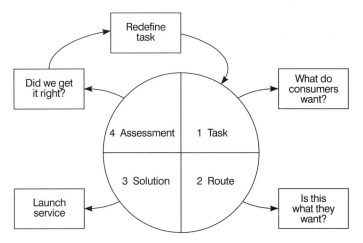

Figure 12.1 Market research and the service development cycle

The market research process

Market research is really just a means of gathering information. The Market Research Society of Great Britain defines it as: 'the means used by those who provide goods and services to keep themselves in touch with the needs and wants of those who buy and use those goods and services'.[1] In product markets, manufacturers rarely come face to face with

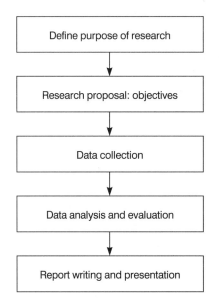

Figure 12.2 The market research process

customers. They are generally separated by the distribution channel. At least in the provision of services, the customer is often present, and therefore feedback often more direct.

However, services cannot rely on the existence of this direct contact to provide them with all the information they need about their consumers. For one thing, the company is restricted to talking to its current customers. It has no means of finding out why people switched to another service or have never considered using their service in the first place. A more systematic approach to gathering the information is required (Figure 12.2).

The company must begin by defining its research objectives. What information does it want to discover? Does it want to know what expectations customers have of the service, or what variables contribute to customer satisfaction?

It then has to go out and collect the data which can be analysed to provide information for presentation to the interested parties.

Data collection

In some cases, the information that is required is already available. This is known as desk research or secondary data. Secondary data can come from information held within the company (internal secondary data) or from externally generated sources (Figure 12.3). The company's own information systems can be a good source of data. If a doctor wanted to know the average length of time that patients had been with his practice, or that he wanted to know what were the three commonest reasons for a patient visiting the surgery, then the best way of finding this out would be to look at his own records.

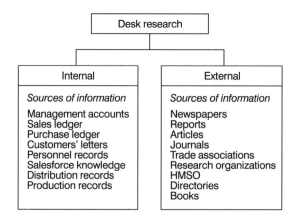

Figure 12.3 Sources of desk research data

Technology has made a significant impact in the back office. Not only in terms of assisting service delivery, but also in helping to develop management information systems of a power not even dreamt of a decade ago. Management are now much more aware of the potential of information. They understand the benefits to be gained from gathering and structuring the information that they process. For example, fifteen years ago the accounts department of a mail order company would no doubt have been able to tell you the age pattern of their debtors, and maybe even the average spend of a customer. Without manually going through order forms, however, it is highly unlikely that there would have been any data on all the items that each customer had ever bought from the company. It would, thus, have been difficult to uncover patterns in their spending behaviour. Nowadays, management will often have these facts available at the touch of a button.

However, there are many management questions which cannot be answered by an exhaustive search of all desk sources. The company must then resort to what is known as field research or primary data. In most instances this will mean commissioning a market research company to conduct the fieldwork.

Observing respondents

Behaviour can be observed where the respondent is aware that he or she is being studied. An article which appeared in *Marketing Magazine* read as follows: 'I stepped into the Supermarket Simulator, and gasped in amazement. In front of me was a bar-shaped handle, and as I took hold of it the rest of the trolley materialised, together with aisles of goods, fellow customers and even assistants stocking shelves. I pressed on the bar and apparently moved forward. Then suddenly the handle recoiled and struck me painfully in the upper midriff. The trolley wheel had jammed, the illusion was complete. It was the year 2000 and I was a respondent entering the Consumer Research Applications Shopping Simulator (CRASS) in order that my entire shopping behaviour should be observed and recorded'.[2]

Observation can also be used where the subjects under investigation have little or no awareness of their participation in the project. One application is known as 'Mystery Shopper' or 'Mystery Customer' research. The researcher attempts to experience the customers' contact with the service, approaches the service encounter posing as a customer and reports back on the treatment received.

This technique can be used to analyse the customers' experience in almost any service setting, e.g. TV rental shops, cosmetic counters, night clubs, car-hire companies. However, it need not be restricted to those services where the customer is physically present. It can be used to evaluate the way in which telephone calls are handled by an organization. Are they answered promptly, politely, effectively etc.?

Business Efficiency Monitoring (BEM), a company specializing in this type of research, believes that the most effective mystery customer surveys have four essential qualities:[3]

- Independence: results are treated with more trust if a third party has compiled them.
- Objectivity: the best surveys are those where the researcher is looking for things that require a 'yes' or a 'no' response. 'Were you greeted when you entered the restaurant?' 'Was the telephone answered before it had rung five times?' This means that there is then no ambiguity in the assessment.
- Consistency: comparisons are usually made across a number of locations. Therefore consistency of approach is essential.
- Qualification: surveys whose results can be quantified provide management with more usable information. These results can be tracked over time to gauge whether or not the quality of the service is improving.

Interviewing respondents

However, trying to gather data by observation is not always the best approach. Observation is useful where the study is concerned with observable behaviour. It is also of use where the behaviour takes place with a predictable frequency. In such cases the researcher can plan the timing of the measurement, and fieldwork costs are contained, e.g. studies of womens' experiences of the health service during pregnancy and childbirth can be timed with relative accuracy.

One of the strongest limitations of the observation technique is that it can only measure observable events. It cannot measure attitudes, opinions, or judgements that influence behaviour. In an effort to understand the reasons why a consumer behaves as he or she does, the marketer needs to explore motivations and attitudes. To do so, the marketer conducts a survey and gathers the data by interviewing respondents.

Interviews can be conducted with respondents face to face, by telephone, by post and most recently by computer. Since the purpose of conducting quantitative research is to be able to provide an accurate picture of the market, all respondents must be asked an identical set of questions. To ensure that this takes place the data are collected by means of a questionnaire. The results of individual questionnaires can then be combined so that an overall assessment can be made.

Applications of market research

Designing a quality service

There are numerous ways in which research can be used to assist in the design of a quality service. The role that it plays depends on the extent or novelty of the service (Figure 12.4).

Figure 12.4 The new service development spectrum

Researching a service which lies on the left of the spectrum will tend to be a multi-staged process requiring considerable investment in terms of time and money. On the other hand, research into service development which lies at the other end may mean no more than an informal observation study.

The completely new service

The research programme that should be adopted for service development in this area is adapted from the model devised by Booz, Allen, and Hamilton for product marketing (Figure 12.5).

Idea generation

The qualitative research that would be conducted at this stage is known as 'brainstorming'. It is run in group discussions and is designed to get respondents to think laterally as opposed to logically about the problem area. The group moderator usually begins with a few 'warm-up' questions to get the creative side of the brain functioning, e.g. 'Can you think of ten uses for a brick?' The research is intended to give the company some idea of what it would take to create the 'ideal' service.

To try to make respondents less inhibited there are some rules. No ideas are laughed at no matter how silly they may appear. Nor are anyone's ideas challenged. The more ideas the better at this stage.

Quantitative research takes the form of 'gap analysis'. This research is pivotal in the delivery of a quality service. It highlights the 'ideal'

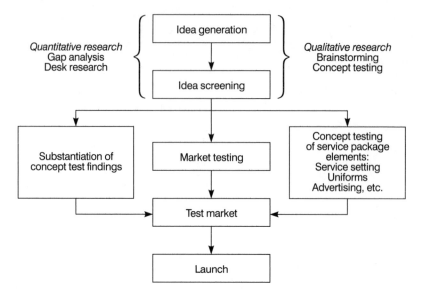

Figure 12.5 Market research and the new service development process

service positioning. To undertake this analysis requires some knowledge of the market since a list of salient attributes is necessary for the questionnaire.

Parasuraman, Zeithaml and Berry[4] have developed a model for evaluating service quality (SERVQUAL). Their research shows that there are five basic dimensions of service quality that should be tested: reliability; responsiveness; assurance; empathy; and tangibles. Unless previous research has shown otherwise, all areas should be investigated in the design of an ideal service.

Indeed, they would suggest that the first service quality gap (Gap One) is caused by a misunderstanding on the part of the company of what it is that the consumer needs/expects from the service. Zeithaml[5] argues that this gap is narrowed through market research.

In designing a service, the company must research the customers' expectations of service performance. It must discover which features are more/less important, and what levels of these the customer expects. It should seek to understand, in situations of service recovery, what consumers' expectations of the company would be.

Screening

The first stage of research may have generated dozens of ideas. So how does the company begin to take this list down to a more manageable size?

Quantitatively, it can analyse any desk research that is available. This might provide information on potential market size, similar services already in place overseas, etc.

The company can also attempt to rank the positions highlighted by the gap analysis. Which ideas are most compatible with the company's:

Strategic goals?
Financial objectives?
Technical know-how?
Legal and environmental constraints?

Qualitatively the ideas can be screened using concept testing research. Ideas generated in the first stage are now evaluated again in the group setting. The following diagnostic questions illustrate the nature of the testing.

- Do they understand the concepts?
- Are they believable?
- What do they perceive its attributes to be?
- What are its perceived advantages/disadvantages over current market offering?
- Which of the concepts is the most interesting?
- Would they use this service?
- Who is the target market?
- Would it cannibalize?
- Could the ideas be improved in any way?

Market testing and test market

This research takes the preferred concept from the previous stage and tests it quantitatively. Until now the financial commitment to any development has been minimal. The results of research at this stage, however, will determine whether or not to proceed to a launch. New services that get the thumbs-up at this stage then require substantial investment. Therefore it is important that this research is sensitive and accurate.

If the testing were for a consumer product, some samples would be mocked up, and consumers would try it. The respondents would be aware that they were taking part in product development research. The purpose of the research would be to estimate market penetration, and repeat purchase levels at various price points.

In many cases, products that test favourably in the market test are taken through one final stage of research – the test market. This is where a limited proportion of the total target market is exposed to the new product, e.g. one TV area. All elements of the marketing mix are in place. Consumers are unaware that they are being researched. They see the promotions, and go out and buy the product through its normal distribution outlet. The test market is monitored by analysing sales using a range of measurement tools.[1]

However, this process is not quite so straightforward for a service. To design a market test environment that closely approximates the finished service requires some creativity. There is still a lack of knowledge about precisely how to proceed at this stage in the development process for a service.

It may be more appropriate to combine the market test and the test market to conduct an 'open' test market. This would be similar to a test market in that the service would be available in its normal market environment. However, unlike a normal test market where the target consumers have no idea of their complicity in the research, in an open test market the consumers' attitudes and opinions are openly and systematically sought.

For example, a company wishing to set up a chain of nursery schools could develop a service based on the results of its concept testing research. It could launch one establishment and research its success before proceeding to its optimum market penetration. At this stage, it may be possible for the company to employ a number of research techniques that have been used in the past to assess performance. Consequently, these have been deployed **after** service consumption.

One such piece of research would attempt to segment service attributes into satisfiers, dissatisfiers, and criticals.[6] In doing so, the service provider would gain a clearer understanding of how to allocate operational resources to deliver satisfaction.

Satisfiers are those elements of service delivery which when performed beyond what the consumer considers adequate, have a positive impact on perceptions. Yet when they are neither in evidence, or are poorly performed, they do not depress perceptions of service quality. These are often elements of service delivery that the customer does not expect. For example, a regular user of a particular car hire company, may consider performance beyond the adequate, if the next time he rings to book a car, the receptionist remembers his preference for car model, collection and delivery details, etc. However, if none of this happens, it will not result in the customer having lower perceptions of service quality.

Dissatisisfiers are those elements of service delivery which when performed at a level below that which the consumer believes to be adequate will result in dissatisfaction. But any performance above that level that the consumer considers to be adequate, will have little impact on perceptions of service quality. So, to continue with our example of car hire, if the customer has arranged for the car to be at his office at 5 pm, and the car is delivered at 7 pm, then this is likely to result in dissatisfaction. If, on the other hand, the car is delivered at 3 pm, this is not likely to raise perceptions of service quality if the customer is in no position to use the car before 5 pm.

Criticals are those factors that can act as both satisfiers and dissatisfiers. Good performance on these factors can improve perceptions of service quality, and conversely, poor performance can detract from it. So, for example, if empathy is a critical factor, then polite service may raise perceptions of service quality and impolite may depress them.

Throughout this discussion of satisfiers, dissatisfiers, and criticals, reference has been made to **levels** of performance. This is similar to the zone of tolerance referred to in Chapter 11.[7] In order to establish this zone of tolerance two measures of expectations must be taken:

- Desired service: what the customer believes the service should be (and can be)
- Adequate service: what is the minimal level of service acceptable to the customer.

The width of the zone (difference between desired and adequate) is often determined by the customer's involvement in the service. So for a service where the customer is highly involved the zone may be quite narrow, whereas for those where the customer is not involved, the zone will be wider. In addition to the overall service having its zone of tolerance, individual attributes of the service will also have theirs.

Running concurrently alongside the market testing other pieces of qualitative concept testing research may be conducted. These would examine the appropriateness of service package elements. Some of these findings may be substantiated with quantitative research, e.g. advertising is an area that companies often test in advance of any launch.[8]

Launching a new brand into an existing market

In many ways the development process is similar to that for a completely new service. It would begin with a qualitative and quantitative assessment of the ideal service. In addition to this, qualitative research would be conducted to examine the relevance and appropriateness of the brand name to the particular service market.

If the results were positive, the company would then complete the process described by Figure 12.5 (see Chapter 9 for a further discussion of brand image development).

Fine-tuning an existing service

Service sector research again differs from that which would be conducted for a product. There are two reasons for this. First, the organization can witness the consumers' experience, i.e. it can observe or interview customers during and after the service encounter. And second, frontline staff will witness the customers' interaction with their company on a daily basis. They then become a good source of development ideas. Both approaches focus on the critical incident. They are examining the areas of both service process and service outcome (Figure 12.6).[9]

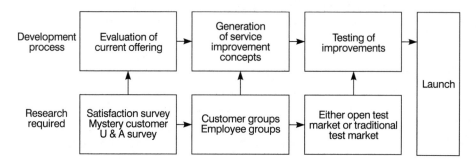

Figure 12.6 Using research to fine-tune a service

The process begins with an evaluation of the current service. This can take the form of a Satisfaction survey (see 'Measuring satisfaction' below) and/or a mystery customer survey (see 'Mystery customer research' below). This research might highlight areas where the service can be improved.

However, there has recently been a suggestion that research conducted with the purpose of improving service delivery should measure Performance against Importance and not against Expectations, as is practised in customer satisfaction research.[10] Why so? First, in services where expectations may not be clearly formulated, benchmarking Importance may be a more relevant approach. Second, studies have shown that the Expectation variable is insignificant in the determination of satisfaction, and that satisfaction judgements are overwhelmingly determined by the customer's perceptions of Performance. The combination of Importance Performance information act together to determine priority areas for improvement (see Figure 12.7).

In addition, consumers' and employees' opinions can be sought. There are few people more likely to have ideas about the way in which the service could be developed. This information would normally be gathered through *ad hoc* group discussions, although more recently many service companies operate their own qualitative consumer panels. Here, the same

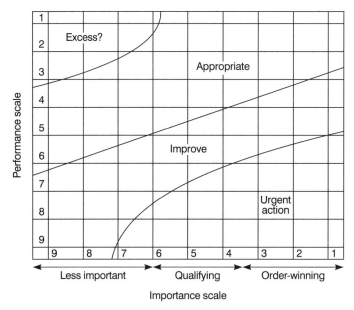

Figure 12.7 Segmentation of areas for improvement using Importance/
Performance criteria. *Source*: Slack (1994)[10]

consumers attend a monthly group discussion to talk about their service experiences over the past few weeks and to pass comment on proposed service improvements.

Underpinning the process should be informal research. Traditionally this would have meant monitoring customers' letters to pick up on any complaints or suggestions. Nowadays, the use of 0800 telephone lines for the customers' 'voice' is becoming increasingly popular and this would be another source of information. The company should also seek to create a culture that encourages employees to become involved in the development process. Employees should know who to inform of any development ideas that they have. The generation of these ideas should also be integrated into the company's career structure or reward system.

Measuring satisfaction

The company cannot sit back and relax once the service has been launched. Researching the consumer view must continue. The company will want to know how it is performing in the market. It will need to know if its customers are satisfied and if not, what it can do to put right the situation. So how does a company monitor customer satisfaction?

A quantitative satisfaction survey based on multiattribute analysis provides a useful starting point.

Satisfaction survey

Suppose that MBA students as they join a Masters course are asked to describe the factors that influenced their choice of educational establishment. Their list would probably contain the dimensions in left-hand column of Table 12.1.

They are then asked to rank the list of attributes:

Most important   = 5
Least important   = 1

This is shown for a hypothetical student in column 1, Table 12.1.

If the list had contained eight attributes and not five, then the scale would have been: most important = 8, least important = 1.

Finally they are asked to state the degree of importance that each holds for them. Using, for example, the following scale:

Very important   5
Fairly important   4
Neither important or unimportant   3
Fairly unimportant   2
Very unimportant   1

This is column 2 in Table 12.1

Table 12.1 A multiattribute expectation/satisfaction matrix

	Pre-consumption expectations			Service experience score			Post-consumption satisfaction		
Attribute	(1)	(2)	(3) ((1)×(2))	(4)	(5)	(6) ((4)×(5))	(7)	(8)	(9) ((7)×(8))
Reputation	5	5	25	4	5	20	4	4	16
Standard of lecturing	4	4	16	5	5	25	5	4	20
Quality of materials	3	3	9	2	3	6	2	3	6
Sports facilities	2	2	4	3	4	12	3	3	9
Location	1	2	2	1	2	2	1	3	3
Expectation score			56*			65			
Satisfaction score									54

*Maximum possible score = 75 (where the individual gives each attribute in column 2 a score of 5)

The validity of using an importance scale has been called into question because of the ambiguity and somewhat imprecise meaning of the word. Wilkie and Pessemier[11] and Oliver[12] suggest instead, that each attribute should be measured on the semantic differential that suits the word best, e.g. good–bad, attractive–unattractive. This may be true for academic works. However, if different attributes have different scales the questionnaire becomes more complex and difficult to administer. The choice between the two methods should be based on the depth of diagnostic information required from the survey.

In this case the student had an *Expectation score* of 56 out of a possible score of 75. This maximum would occur where the student had given an importance rating of 5 to each of the variables.

The same two questions are asked at the end of the MBA course to give a *Revised expectation score* or a *service experience score* (columns 4 and 5). In situations where the service takes some time to consume, this revised score must be calculated since experience of the service will often change what it takes to make the customer satisfied. In this case the student took up sport during the course and so its importance increased and its ranked position rose. Notice that his expectations have now been revised upwards to 65.

Finally, to compute a *satisfaction score*, the following two questions are asked of the same list of attributes:

Q1 A ranking of the attributes (column 7, Table 12.1):
Most important   = 5
Least important   = 1

Q2 How did the service perform against expectations (column 8, Table 12.1)?
A lot better than expected	5
A little better than expected	4
Just as expected	3
A little worse than expected	2
A lot worse than expected	1

Models have been developed where the respondents have instead been asked to discuss their degree of satisfaction. As in the following scale:

Q3 The degree of satisfaction.
Very satisfied	5
Fairly satisfied	4
Neither satisfied nor dissatisfied	3
Fairly dissatisfied	2
Very dissatisfied	1

Many writers prefer the earlier scale. This is because on the one hand, this scale has been shown to be independent of the level of expectations, and at the same time to be highly correlated with satisfaction.[13] However, in many senses it is more important that the service results in satisfaction than that it lives up to expectations. Indeed the earlier scale tends to ignore the possibility of expectations being revised during the service process.

The satisfaction score for this student is 54. He is therefore dissatisfied. To achieve satisfaction the score has to be equal to, or greater than, the expectation score (see Figure 12.8).

Figure 12.8 The measurement of expectations/satisfaction

However, the validity of this somewhat blunt approach to the measurement of satisfaction has recently been questioned. We have previously discussed the relevance of measuring expectations in the context of services. Furthermore, concentrating solely on outcome satisfaction and failing to measure satisfaction during the process of consumption may result in inaccurate readings of customers' attitudes.[14] This is particularly true if you believe that after consumption cognitive dissonance will be evident.

Finally, the usefulness of the information provided by these satisfaction studies has also been questioned. What is the meaning of any recorded difference between Expectations and Performance? What is the difference between 80 per cent of your customers being 'very satisfied' and 70 per cent of them feeling 'very satisfied'? These surveys cannot say, for example, how much more likely than a Very Satisfied customer is a Satisfied customer likely to switch. So in quantitative studies, companies are simultaneously recording high satisfaction ratings and declining loyalty[15] and high switching behaviour among satisfied customers.[16]

In an attempt to provide more powerful satisfaction data, it has been suggested that emotional responses to the service performance and the quality of the satisfaction should also be captured.[14,17] Three satisfaction types have been suggested:

- Those who are *resigned*. This is typified by those who will repeat purchase because there is nothing better on the market and they don't feel that they can expect any more from the service provider.
- Those who are *stable*, i.e. are happy with the current situation and *expect everything to remain as it is*.
- Those who are *demanding*. This final group are constantly revising their expectations upwards, and believe that to succeed, the service provider will need to keep pace with their changing requirements.

A knowledge of what type of satisfaction your customers have and what emotional response your service brings will help you design your service offering.

Mystery customer research

Another way in which companies measure satisfaction is with mystery customer research. The company that designed a service which was intended to deliver satisfaction could measure its performance against these standards. Suppose a chain of hotels understood the major variables that contributed to quality to be:

- The cleanliness of the room
- The responsiveness of room service
- The peaceful atmosphere
- The accuracy of their bill

It designed a service to meet these criteria and in the process set standards for employees to achieve. The hotel could then send round mystery customers to check on performance. Companies are encouraged to inform employees that they are conducting research of this nature. Otherwise they could be accused of 'spying' on them. Researchers are encouraged to report the findings in such a way that individual employees cannot be singled out.

The weakness of this technique for measuring service performance is that time will have passed since consumers were first asked about the variables that were important for the creation of a quality service. Even if this 'ideal' service had in fact been delivered, the customers' views of what constitutes quality may have changed.

The mystery customer survey can be used as a proxy for a satisfaction survey. It is certainly a useful supplement to such a survey. But perhaps its most important contribution is in the evaluation of employee performance.

Evaluating dissatisfaction

In the case of our MBA student, the customer was dissatisfied. An organization hoping for a long life has to understand the reasons why this has happened. There are several ways that the organization might choose to do this. It could conduct follow-up interviews with satisfaction survey respondents whose results showed that they were dissatisfied. The objective of this would be to understand in more detail the reason for their disappointment.

Another source of information about dissatisfaction comes from the complaints that customers make. All complaints that are made to the company should not only be dealt with expediently, they should also be recorded so that management can utilize them strategically.

Frontline employees could be questioned about the complaints that they receive. It is best to do this formally and systematically to ensure that all verbal complaints are recorded. They are more likely to be recorded if the employee receiving the complaint is empowered to act to put it right. Those charged with the achievement of customer satisfaction are more likely to pressure management to enable them to deliver it. However, the empowerment cannot be divided solely between management and the frontline worker. All employees should be empowered. Otherwise it would be all too easy for those at the frontline to blame back-office staff, e.g. if a waiter often gets complaints about the temperature of the food that he serves, he could point the finger at the kitchens saying that they often forget to tell him when an order is ready. Neither group of employees really cares about the customer. If instead they were driven by a desire to make customers happy (by tying pay to customer satisfaction?) there would be less finger-pointing.

The effective monitoring of complaints is not a sufficient measure of dissatisfaction. Only a tiny proportion of dissatisfied customers actually complain. Most of them do not take the trouble to inform the company of their dissatisfaction, but they often take the trouble to inform their friends. Therefore in addition to analysing complaints, the company should actively attempt to monitor levels of dissatisfaction, and understand in detail the reasons for the dissatisfaction.

One category of dissatisfied customers who should not be forgotten, are those who are so dissatisfied that they reject/leave the service. In all cases where the company can identify such individuals their reasons for leaving should be sought. Knowing what caused their dissatisfaction, and acting on it may prevent another customer leaving in the future.

Monitoring corporate image

For many service companies, projecting the right image is fundamental for securing market success (see Chapter 11). A company will have adopted a market positioning that it expects has the greatest potential. To realize that potential, the company must project an image that fits this positioning.

Having developed the appropriate image, the company should set up an Image tracking study to check that this is indeed what is being communicated about its service. This research is generally quantitative and employs an identical questionnaire for each successive piece of fieldwork.

The tracking begins with a benchmark study which is conducted before the image is launched. This defines the scope of the task. The company knows where it currently stands, and it knows where it wants to go. It now has to monitor its progress towards this goal. The tracking would normally contain questions in the following areas:

- Awareness of the company (spontaneous and prompted)
- Awareness of any specific communication exercises, i.e. advertising, publicity (spontaneous and prompted)
- Image of the company using a battery of statements that reflect the company's intended image (spontaneous and prompted)
- Buying behaviour (past behaviour and future intentions)
- Reasons that govern choice of brand

This study is repeated at frequent intervals. The timing of the fieldwork should be spaced so that enough time has elapsed between each survey to allow some image shift to take place, but it should not be done so infrequently that those charged with altering the image feel no sense of urgency. In most cases, two surveys a year would probably suffice.

In addition to a quantitative tracking survey, the company might conduct a qualitative image study to flesh out its understanding of consumers' opinion. Projective techniques are often used to unlock this information. For example, the respondents are asked to say what sort of person, animal, flower, car, or chocolate bar best describes the company.

To give a context for the findings of both the qualitative and the quantitative research, the company should be analysed alongside its competitors.

Understanding employees

Most service companies sink or swim on the strength of their employees – particularly those at the frontline. These individuals often provide the only unique benefit that a company offers. Companies therefore need their commitment and motivation in order to deliver quality service. By listening to what they have to say about their jobs, and understanding their needs, the company creates the opportunity to build their loyalty and effectiveness.

The company should seek information from them on two accounts. It should ask them to represent the case of the external customer, e.g. what do they think it is that the customer wants, what do they like/dislike, what problems do they face in their purchase/consumption of the service?

Employee appraisal

The company should also treat employees as their own internal customers (see Chapter 7). Taking the job that the employee does as the product, the company should seek the same sort of information from them that it would seek from an external customer:

- Are they satisfied with their job?
- What could be done to improve it?
- What could be done that would put them in a position to offer a better service?
- What are their aspirations?
- Do they have skills that are underutilized?

This sort of information should be collected at an individual employee level. It can be gathered in the form of an appraisal. As well as evaluating past performance and achievements, such an appraisal should encourage employees to set their own objectives for the next few years. In their book *In Search of Excellence*, Peters and Waterman[19] note that human beings are more likely to overrate rather than underrate their potential.

Performance appraisal

The employee should also expect to be evaluated in terms of his or her performance. The employee appraisal often focuses on what the company can do for the employee. The performance appraisal, however, takes the employee as the focus and asks – what is the employee doing for the company?

Given human variability and heterogeneity in terms of service perform-ance of the service employee, his or her performance should be measured in terms of the variables that contribute to customer satisfaction. These are the things that really matter, and they should be measures of effectiveness, not of efficiency. In addition to the methods of measurement discussed in Chapter 10 ('Performance measurement'), performance can be measured through a customer satisfaction survey or by means of mystery customer research.

Employee group discussions

The views of employees' should also be encouraged at group level. Their views as both internal customers and as another mouthpiece for the views of customers should be sought. The kind of information that a forum of this nature throws up often never surfaces using more direct methods of questioning. Once the employees relax, the discussion can become more like a Tupperware party than anything work-related. Group discussions like these can be a powerful way of encouraging a team-spirit. If the group is successful in this respect, respondents will feel energized. They will feel a sense of belonging, and so the discussion becomes a socialization mechanism.

Using the applications of market research

All too often funds are deployed on research without sufficient thought being given beforehand to how useful the findings will be. Such projects produce information that is rarely acted upon. Needless to say, none of the research suggested in this chapter is of that nature. Only the bare minimum in terms of research has been described.

So what should the company do with all these findings? Why did it bother to conduct the research? In the first place, research was conducted to help design a quality service that matched customers' needs. In doing so, it helped to set performance standards for employees to meet. It then proceeded to monitor the satisfaction that was being achieved, and to evaluate the performance of its staff. This analysis is then used to determine which improvements, if any, are required to maintain the provision of excellent service.

Summary

This book has focused on the development of principles which help to build excellent service. But what exactly *is* excellent service? And how does a company ever know whether or not it is achieving this goal? Indeed, how does a company design an excellent service in the first place?

In all of these cases the answer lies in asking consumers. They can describe what they mean by 'excellent service'. A service which meets these requirements can then be designed. Performance can be measured against these variables to evaluate service delivery against their expectations.

Customer involvement in the development of excellent service is an ongoing commitment. There should be continuous monitoring of both performance against standards and of the relevance of the standards themselves. These standards often change over time as expectations develop.

The consumers' voice can be listened to in many ways. It can be heard informally, e.g. management chatting to customers, or reading customers' letters of complaint, or, more formally, a variety of market research techniques can be employed.

There are many elements of service design and delivery that should be monitored and evaluated using market research. This chapter is designed to be of practical help in this respect. It aims to provide a basic overview of the market research process. It looks at the techniques involved, and then examines some relevant applications of these techniques.

References

1. Chisnall, P. (1996) *Marketing Research*, McGraw-Hill, New York.
2. Knight, D. (1992) 'Shopping in the new millennium,' *Marketing Magazine*, 19 March.
3. Joliffe, S. (1992) 'Quantifying customer service via mystery shopper surveys', Conference Paper Presented at the Market Research Society Conference, March 1992. Market Research Society.
4. Parasuraman, A., Zeithaml, V. L. and Berry, L. L. (1988) 'SERVQUAL: a multiple item scale for measuring consumer perceptions of service quality', *Journal of Retailing*, **64**(1), 13–37.
5. Zeithaml, V. (1996) *Services Marketing*, McGraw-Hill, New York.
6. Johnson, R. and Lyth, D. (1988) 'Service quality: integrating customer expectations and operational capability, *Proceedings of the QUIS Symposium*, University of Karlstad, Sweden, August.
7. Johnson, R. (1995) 'Managing the zone of tolerance: some propositions,' *International Journal of Service Industry Management*, **6**, No. 5, 53–71.

8. Cowley, D. (1989) *How to Plan Advertising*, Cassell, London, Chapter 9.
9. Hoffman, K. D. and Bateson, J. E. G. (1997) *The Essentials of Services Marketing*, Dryden Press, New York.
10. Slack, N. (1994) 'The importance–performance matrix as a determinant of improvement priority', *International Journal of Operations and Production Management*, **14**, No. 5, 59–75.
11. Wilkie, W. L. and Pessemier, E. A. (1973) 'Issues in marketing's use of multi-attribute attitude models, *Journal of the Market Research Society*, x, 428–441.
12. Oliver, R. L. (1980) 'Product dissatisfaction as a function of prior expectation and subsequent disconfirmation: new evidence.' In *New Dimensions of Consumer Satisfaction and Complaining Behaviour* (Day, R. L. and Hunt, H. K. eds), Indiana University, Bloomington.
13. Oliver, R. L. (1981) 'Measurement and evaluation of satisfaction processes in retail settings', *Journal of Retailing*, Fall, 25–48.
14. Cottam, A. M. (1998) *The Experiential Nature of Service Consumption: An Investigation of the Formation of the Determinants of Customer Satisfaction*, unpublished PhD thesis, University of Manchester Institute of Science and Technology.
15. Gierl, H. (1993) 'Zufriedene Kunden als Markenwelchsler', *Absatzwirtschaft*, **36**, No. 2, 90–4.
16. Reichheld, F. F. and Aspinall, K. (1994) 'Building high-loyalty business systems', *Journal of Retail Banking*, **15**, No. 4, 21–9.
17. Strauss, B. and Neuhaus, P. (1997) 'The qualitative satisfaction model', *International Journal of Service Industry Management*, **8**, No. 3, 236–249.
18. Market Research Society (1998) *Code of Conduct. The Research Buyer's Guide*, Market Research Society, London.
19. Peters, T. and Waterman, R. H. (1983) *In Search of Excellence*, Harper & Row, New York.

Index